BEING EQUAL DOESN'T MEAN BEING THE SAME

Why Behaving Like a Girl Can Change Your Life
and Grow Your Business

By Joanna L. Krotz

With a Foreword by CEO Sheila C. Johnson,
Entrepreneur and Philanthropist

Published by Motivational Press, Inc.
1777 Aurora Road
Melbourne, Florida, 32935
www.MotivationalPress.com

Manufactured in the United States of America.

ISBN: 978-1-62865-250-5

CONTENTS

For all the women at all the jobs who hold back, hold in and hold on while dreaming about being the leader. Take the leap.

And for Wayne, who knows a thing or two about what it takes for women to make that leap.

Don't Wait to Act
By Sheila C. Johnson

In 35 years of entrepreneurship, I've amassed a broad portfolio. I cofounded Black Entertainment Television, became founder and CEO of Salamander Hotels and Resorts, purchased an ownership stake in the Washington Mystics, Wizards and Capitals, and produced several acclaimed independent films, including Lee Daniels' *The Butler*.

But across these varied industries, one common feature stands out: When I sit down at a high-level meeting with my peers, I am often one of the only women in the room.

Sadly, this isn't unusual. In fact, across the Fortune 1000, only 5% of companies are led by women CEOs. Last time I checked, women made up 50% of the population. Yet across the private sector, we are underrepresented at the highest levels of leadership.

I want to help change that. And I firmly believe that organizations from Wall Street to Silicon Valley can and should do more to ensure women get a fair shot at rising to the top.

But why should we wait for others to act? The fastest way to get to the top is to build our own ladders. It's time to encourage, enable and empower more women to launch the enterprises we aspire to lead.

Entrepreneurship is one of the most compelling ways for women to live our fullest, most stimulating, most challenging and most exciting lives. Running a business is incredibly hard work, but it's also incredibly rewarding, as a pathway to personal growth and fulfillment, and to financial security and success.

Women-led businesses can also have a transformative impact on the market. Every day, women see market opportunities that others may overlook or miss. And that means that when women are underrepresented in business, everybody loses. Think of all the products that go un-invented, services that go unimagined, perspectives that go unconsidered, voices that go unheard—not to mention the diversity of management styles that women CEOs could bring to the table.

But it's not just the market that loses. America's private sector leaders help shape our economy, our public policy, and—by extension—our values as a society. If we want to accelerate progress on issues such as equal pay, supportive policies for working parents and families, or even equal representation in government, we need to put the reins of business leadership into more women's hands.

So, what's the holdup? If women have so much to offer, why is a Y chromosome still considered a business advantage?

We've all heard the old excuses—that men are just more ambitious than women, hungrier for that next opportunity, bolder about putting themselves out there, and quicker to speak up and ask for a chance to prove themselves. But I know there are plenty of vivacious, ambitious, talented women entrepreneurs who are just as hungry to prove their mettle.

The fact is, women face particular challenges in realizing our entrepreneurial aspirations.

Some of these challenges come from external forces. Repeated studies have shown that it's harder for women to secure the financing to get a great idea off the ground, much less to build it to scale. Consider that even though women-owned businesses now account for 30% of all businesses, they contribute a mere 4% of business revenue. With so much entrepreneurial energy out there, shouldn't women be driving more growth, and reaping more of its rewards?

At the same time, women also grapple with attitudes and behaviors of our own that can prevent us from reaching our fullest potential. For example, we may find it difficult to delegate. Or, we may be uncomfortable with risk. (And, let's be honest, sometimes delegating an important task can feel like a risk in itself!)

If we acknowledge these discrepancies—rather than pretending they don't exist—we can find ways to overcome them, so that we can begin to break down barriers for the next generation of talented, aspiring businesswomen. That's exactly what Joanna Krotz has done with *Being Equal Doesn't Mean Being the Same*.

Ms. Krotz has devoted her career to advising women and documenting their progress as a business reporter, editor and columnist. This thoughtful guide, designed expressly for women entrepreneurs, offers valuable insight into the unique strengths and weaknesses women bring to the table—and how to leverage all that we have to our full advantage.

Through extensive research and dozens of interviews with successful women of all ages, Joanna Krotz has zeroed in on the gender distinctions that can make or break women in business and developed smart solutions for coping with societal pressures and double standards. Interspersed among the book's inspiring stories of entrepreneurship are practical tips that can help women capitalize on their strengths, avoid common pitfalls, and shatter glass ceilings on their way to the top.

Whether you're already juggling numerous ventures, or just beginning your career as an entrepreneur, I hope this book inspires you to be bold, to seize opportunities and to take on new challenges with confidence. You are the trailblazers and changemakers who will write the next chapter of women's empowerment. I can't wait to see what you create.

INTRODUCTION

The Distaff Disconnect: Why I became a passionate advocate for women-led businesses

Before the turn of the 21st century, during the so-called "second wave" of feminism, I actually drank the Kool-Aid. I thought women could, should and would change the world. Catch phrases at the time were all about how the personal is political. It made a lot of sense to me—then and now—because I could look around and see palpable, tangible, unacceptable gender inequities in the home, in the workplace, in government and boardrooms, in schools, at all levels. More clearly, I could see that women's ways of thinking, talking, working and relating were often dismissed, not valued.

I figured that by working in media, I could develop messages and stories that would help bring about change for women, and for men too, that would redefine perceptions. I've been a top editor and manager at a string of national magazines, including at Time Inc., Meredith and Hearst, and I've been a commentator and editor at a bunch of online publishers, including MSN. I've spent years tracking and analyzing gender-based elements in the workplace, the culture, leadership and entrepreneurship. Over those years, I've interviewed hundreds of small business owners, male and female, hearing their stories and struggles. I've also run my own small business for more than a decade, a New York-based custom content provider, which keeps me honest about ownership hurdles and triumphs.

My personal has indeed been political. It's been a tricky odyssey, a challenging journey of navigating between the Scylla of battling for recognition and the Charybdis of staying optimistic despite slow progress and setbacks. For sure, women's roles have changed—dramatically— over the past few decades, most everywhere you look. But honestly? I thought we'd be much further along by now in securing women's parity and prosperity.

Some benchmarks to prove that point: Two decades ago, at the United Nation's Beijing women's conference in 1995, world leaders pledged to work toward achieving 30% women members in their national legislatures and parliaments. Today, a scant 44 legislatures among those 190 countries have met that 30% goal. The US is not one of them. The 114th Congress, elected in 2014, boasted a record number of women. Sadly, that added up to only 104 among the 535 members of Congress, or 19% women in the House and 20% women in the Senate.

Don't forget, women today account for half of the US population. Who represents us? Consider Congressional hearings on reproductive rights that consist of all-male committees and exclusively male expert witnesses called to testify about what women need or should have. Consider the male-led majority in the House and lobbyist groups during the 2010 healthcare reform debate that continues to rage a half-decade later, insisting on "gender rating," or requiring that women pay higher fees than men for similar medical services because "women go to the doctor more." Restrictions on women's healthcare are fast becoming law, mandated by male-dominated state legislatures across the country. In August 2015, presidential candidate Jeb Bush—presumably running to be president of all the people, not just men—announced, "I'm not sure we need half a billion dollars for women's health issues." Public indignation forced Bush to walk back that statement, but you know, first utterances out of people's mouths are usually what they really believe.

Where are the legislators and policymakers who understand women's lives, needs and rights? How far have we really come? Think how the thinly veiled real beliefs about women's advancement, like Jeb Bush's front-line throwaway, reverberate in workplaces and corner offices nationwide.

I believe we've now shifted from first generation discrimination into what many researchers call "second generation bias." What is that? The Center for Gender in Organizations at Simmons School of Management in Boston defines it this way: "Distinct from first generation discrimination involving intentional acts of bias, second generation gender practices seem unbiased in isolation, but they typically reflect masculine values and the life situations of men who have dominated in the public domain of work."

In other words, whereas workplace and other discrimination against women used to be blunt, blatant and condoned, nowadays it's subtle, intangible and, speculates Simmons, even occasionally unintentional.

What does this mean in practical terms? First, despite women's inroads into dozens of professions, men still make the rules and decide the teams. Second, challenges for women have moved beyond getting hired. We've pretty well accomplished that. Hurdles to clear now involve being valued and promoted. It's all about advancement.

By the career metrics men use—who gets the fancy executive suite, big cheese title, multimillion-dollar salary and power seat at the table— women are hardly fast tracking. As of 2015, only 23 CEOs in the S&P 500 are women, or less than 5%. Likewise, only 25 women are Fortune 500 CEOs. Worldwide, a puny 8% of women CEOs steer companies with revenues of $500 million or more.

When you do the math, it's crystal clear that men continue to run things in government and business and academia and so on.

But simply turn the page—literally to check out the extraordinary facts of women's rising economic power in the chapters that follow and metaphorically by taking a look at the future hurtling toward us—and you'll discover real and unprecedented expansion of women's leadership. Change is looming.

We now have an entirely new playing field that tilts toward women's economic power and skills. For about a decade, business media with serious male gravitas have been broadcasting the upsurge in women's economic influence, beginning with an entire issue from *The Economist* in 2006 called "womenomics" that concluded women would drive global growth in the coming years. From *Fast Company* in 2011: "Women dominate the global marketplace." And in 2012, writing in *Time*, no less than President Bill Clinton distilled the essence: "Women rule."

What's shifted? The transformation began with women flexing their consumer muscle and lucrative purchasing power as CEO of the family amid a rising global middle class. Increasingly, however, the ripple effects of that economic impact are being bolstered and driven by women entrepreneurs.

Around the world, women are launching and growing their own businesses in never-before-seen numbers. In Western nations, it's typically because women are walking away from male-run companies, weary of being undervalued or overlooked, and/or seeking greater control over juggling work and childcare. Among younger well-educated women, startups are being launched to find purpose as well as profit in the burgeoning "fourth sector," or social entrepreneurships. In developing nations, it's usually because women have few other options to sustain themselves and families. Whichever the route, on every continent, women are now buying and selling new and different categories of products and services. They're creating new marketplaces, new classes of customers and significantly greater GDP for their regions and the world. And as we've all learned, money talks. Economic power has a way of leading to political clout.

Change happens by degree. Solutions surface locally. Opinions get shaped one person or two at a time. Focused on the day-to-day, struggling with challenges and hurdles, women entrepreneurs mostly aren't aware or thinking about the reach and influence of their *collective* power and what they might achieve by banding together. But that perception, too, is shifting as women's business groups set up international networks, enabled by social media and technology that allows cheap new ways to connect in far-flung locations (check out the "Resources" chapter in the back to see how far we've come in forging such helpful connections).

In the early 20th century, British and American suffragettes rewrote the rules of society forever by demanding that women have a voice and a vote in issues that affect their lives. It got messy and took a while. Men weren't comfortable seeing women at the ballot box. Similarly, a century later, women are demanding greater power in business and across society. This is also taking a while. Again, men are uneasy seeing women take charge. But more and more women are no longer waiting around for male approval or recognition. Instead, they're taking the reins, launching their own enterprises and leading on their own. Increasingly, women are gaining control of markets, influencing economic growth and investing in lives of purpose and satisfaction.

As the number of female-owned firms grows, it's become clear that women bring unique and characteristic strengths to running a business that are especially relevant in the current climate of more precious resources, ubiquitous technology and global brands and customers. Simultaneously, however, it's also clear that women have some characteristic gender weaknesses that often handicap their growth.

Those are my reasons for reporting and writing *Being Equal Doesn't Mean Being the Same:* first, to trumpet and describe women's special strengths in an era of absolutely unprecedented opportunities for women in order to encourage them to become leaders and launch businesses; and, second, to accurately pinpoint weaknesses women often demonstrate and must improve on in order to overcome threats to their success. I cover all this, including remedies for the weaknesses, in the pages that follow.

This is a hands-on guide with authentic, practical advice and dozens of real-life profiles for the ways women prefer to work, manage and create. Most business guides for women seem to dumb down male-oriented organizational blueprints or else lift up pink-tinged emotional exhortations for "empowerment." I've yet to see either of those approaches work well, mostly because they start from the default position of male success. By contrast, *Being Equal Doesn't Mean Being the Same* provides specific and contemporary female-friendly tools that will aid women to grow their kind of thriving businesses—which are categorically different than companies run by men. As you'll see in the chapters that follow, women are poised to dominate the global marketplace, especially if they're true to themselves.

Around the world, one business at a time, women's entrepreneurship is changing women's future. Lately, I've been eyeing that Kool-Aid one more time.

Joanna L. Krotz
New York City

PART I

LOOKING THROUGH A GENDER LENS

When a university recently invited me to give a keynote address at a conference, they asked what fee I expected. I wasn't quite sure how to respond. The best advice I got—from my husband—was: "Just tell them to give you 77% of whatever they're paying the male keynote speaker." That response resulted in a generous honorarium.

— *Ruth Rosen*

Professor Emerita of History, University of California, Davis
Author, "The World Split Open: How the Modern Women's
Movement Changed America"

1

Past: Rosie the Riveter Had Nothing on Madam C. J. Walker

The very idea of women taking charge of family income and decisions has been fueling controversy and political upheaval in America since at least the 1700s. When women are the breadwinners, society sees inadequate males, not thriving females. Throughout the eighteenth and nineteenth centuries, women who worked outside the home were considered déclassé or objects of pity, with an occasional pass for teachers. Typically, early workingwomen were compelled by economic necessity not choice. "…Women owned businesses in the face of prevailing social ideas that the unsavory world of business was unsuitable for women's gentle and frail natures," reports an online exhibit of the National Women's History Museum.

Choosing to work meant women were impoverished, abandoned, widowed or, very often, African American. Many free black women and former slaves leveraged skills they'd honed as domestics and on plantations to develop prosperous businesses. Let's also remember that at the time women were not permitted to own property or secure bank loans, which remained the sole province of men and husbands. That included intellectual property, such as patents.

Yet during those eras, untold numbers of women ran sprawling multi-enterprise farms and plantations, launched printing, manufacturing, ironworks, construction and import/export companies, created catering, millinery and dressmaking services, produced lucrative beauty and home remedy businesses, operated taverns and hotels, boarding houses and brothels, became bankers, inventors and even, in 1868, respected publisher of the Midwest's first weekly law journal. No doubt, most women who took in laundry or hired out as servants and clerks dreamed about being supported by an upstanding man. Nevertheless, the "female pariah" image portrayed in history books and popular culture could use some fresh paint. Hundreds of women started and operated flourishing businesses across the expanding nation. Most were married, some with husbands and children as partners or employees. Several defied obscurity by piloting companies into multimillion-dollar enterprises, despite property, tax and estate laws that often stripped their achievements.

Tantalizing clues trace lives of action and purpose. Business owners were also wives and mothers, philanthropists and social activists, churchgoers and community pillars. These were hardly women living on the margins, aching for respectability and social approval. But like so many trailblazing women in the arts and sciences, early women business leaders have been overlooked and under-recognized. We have no true notion of the numbers of pioneering women business owners nor the reach of their success simply because records and historic studies only document men. Detailed accounts of American mythmakers like Benjamin Franklin, Alexander Graham Bell, Andrew Carnegie, Thomas Edison, Henry Ford and dozens of other inventive entrepreneurial men abound. Where are the women?

Even today, with women the victor in extended battles for legal and financial rights, the "historical inattention paid to female entrepreneurs and their initiatives" remains scarcely improved, according to a 2012 issue devoted to women's entrepreneurship by scholarly journal *Entrepreneurship Theory and Practice*. For centuries of American history, from colonial times straight through the 1950s, when it comes to understanding or merely reporting on women in business, you can pretty much write your own fables. Which is why that early outcast stereotype lives on. "Women don't have a head for business" and "shouldn't bother their pretty little heads with money," right?

So let me tell you some stories about women we do know a bit about and who clearly deserve our homage. Their determination, success, smarts and creativity as well as their admirable ability to fight through obstacles holds lessons for us even now. The famous Fred Astaire – Ginger Rogers line comes to mind, about Rogers doing everything Astaire did, only backwards and in high heels.

Turning a problem into a solution

Surely the best known, relatively speaking, is Madam C. J. Walker, one of America's first self-made female millionaires and a legendary African American entrepreneur. In the early 1900s, she created Madam Walker's Wonderful Hair Grower, a hair conditioning and scalp product for black women that she manufactured, marketed and sold across the US, Central America and the Caribbean. "I got my start by giving myself a start," Walker said in later years, explaining her success.

Madam Walker's improbable rise and splendid life is celebrated in detail only because her great-great-granddaughter, A'Lelia Bundles, a network TV news producer, spent decades of holidays and weekends poring over family albums and account books, digging through attic trunks, visiting historical societies and courthouses and traveling to talk to anyone with past connections to her ancestor. In 1991, Bundles published a young adult book about Madam Walker and, in 1998, spearheaded a successful campaign to persuade the US Postal Service to include Walker in its Black Heritage commemorative stamp series. Eventually, Bundles wrote a full-scale best-selling biography, published in 2001, called *On Her Own Ground: The Life and Times of Madam C. J. Walker.*

Born Sarah Breedlove in 1867 in Delta, Louisiana, Walker was the first child in her family to be born into Emancipation. Her sharecropper parents farmed the same cotton plantation they'd worked as slaves. She had virtually no education and faced a bleak and miserable future as Reconstruction faded and the local Ku Klux Klan grew bold. "Orphaned at seven, married at 14, widowed at 20 with a two-year-old daughter, it seemed that Sarah Breedlove McWilliams was destined to remain a poor, uneducated washerwoman," writes Bundles.

Walker reshaped fate by moving with her young daughter to St. Louis in 1888, joining her older brothers who had set up as barbers. For years, she worked as a washerwoman and cook in St. Louis, living in boardinghouses and earning roughly $1.50 a day while saving enough for her daughter to go to city schools, a huge priority for Walker.

"Madam C. J. Walker was a resilient child who overcame a life of extreme difficulty," says Bundles, now in her sixties and living in Washington D.C. "That breaks some people and inspires others. It was a matter of survival for her and instead of being destroyed, made her stronger." At critical moments in St. Louis, when Walker was at the end of her rope, "she was fortunate to have been embraced by women of the African Methodist Episcopal Church," points out Bundles. "These were middle-class women who had a lifting-as-we-climb philosophy and Madam Walker benefited from their mentoring. Like most mothers, they wanted their daughters' lives to be better."

Walker's history began its turn with the new century. Like many women of the day who lacked hot and running water and washed their hair infrequently with caustic soap made from lye, Walker suffered a scalp condition called acacia. Her hair began falling out. As a result, in what has become an enduring theme among women entrepreneurs, Walker transformed her own problem into a solution. Her first step, perhaps unconsciously, was to become an apprentice in her chosen field, also a familiar pattern among women who start businesses.

Defying the odds

In 1905, Walker moved to Denver to work as a sales agent for a flourishing entrepreneur named Annie Turnbo Malone. A black woman from the Midwest, Malone had started a pioneering hair care business back in the late 1890s, well before Walker even thought about launching a business. By 1905, Malone's gentler, more healing shampoos and treatment products, called, wouldn't you know, "The Great Wonderful Hair Grower," were already well established.

Early details about her life remain sketchy. Born in 1869 in Metropolis, Illinois, also to former slaves, Malone, again like Walker, was orphaned young and sent to live with siblings. She is thought to have dropped out of high school owing to illness yet managed to acquire a fair knowledge of chemistry to go along with an early interest in hairdressing. Inspiration for the products she developed came from an aunt who was an herbal practitioner.

In 1902, sensing opportunities in the bustle around the 1904 World's Fair, Malone moved to St. Louis, which proved prescient. Business began to boom. Expanding at a time when African Americans and women—so two strikes against her—were forced to devise end runs around conventional marketplace practices, Malone systematically invented modern marketing and distribution methods, with Walker later following suit to more spectacular effect.

Banned from drugstores because of her race, Malone recruited agents to sell door-to-door and trained staff to travel widely, offering free treatments and demonstrations at churches and community centers. She used African American newspapers to advertise and polished her profile by hosting press conferences. Becoming an activist in national black politics, she cultivated social and business networks from church congregations and women's clubs around the country. She also shared her largesse. Malone founded a home for children, a beauty college in St. Louis, and donated generously to African American causes and colleges, including Howard University and Tuskegee Institute.

By 1915 or so, the Great Wonderful Hair Grower company employed about 200 people and Malone created opportunities and jobs for thousands more women through her school and franchised retail locations throughout North and South America, the Philippines and Africa. By the mid-1920s, before the 1929 market crash and other troubles eroded her empire, her worth was estimated at $14 million. Annie Turnbo Malone, daughter of escaped slaves, was the first citizen in St. Louis to tootle around in a Rolls-Royce.

Pushing the known limits

When Walker joined the company as a Denver sales agent in 1905, Malone was just beginning the national expansion she managed over the next five years. Walker had likely tried Malone's superior shampoo and restorative treatments. Just as likely, Walker would have embraced Annie Malone as an inspirational role model. Eyeing the future, and after marrying third husband, newspaperman Charles J. Walker, in 1906, Sarah Breedlove founded the Wonderful Hair Grower enterprise—bypassing Malone's "Great"—and also changed her name. Madam C. J. Walker emerged. For a while, the Walkers worked on the business together.

In the high-flying next decade, Walker grew the company into an international powerhouse, using selling and marketing methods that built on those of Malone. Along the way, Walker decided her husband didn't think big enough and they divorced: "When we began to make $10 a day," she said, "[Charles Walker] thought that was enough, thought I ought to be satisfied. But I was convinced that my hair preparation would fill a long-felt want. And when we found it impossible to agree, due to his narrowness of vision, I embarked on business for myself." Charles also was ditched for having an affair with one of Walker's agents.

After moving to New York, Madam Walker wisely retained her manufacturing business in Indianapolis, which was handy to shipping outlets. Astute about hiring, she put loyal and skilled supervisors in place to oversee production while she continued to travel, recruit agents and promote herself and her product. She networked continuously, well before anyone had a term for it.

The very model of a modern entrepreneur, Madam C. J. Walker worked on her business, not in it. There are critics, often among the black community, who respect Walker's journey but also view her as something of an upstart who swiped Malone's formula, copied her innovations and somehow achieved success she didn't rightfully earn. Imagine harnessing such arguments to dismiss the accomplishments of, say, Apple's Steve Jobs or McDonald's Ray Croc, who are universally admired for their creative and commercial acumen and who each built global companies on the foundation of other people's inventions. Both Jobs and Croc remained rather ruthless leaders who expertly curated what's-next options, unleashed the talent of freethinking individuals, scaled to mass market without sacrificing quality and, perhaps most importantly, served up the next must-have with style and affordability. Just as Madam Walker did.

Certainly, A'Lelia Bundles' biography and continuing advocacy has been the prime mover in resurrecting the Madam Walker story. But Malone also ended up penniless and embittered, dying in 1957 at age 87 in Chicago, the victim of mismanagement, a vindictive divorce, crippling tax troubles and a nasty employee lawsuit. By contrast, Walker died years earlier, in 1919, at the height of her fame and wealth. She was 51, feted by Harlem society and ensconced in both a New York City mansion and Villa Lewaro, the eye-popping palatial estate she built in Irvington, New York, not far from Hudson Valley neighbors Jay Gould and John D. Rockefeller. She also had recently visited the White House to protest then widespread national lynching. After her death, Walker's company continued to prosper for decades. For sheer storybook appeal, Malone can't come close. That has helped push Malone's groundbreaking contributions to African American culture and the black beauty and cosmetics business off the radar, except in St. Louis, where the annual Annie Turnbo Malone parade has been held for a century.

Responding to critics who accuse Walker of living in Malone's reflected glory, biographer A'Lelia Bundles offers a contextual, less gendered explanation, saying, "It's a little more complicated than people think." First, Malone and Walker weren't the only ones in the black beauty culture market. There were other competitors, notably Amanda Lyles Weir, who ran a successful salon and hair care business in the 1890s in St. Paul, Minnesota, and the younger Sarah Spencer Washington, born in 1889 in Virginia. "Madame Washington," as she preferred to be called, studied for a time at Columbia University and also became a millionaire. She launched a hairdressing and beauty training business in Atlantic City, New Jersey, in 1913, which grew into the Apex News & Hair Company. Ultimately, the enterprise sold dozens of creams, perfumes and cosmetics products and, in addition to the Atlantic City manufacturing base, included a New York office, beauty colleges in 12 states and some 30,000 sales agents around the world,.

In other words, Walker was hardly cannibalizing Malone's business. Demand was much greater than that. As for Malone's supposed secret formula, as Bundles reminds us, Madam Walker's brothers were barbers. Walker most likely first learned about the scalp conditioner from them. "Early 19th-century medical texts described a basic ointment made from sulfur that was used to cure skin diseases. Most pharmacists mixed it up," explains Bundles.

A brilliant marketer and hard-driving visionary, Walker always claimed her hair conditioner formula came as a spiritual revelation: "God answered my prayer, for one night I had a dream, and in that dream a big black man appeared to me and told me what to mix up for my hair. Some of the remedy was grown in Africa, but I sent for it, mixed it, put it on my scalp, and in a few weeks my hair was coming in faster than it had ever fallen out. I tried it on my friends; it helped them. I made up my mind I would begin to sell it."

Early tutoring in lifting-as-we-climb, nowadays called "paying it forward," infused Walker's business dealings and her life. "The critical divergence for Madam Walker, compared to Malone," explains Bundles, "was the point when Walker realized tremendous success selling products, as much as $10 a week, which was a bunch of money at the time." Walker figured out that if she could make the conditioner more inexpensively, she could sell lots more, which meant she could hire more agents and encourage other women to become independent. "That began to mean more to her than the product itself," says Bundles. "She enjoyed empowering other women and that was part of what spurred her on."

In "doing good while doing well," as the 21st century has it, Walker might qualify as the nation's prototype social entrepreneur. The flamboyant, self-made male magnates of her era, such as J. D. Rockefeller, J. P. Morgan and Cornelius Vanderbilt, only turned to good works and philanthropy in their later years, presumably when closer to meeting their Maker. First, they pursued fortune and power with relentless and single-minded focus. Even Andrew Carnegie, who died in 1919, the same year as Walker, didn't begin his breathtaking charitable works in earnest until he retired in 1901 at age 66. Only then did Carnegie preach his oft-invoked "gospel of wealth," which taxed the wealthy with a moral obligation to give back to the community. Walker, on the other hand, with neither the men's opportunities nor education—and perhaps that's the key—began her drive to help other women early on. "I am not satisfied in making money for myself," she said. "I endeavor to provide employment for hundreds of the women of my race."

Establishment validation for Madam C. J. Walker arrived when business historian and Harvard professor Nancy F. Koehn wrote up Walker's complex achievements and performance as a Harvard Business School case study. Most Fortune 500 CEOs would be thrilled to become such a model. The studies, of course, are famously used as course templates to teach MBA students at Harvard and other schools how to run a business. Koehn had stumbled on the Walker tale while looking into early 20th-century beauty businesses to research the rise of Estée Lauder for a book she published in 2001, *Brand New: How Entrepreneurs Earned Consumers' Trust from Wedgwood to Dell.*

Announcing the new case study back in June 2007 on *HBS Working Knowledge*, the faculty's online forum, Koehn posted, "I think much of Walker's business model and her animating vision is a product of the constraints that she faced.... In a market in which there weren't many realms where women could play, she found a way. She lived on a fascinating threshold between the end of slavery, the beginnings of the great migration northward by African Americans, and the opening up of consumer capitalism."

Spotlighting forgotten pioneers

Absent A'Lelia Bundles' biographical work, few of us, and certainly no Harvard professor, would ever have heard of Madam C. J. Walker. The lives of most early women entrepreneurs are barely noted, much less chronicled. During the 19th century, as the nation expanded west, through the beginning decades of the 20th, as America consolidated its economic might, hundreds of women coast-to-coast risked starting and steering businesses. But their stories surface only in sporadic bursts, typically unearthed by women's history buffs, bloggers and academics.

The pity of losing so many historic examples means we, the successors, can neither learn nor profit from early trials and errors. Specifics that do survive, however, fill in blanks for today's businesswomen. Surfacing those stories combats the widespread arguments that women entrepreneurs are handicapped by a lack of role models. Not exactly. There were lots of female forbears. We just don't hear enough about them.

As remedy, here's a fast-track sampling of women owners from colonial through modern times who particularly stand out. Puncturing another stereotype, most of these women had families as well as businesses.

In 1738, circumstances forced sixteen-year-old Eliza Lucas Pinckney to assume control of her well-to-do British family's three plantations in the South Carolina Lowcountry, including all plantings, slaves, livestock and the bustling big household. Against all odds, the teen thrived, becoming a serious student of botany. She began experimenting with planting indigo. Prized for its blue dye and widely cultivated in Asia, indigo had never before been grown in North America. It took Pinckney three painstaking years to successfully extract any dye, but her first 17-pound export to England "almost single-handedly boosted the economy in South Carolina," according to Stephen and Maxi Farnsworth, who write a Palmetto State blog. Pinckney's major cash crop made South Carolina the wealthiest of the colonies.

As the American Revolution loomed, the honor—and the risk, since the British deemed it treasonable—of producing the first printed copies of the Declaration of Independence with all the signers went to Mary Katherine Goddard, America's first woman publisher. Owner of the *Maryland Journal,* Baltimore's first newspaper, Goddard was also first to offer use of her presses when the Continental Congress legislated widespread distribution of the Declaration in January 1777.

During the Civil War era, former slave Elizabeth Keckley was the earliest fashion designer to achieve celebrity status by dressing the First Lady. A talented seamstress, Keckley rose out of a tradition of early black dress designers, many of them slaves, who were seamstresses for wealthy women. Keckley managed to save enough to buy her and her son's freedom for $1,200, and then moved from St. Louis to Washington D.C. in 1860 to join the capital's growing middle-class black community. She set up a dressmaking business and elite clients followed, including Varina Davis, wife of Jefferson Davis, and Mary Anna Custis Lee, wife of Robert E. Lee. Soon, Keckley was hired to personally dress First Lady Mary Todd Lincoln, a widely known fashionista of her day. After traveling with the First Lady, becoming close to her and privy to Lincoln family secrets, the dressmaker published "a tell-all book about the first family in 1868," according to writer KeriLynn Engel, who maintains a well-researched "Amazing Women in History" blog. Keckley plummeted from favor faster than a comet, and died poor and unknown in 1907.

About the same time, Myra Colby Bradwell, born in 1831 to Vermont abolitionists, was moving around the Midwest as a schoolteacher. Just before the Civil War was declared, she settled in Chicago, with husband, James, who was established as an Illinois circuit court judge and state legislator. In 1868, Bradwell founded the *Chicago Legal News*, serving as both editor and business manager for the region's first weekly law journal. She turned the publication into a must-read for the local legal profession while also making sure to cover news of women's rights and the growing suffragette movement. Her husband's legal influence led to a special exemption for Bradwell to operate the business despite a state law that banned married women from entering into contracts. In 1869, after passing the state exam with honors, Bradwell was still refused admission to the Illinois bar because she was a woman. Despite her appeals, that ban held firm for nearly a quarter-century, until she was finally admitted in 1892.

If cities east of the Mississippi set tough barriers for 19th century businesswomen, such restrictions looked nearly progressive compared to society in the west. Born in Germany in 1829, Amelia Dannenberg immigrated with husband Joseph to San Francisco. Women in business weren't tolerated, with teachers often the only exception. Being Jewish, Amelia Dannenberg had additional hurdles. Nevertheless, working with her husband, in the 1850s, she began importing and manufacturing infants' and children's clothing and furnishings, winning an award for quality from a trade fair in 1869. In the 1870s, Dannenberg expanded to men and women's clothing.

As testament to her huge success, and perhaps foreshadowing the rise of today's "wellness" sector dominated by women entrepreneurs, most of us have heard of Lydia E. Pinkham and her "tonics" for women that relieve menstrual and menopausal symptoms. That legacy is largely owed to Pinkham's aggressively canny marketing and her early emphasis on health education. She boosted the old-style patent medicine, called "Vegetable Compound," into a corporate phenomenon that's still sold under her name today, though the formula has changed. Born into a Massachusetts Quaker family in 1819, Pinkham was an early abolitionist and feminist. Like many of her day, she was pushed into brewing home remedies because doctors were expensive and generally clueless when it came to "female complaints." Pinkham's recipe proved popular and, supposedly, when her husband fell on hard times, one of her sons suggested going into full-scale business in 1875. The rest is history. Pinkham was the first marketer to run ads urging women to write with questions. Every such letter received a personal response, including medical news, advice and, naturally, suggestions for using her product.

In 1896, as the nineteenth century wound down and the Klondike Gold Rush ramped up, serial entrepreneur Belinda Mulrooney was dubbed "the richest woman in the Klondike." She made a fast fortune as some 100,000 prospectors raced to the Klondike region in the Yukon territories of northwestern Canada to find gold, though she never staked so much as a single claim. After an ice cream parlor she launched in San Francisco burned to the ground, Mulrooney took a turn as a steamship stewardess on routes running from California to Alaska. When gold was discovered, first in Juneau, instead of becoming a prospector, she used $5,000 in savings to buy things like silk underwear, hot water bottles and bolts of cloth. She traveled to the Klondike and sold the supplies for six times what she paid. Leveraging her wealth and, like any rising entrepreneur, diversifying her assets, Mulrooney went on to buy and sell mining claims and build restaurants, roadhouses, hotels and mansions. By the time of her death in Seattle in 1967, Brenda Mulrooney had earned and lost several fortunes, married and divorced multiple husbands, and bequeathed as many larger-than-life yarns as the original Forty-Niners.

Modern, motivated and memorable

Dozens more stories and hundreds more women leaders are shrouded by the years when women's feats went unnoticed. As we move into the

20th century, pioneers don't suddenly emerge. The women simply become more recognizable.

There's Martha Matilda Harper, another turn-of-the-century social entrepreneur who opened doors to Rochester, New York's first public hair salon. She offered independence to women by only hiring former servants. Harper hung out with the Susan B. Anthony social reformer crowd and, oh yes, also devised an entirely new business model known as retail franchising, eventually overseeing more than 500 franchised Harper shops worldwide. Olive Ann Beech, a leader in aviation, cofounded Beech Aircraft in Wichita, Kansas, in 1932, with her husband Walter. When he could no longer run the company, she did, spearheading expansion and joining the Raytheon Board when the companies merged.

Modern entrepreneurial stars include the inimitable Estée Lauder, catalog royalty Lillian Vernon, Debbi Fields and her break-the-mold cookies, the extraordinary Lucille Ball, who introduced both technical and cultural innovations into TV comedy and became the first woman to run a Hollywood studio. Let's also offer a nod to the late Muriel Siebert, the first woman among nearly 1,400 men to own a seat on the New York Stock Exchange.

In fact, past role models are everywhere, ready to lend us lessons and encouragement. We simply need to do a little digging.

Why can't a woman be paid like a man?

Historic restrictions on women workers and business leaders eased as the 20th century gained traction, as we all know, especially in the tumultuous 1960s and '70s. Change has been unmistakable. We have women on the Supreme Court, women astronauts and surgeons, female Presidential candidates, women CEOs in the Fortune 500—well, all 23 of them, anyway—and a generation of rising female technology wizards, as you'll learn in chapters that follow. Women in the US today also outstrip men in educational achievement, long accounting for more undergraduate degrees, and, since 2010, earning more doctoral degrees than men. Never mind that studies show women face a stiffer wage penalty than men when rising costs push students to drop out of college to look for work. That means women opt to stay in school even as their loans and interest payments balloon, making crippling student debt a particular woman's issue. Still, all those degrees have been a nifty woman's first. The firsts go on and on, and undoubtedly will keep piling up for decades to come.

The problem is that the pace of change remains glacial. Despite more than a century of social evolution and political activism, women never seem to reach parity. Women continue to earn less than men in all ten fields monitored by the US Bureau of Labor Statistics, as of July 2015, including management, professional, service and farming sectors. The gap, on average, runs about 80 cents earned by women for every dollar paid to men, with women's pay considerably lower in certain sectors, such as sales. Women of color fare even worse. African American women earn only 64 cents and Hispanic women a scant 54 cents to a white male's dollar.

Yet in September 2014, the Republican-led Congress failed to pass the Paycheck Fairness Act requiring employers to pay women the same as men for the same jobs—*for the fourth time.* Six months later, in March 2015, Sen. Barbara Mikulski (D - MD) and Rep. Rosa DeLauro (D - Conn) yet again introduced the legislation. It was referred to a House committee for "study." GovTrack.us, the US Congress tracking group, rates the bill a 1% chance of being enacted.

Admittedly, little about this issue is easy. Many entwined threads weave the complicated tapestry of women's entrance into business and executive suites, including the demands of family and childcare, deep-rooted social conventions, women's comfort levels and sense of identity, male legislative and economic power and all the other stuff. But when you pull the root thread of that tapestry, the real culprit for the never-ending gender pay gap turns out to be labor policies established during World War II, which unintentionally sanctioned treating women as second-class citizens. Over time, women's lower status became entrenched and institutionalized.

It began with a federal directive designed to do just the opposite. The National War Labor Board, made up of representatives from labor, government and management, was formed in January 1942 to smooth any industry problems that might slow war production. Women were streaming onto factory floors to replace men who had been called up to serve. By the mid-1940s, the workforce consisted of 45% women, up from 24% in the century's early years. Images of patriotic "We Can Do It" Rosie the Riveters flooded wartime culture, but those women earned only about 60% of what men did for the same jobs.

In response, and bowing to union concerns that paying women lower wages would permanently undercut salaries for returning men, in November of that year, the NWLB came up with a mandate that reverberates to this day: "Equal pay for equal work" for women workers who replaced men. However, then came a kicker of a caveat. Presumably playing to the tenor of the times and trying to be equitable, the Board stipulated an exception:

> Where the plant management, in order to meet the necessity of replacing men by women, has rearranged or lightened the job, perhaps with the employment of helpers to do heavy lifting or the like, a study of job content and job evaluation should afford the basis for setting "proportionate rates for proportionate work."

Such "study" and subsequent judgments were left to employer discretion. From the get-go, employers had an unregulated loophole that allowed them to create lower-paying and de facto "female tracks." Over time, that loophole solidified into institutionalized justification for women's unequal pay.

After the war, federal and civilian policies permitted employers to fire women to ensure that returning veterans had jobs to support their families.

With that dispensation, many companies reinstated prewar policies and refused to hire women, whether out of flag-waving, discomfort or both. Companies that continued to hire women just reclassified jobs, dropped the pay permanently and never looked back.

Hardly feeling Rosie

Two decades after Rosie the Riveter flexed her muscles, women accounted for 37% of the workforce and still earned only 59 cents to every male dollar. By then, "proportionate" terminology had segued into "comparable pay for comparable work"—and that's been the slippery slope down which equal pay has slid ever since. What exactly is "comparable work"? No one seems to know. Later legislation certainly moved in the right direction but passed only as compromise measures. That includes the 1963 Equal Pay Act (actually only an amendment to another labor bill because the business community protested supposed new costs, like women's rest rooms) and the 1964 Civil Rights Act, which banned sex discrimination. Since women's large-scale entry into the workforce in the 1940s, and after 75 years of progress, only 20 more cents, on average, has been added to that "comparable pay" for women, or 80 cents to the male dollar. In fact, we seem to have hit the wall: That 80-cent ceiling has been in place since 2009 or so.

One of the most popular explanations for the pay gap, put forward by opponents every time they vote down the Paycheck Fairness Act, is that women simply work in lower-paying fields, such as social work and education. "There's a disparity not because female engineers are making less than male engineers at the same company with comparable experience," announced the Republican National Committee, justifying their fourth vote to block the bill. "The disparity exists because a female social worker makes less than a male engineer." But the gender pay gap gets widest, according to Harvard labor economist Claudia Goldin, in some of the highest-paying fields. Goldin has found that female financial specialists earn 66% of what male counterparts do. For female doctors, it's 71%, and notches up to 82% for female lawyers and judges. The gender pay gap is hardly a chimera of women's "softer" work. Over time, whenever a field becomes female-dominated, say nursing or teaching or that social work example, salary levels typically drop. That industry turns into a "girl ghetto," like the World War II "female" jobs.

At that point, it's not only women who are being shortchanged. "A persistent wage gap not only cheats women and their families out of the earnings they deserve, but artificially constrains the purchasing power of women, and therefore hampers the American economy as a whole," reports a recent Joint Economic Committee Congressional report, called "Invest in Women, Invest in America."

Following the money

The pay gap is both metric and proxy to represent women's lack of advancement—a swift formula that lets us do the math. Distilling the range of intangibles into the 80-cents-to-the-dollar ratio is a simpler way to deal with the kaleidoscope of attitudes and issues raised by gender inequality. Some industries, of course, pay women very well. Numbers of individual women are commanding multimillion-dollar paychecks. But the pervasive attitudes and climate that women face in today's workplaces go much deeper than comparing the zeros in any salary.

In a 2011 study, nonprofit researcher Catalyst, which has tracked women in business since 1962, took on the received wisdom that women don't advance on the job because "women don't ask." That is, women lack confidence and ambition. Supposedly, those "feminine" failings, stubbornly unacknowledged by women advocates, are the dirty little secret to explain why progress has stalled. This oft-told narrative recognizes that the country's history of sex discrimination led women to grow up culturally and politically challenged (read: not like men). As a result, it's not women's fault. Yet by now, according to this reasoning, prejudices have fallen away and opportunity is rife. So women are simply failing to step up to the big boy chairs—as they must do to reach the top. Bottom line, it's a girl problem.

But the actual dilemma is that such rationales, dished out by politicians, academics, corporate diversity officers and so on, turn out to be a shibboleth. In a study called, "The Myth of the Ideal Worker: Does Doing All the Right Things Really Get Women Ahead?" Catalyst looked at how women fared when they adopted all the universally accepted strategies for building a career. That includes: "Let your boss know you're ready for that challenging assignment. Make your career ambitions and willingness to put in the requisite time and effort clear. Don't just build a relationship with your boss; make sure to build one with your boss' boss as well."

Catalyst found that "the strategies adopted by high-potential women had little bearing on the rate at which they advanced to leadership. Conversely, men who applied the most proactive career strategies advanced further than other men." In sussing out the results, Catalyst concluded that women were paid only for proven performance—which meant they had to remain in lower-paying positions and wait to be promoted, because if they jumped to new jobs, employers couldn't be sure of their abilities. "Women who changed jobs two or more times post-MBA earned $53,472 less than women who rose through the ranks at their first job," reported Catalyst. Men, however, were paid for potential: "…Men who had moved on from their first post-MBA job earned $13,743 more than those who stayed with their first employer."

"This study busts the myth that 'women don't ask,'" said Ilene Lange, when the findings were released and then CEO at Catalyst. "In fact, they do! But it doesn't get them very far. Men, by contrast, don't have to ask. What's wrong with this picture?"

Indicators that keep lagging

Other widespread arguments contend that slowly and inexorably women on the job are being treated the same as men. So it's only a matter of time and generations, goes this thinking, until gender bias withers away altogether. But that also turns out to be myth, even among groups noted for their objectivity.

In 2012, researchers at Yale University asked 127 physicists, chemists and biologists at six major research institutions to evaluate identical resumes of two imaginary applicants. The only difference in the resumes was male and female names. The upshot? The male candidate consistently scored higher on several criteria, including competency. He was more likely to get the job and, if the woman was hired, her salary was fixed at almost $4,000 less than the male received. Most tellingly, and sadly, women scientists were as equally biased as the men. Microbiology professor Jo Handelsman, a science education expert and, currently, associate director at the White House Office of Science and Technology Policy, had developed the study to test her observations in the field. When the results were published in the *Proceedings of the National Academy of Sciences,* she said, "Whenever I give a talk that mentions past findings of implicit gender bias in hiring, inevitably a scientist will say that can't happen in our labs because we are trained to be objective. I had hoped that they were right."

But that bias looks genteel compared to the rough and tumble environment outside academia, especially throughout Silicon Valley. Within the young, male-dominated technology industries—STEM for short, or science, technology, engineering and mathematics—it seems still to be the 1960s with workdays lifted straight out of the *Mad Men* TV series, only now they smoke e-cigarettes. Touted as our country's most advanced and forward-looking industry, tech companies and their institutions carry on with blatant sexual discrimination in hiring, promotion and workplace practices, even extending to sexual harassment.

Women now occupy nearly half the jobs in the country, but hold less than a quarter of STEM positions, according to the US Commerce Department. One bright note is that women with STEM jobs earn 33% more than women with comparable positions in other industries. But then, they're putting up with more. Consider it combat pay.

Early in 2014, women at a series of well-regarded Silicon Valley companies alleged instances of unsettling sexism. When other women in the industry called for investigation into the accusations, the tech blogosphere erupted in virulent anti-female invective. Responding to the hostile atmosphere, without coming down on whether or not the original allegations were true, nine women programmers and developers put up a blog page in May 2014 called "AboutFeminism.me" to ask for change, call the industry to account and accept the fact that girls not only can, but want to code.

Sabrina Majeed, a product design manager at BuzzFeed, says the posting grew out of a conversation initiated by colleague Divya Manian, then at Adobe and now at Apple, "who reached out to me and the seven other women to start the conversation. Originally, we were going to write a series of blog posts individually. But after thinking about it, we thought it would have a stronger presence and reach if we collectively wrote something together."

The post describes in shocking detail what women programmers experience on the job:

- We've been harassed on mailing lists and called "whore"/"cunt" without any action being taken against aggressors.

- We get asked about our relationships at interviews, and we each have tales of being groped at public events. We've been put in the uncomfortable situation of having men attempt to turn business meetings into dates....

- We're constantly asked "if you write any code" when speaking about technical topics and giving technical presentations, despite just having given a talk on writing code. We've been harassed at these same conferences in person and online about our gender, looks and technical expertise.

- We get asked if we're the event planner or executive assistant on a regular basis.

- We regularly receive creepy, rapey e-mails where men describe what a perfect wife we would be and exactly how we should expect to be subjugated. Sometimes there are angry emails that threaten us to leave the industry, because "it doesn't need anymore c**ts ruining it."

- We have watched companies say that diversity is of highest importance and have invited us to advise them. After we donate much of our time, they change nothing, do nothing, and now wear speaking to us as a badge of honor. Stating, "We tried!"

- We've experienced a staggering earnings gap in our field, which, being freelance and project-based makes it challenging to ascribe blame. We've been told repeatedly that accomplishments were due to our gender and our role as the "token woman."

Promises, promises

In 2012, Ellen Pao, formerly a junior partner, brought a sex discrimination lawsuit against Kleiner Perkins Caulfield & Byers, the prestigious Silicon Valley venture capital firm. Three years later, when the suit finally wound up before a jury, the courtroom dripped daily and salacious details about office affairs, women partners excluded from client meetings, male partners soliciting women subordinates and more, much to the Valley's consternation. Pao lost her case on all counts and was directed to pay Kleiner Perkins's legal costs of more than $275,000. But she seems to have won the war of perception, and timing is everything.

Two other sex discrimination suits have since been filed, one by a former engineer suing Facebook and the other a class action suit by a former female software engineer against Twitter. All the negative media scrutiny of its tone-deaf culture—Twitter actually hosted a "frat party" for employees midway through the lawsuit—has stung the industry and forced reevaluation. Lately, Silicon Valley kingmakers have tried to project a more equitable and diverse profile. But so far, few are backing up the talk with any serious walk.

Tech giants Google and Facebook released their first-ever workforce diversity reports in 2014. At Facebook, despite COO Sheryl Sandberg's Lean In advocacy for women in the workplace, only 30% of its 7,000-plus workforce was female, and the male workers were also overwhelmingly white. Facebook promised to up its game but those numbers haven't budged in 2015. Women still account for about 30% of Facebook staffers despite the company increasing its headcount by a whopping 59%. Google likewise released its first workforce diversity figures in 2014, and also reported 30% women overall, and, yes, further pledged to do better. In 2015, women still number only about a third of the company. At Twitter, about 70% of employees are men (seeing a pattern here?), although that rises to 90% male for significant technology teams. Apple and Intel, testing which way the wind is blowing, have done a bit better, with women numbering more than four out of 10 of Intel's new hires in 2015, up from about three out of 10 in 2014, and Apple boosting its women hires by 65% worldwide, to 11,000.

It takes more than reshuffling numbers to generate change, though. As we've seen, gender bias is subtle and endemic and simply hiring more females doesn't change minds or hearts or promotions. Although nearly three-quarters of the women working in technology say they're "loving their work," women leave the industry at an astounding 52% rate. That's double the rate at which men quit. Most walk away just as they hit mid-level careers—that is, when their talent is most valuable to employers and replacements are most costly. "If current trends continue, by 2018 the industry will only be able to fill half of its available jobs with candidates holding computer science bachelor's degrees from US universities," reports the Center for Talent Innovation, a New York-based think tank.

Preparing to launch

Is it any wonder so many professional women are jumping off corporate ladders and opting out of male-run companies to assume the reins of their time, lives, families and futures?

Instead, like Madam Walker, you might do better in getting started by giving yourself a start. These days, you'll find yourself in excellent company.

2

Present: How Women Entrepreneurs Walk and Talk

In the late 1990s, Lori Gold Patterson was living with her family in Urbana, Illinois, while working for a major foodservice packaging company in Chicago, some 140 miles away. Unusual for a woman at that time, she had a mechanical engineering degree as well as experience working as a systems consultant for Andersen Consulting and head of a product development team at Caterpillar. Patterson had been tapped by the Chicago-based packaging company for a new position as internal change manager, charged with re-engineering processes, bolstering CRM or customer relationship software and more—her dream job. "I was managing three different high-profile projects out of Highland Park, gone from home five days a week and my two-year-old was falling to pieces," she says, looking back. "I was very driven and it was a huge opportunity to do great work, but taking care of the family didn't really exist there."

"One Monday," remembers Patterson, "I was dressed and ready to head out to the car when I realized I forgot something. I kicked off my high-heeled shoes and ran to get it. When I returned, I found my two-year-old had hidden my shoes. I couldn't decide whether he had done it purposely or playfully. Later that week, when I went to pick him up at my mother-in-law's, she gave me some slippers to put on. He laid his body across my feet and started screaming." Patterson gave three months' notice and left, mid-project. It was 1997.

"Coming out of corporate life was a very hard thing," says Patterson today, age 50. "I didn't know any women who had careers after they had chosen to come out." She also didn't know many women of her generation with engineering credentials. "I thought I'd stay at home and I wasn't sure what to do." She began thinking of starting a business. Several lunches later, after talking to women in similar positions, Patterson "recognized that I wasn't the only one doing something so crazy." Soon, her brother left his job in New York as a corporate programmer to return to Urbana, where they'd both grown up. The two founded Pixo, a technology services provider for programming, Web and mobile application development. During its first decade, Pixo also had 11 sweat equity investors while Patterson consciously kept the company small and focused. Recently, she bought out the other owners and beefed up staff to 30. In the past few years, the firm has been expanding rapidly. Her wailing toddler is working on his college degree.

Redefining career and family

Starting a business is killer hard and frequently all-consuming. Yet it's been attracting women at all levels. Far from being Plan B for women who can't make it or a part-time stopgap for stalled careers, women most often start enterprises nowadays because, in a wide range of circumstances, it's so plainly the better option. "The perception of a lot of women is, 'I can't have the flexibility I need in a corporate environment or in another kind of organization, but I can do it if I'm the one setting my hours and my flexibility,'" explains Jamie Ladge, a management professor at Northeastern University, whose research focuses on women's careers and work-life integration. When you're the boss, with or without employees, you have the satisfaction, the privilege and sometimes the indulgence of making your own compromises. No one chooses for you. That freedom can be exhilarating for women–or, uhmm, "liberating." Often, it starts with having a baby.

Some twenty years ago, Samuella Becker had what she calls her "aha moment" and founded her home-based New York public relations agency, TigressPR. "I was a mother and trying to do it all. I had a prestigious position as director of corporate relations for a Fortune 500 company," she remembers. "Sometimes you worked almost all night because of covering different time zones, like London or the West Coast. Then everything you did was changed the next day anyway. It was like a merry-go-round."

At one point, says Becker, "I went three weeks without seeing my son awake because of the workload. I remember mentioning that to my boss and she said, 'You shouldn't have had children.' It was one of those game-changer moments where I thought, you know what, I think I can change this."

Becker walked out, becoming an independent PR consultant, and surprise, surprise, agencies that required unbearable hours with endless rounds of edited work for fulltime staffs were happy to hire an outside contractor from 10 am to 3 pm. Today, Becker still runs her thriving business from home and manages a diversified client roster, including a global art studio greeting card company, lawyers, authors and skincare salons and spas. Along the way, she earned an MBA, an unusual move for a PR consultant, because she wanted a credible handle to represent corporate clients. Leveraging her skills, she had her degree partly subsidized by taking on the job of communications director for Pace University's entrepreneurship program for a few years. "I always said yes to any potential client and that was the big difference in my career," explains Becker.

Similar stories are legion among women owners.

Change but far from enough

Let's be clear. The current American workplace is an entirely different playing field compared to mid-20th century. Better educated and skilled, shaped by a half-century of advances and freedoms, women today have their pick of unparalleled options. No matter that men still relinquish power only reluctantly. Starting with the 1940s wartime reformation, once women integrate any working ranks—in construction, sports, politics, finances, unions, symphony orchestras, the presidential cabinet and on and on—the genie never goes back into the bottle.

Ongoing challenges do not belie the dramatic inroads women have made across the business landscape. Likewise, urging women to start their own enterprises has nothing whatsoever to do with whether selected women can perform as leaders of global conglomerates or commanders of corner offices.

Of course they can. But, same as most men, the majority of women have neither the chops nor the drive to ascend to Fortune 1000 CEOs (though we know women have a much lesser shot at it). It's precisely *because* of all the choices women fought for and secured, not despite them, that so many women now are questioning how best to expend their well-honed talents, energy, passions and abilities. Why keep struggling for pay and parity within rigid corporate precincts when the lines keep wavering, the goalposts keep moving and the battle is never won?

It might just come down to time and money. How much of each is important to you? How much of each are you willing to sacrifice? How well can you adjust to the corporate sandbox, which hands men the shovels while women get the buckets? How much frustration and lack of recognition can you swallow? "The advice to women who can't seem to succeed in the corporate worlds in which they exist should be to walk away and start your own company," recommends Holly Lynch, an angel investor in women-led companies and founder of 85-Percent, a New York City women-focused marketing consultancy named for the percentage of consumer products purchased by women.

We each have only the one life, typically the one family and, usually, only a couple of decades or so to build a career, though that window is widening with longevity and advances in technology. In many respects, women have a much broader continuum for work and life choices than men, with many more potential roles and transitions. So what's worth doing? With patently difficult paths for women in the corporate arena, and having "leaned in" so long and so hard that thousands of women professionals are bent double, women are increasingly deciding to run their own shows.

What does today's entrepreneur look like?

Even so, all these women starting businesses are neither considered nor popularly labeled "entrepreneurs." Instead, images of the entrepreneur still consistently call up the take-no-prisoner, egocentric, gung-ho risk-taker—the rebellious geek in the garage like Steve Jobs or Bill Gates, or, lately, the cool dude in the startup incubator, like Instagram cofounder Kevin Systrom. "The dominant narrative and optic about entrepreneurship is male," explains Susan Duffy, executive director of the Center for Women's Entrepreneurial Leadership at Babson College. But that pinup of the Boy Wonder Billionaire, feted by Wall Street and romanced by business news media, is bogus as a representative portrait.

"Entrepreneurship is an entire continuum of venture creation and the vast majority of entrepreneurs in the country run businesses that generate less than $1 million in revenue," says Duffy. Only about 6% of men-owned firms and less than 2% of women-owned firms have more than $1 million in revenue, she points out. "We have to remember that the story of entrepreneurship is very broad and people do it a lot of different ways."

Whether Millennial, Gen X or Boomer, the face of the 21st century entrepreneur is as likely to be a woman as a man, according to annual studies from the US Census Bureau and American Express OPEN. In fact, a snapshot study, "State of the Startup," from accounting software company Sage in May 2015 found that women led nearly six out of 10 (57%) of the startups and businesses in operation less than five years. Entrepreneurial is exactly what characterizes all those women.

Startup hopefuls are hardly college dropouts or newbie grads, either. The average age of entrepreneurs in the US has been climbing, owing to the ease of entry afforded by technology, longer and healthier lives and the ongoing effects of the economy, with older workers being phased out and fewer well-paying jobs to be found. Most people start businesses at ages 35 – 45. But entrepreneurs ages 55 – 64 have multiplied in the past few years and now account for more than a quarter (26%) of all new businesses, up from only 15% in 1996, according to the Kauffman Foundation, the private foundation that focuses on entrepreneurship. Perhaps surprisingly, high-tech startups are twice as likely to be founded by someone older than age 50 as opposed to someone younger than age 25. In addition, within the older group, more women than men have taken steps to start a business, according to a Babson study.

Doing the math on women-led businesses

It turns out that when Lori Patterson began thinking about launching her technology services business in 1997, she was in excellent company. That year marked the beginning of a spectacular surge in women-led startups, which climbed at a fantastic clip through 2008 and continues today, though at a slower rate. Women startups in the US jumped a whopping 54% from 1997 – 2014, or 1.5 times the national average. Today, there are almost 10 million women-owned businesses, up from about 8 million in 2007, which generate $1.6 trillion in total sales receipts (all payments to the business) and employ close to 9 million people, according to the National Women's Business Council, the federal advisory council. That's close to four out of 10 of all US firms (36%). Women-owned businesses also are entering the middle market at five times the rate of all active businesses, a nearly 24% increase compared to only 4% for all mid-sized

Often dubbed "the Big Bang of women's entrepreneurship," H.R. 5050 cleared the runway for women business owners. After that, a number of economic, social and technological influences revved the takeoff.

In 1990, as the country went into recession, women were pushed into self-employment more than men. While the widespread downturn collapsed careers for thousands of male and female middle managers, women always have a harder time landing jobs when times are tough and skilled men are available. Many professional women began offering freelance white-collar services, such as consulting, event planning, catering, graphic design, coaching, marketing, accounting and more. Affordable home computers dropped the barriers to business entry and, a few years later, the dot-com revolution minted bushels of money for outsourced and independent contractors who provided entirely new sets of skills, markets and models. The job market was redefined. Middle manager positions never really returned.

Instead, "disintermediation," which dispensed with middlemen, summed up the era's go-to business model, allowing producers to sell directly to customers. No brokers or wholesalers or mid-level supervisors needed. Anyone with a phone and a desktop could effectively work from home without staff or infrastructure. Women could earn income without brushing up their resumes.

Nearly a decade later, the dark years of the Great Recession pushed a new wave of unemployed into entrepreneurship, both men and women. Many of those solopreneurs settled into the jobless New Normal, especially Gen Y and women, who continue to be the first fired and last hired in many industries. Although job data shows more women then men working post-recession, the statistics ignore just how low-paid, low status and dead-end most of those jobs have become. Many men simply wouldn't sign on or settle for these positions. Women often do and must. But for everyone entrepreneurially minded, perhaps the sole upside to the Great Recession has been the corporate embrace of Free Agent Nation, cheap cloud computing that enables real-time remote mobile work and, of course, virtual collaborations.

As a result, women who need flexible schedules because of families and kids, as well as independent-minded younger women, have been able to cut 9 - 5 corporate tethers more easily. The so-called "1099 Economy" now rules, named for the income tax form employers file for outsourced contractors and independent vendors.

Outside the workplace, Boomer women, who tended to marry and have babies later in life than previous generations, faced other challenges. Of course, Boomers were also the first generation of women to earn college degrees on a large scale and build full-sized professional careers. As the new century got underway, a critical mass of Boomer women were therefore reaching middle-management levels. "Having it all"—the mantra of the high-achieving Superwoman to simultaneously be perfect mother, perfect professional performer and perfect wife—provoked hot and controversial debate. Scrambling to manage work and family demands, dubbed "the juggler generation," women experienced stress levels that zoomed off the charts. Pretty soon, the notion of launching your own business and being the producer of your own show looked like a high-IQ way of stepping off the treadmill while still earning income and keeping your hand in the game.

The push-pull of work and family hasn't eased all that much but the need for "work-life balance" has achieved at least lip-service currency in corporate life. Among Millennials, men as much as women, career is something that embraces time for family and other interests. As one 52-year-old mom puts it, only half-joking, "The next generation is going to live to be 100 years old with many, many years for work. I asked my teenage son if he'd be willing to take ten years off his career to raise kids. The answer, 'Yes, absolutely.'"

All in all, starting a business has blossomed into a solution that suits millions of women like never before. "For the first time, we're seeing a critical mass of women in the marketplace who have been successful in the corporate arena for 20 to 35 years," says Carla Harris, a prominent Morgan Stanley investment banker and current chair of the National Women's Business Council, which advises Congress and the White House on women's entrepreneurship. "These women are looking for ways to extend the professional runway into entrepreneurship and becoming investors. Women now have functional expertise across the business spectrum, including in marketing, operating and financial exposure. They're eligible for board service and have a wealth of knowledge and experiences."

Professional women nowadays are uniquely positioned. They are leveraging unprecedented resources and skills, innovative markets and models, cheap and efficient tech tools as well as untold legions of online experts and communities that can be tapped everywhere at any time. Women with less education and fewer skills surely have a harder time. But even so, a growing number of marketers and private and public partners have joined forces to help lift and support women's opportunities in business startups.

What women owners bring to the table

Unlike male counterparts, most women prefer to launch businesses that generate modest revenue, provide professional satisfaction and operate under the radar. Typically, women owners don't seem to scale up or go for the brass ring. Three primary reasons account for why women-owned businesses are starting so fast but tend to have lower survival rates, growth rates and profits than male-owned firms.

First, for women who are established with marketable skills and some financial safety net, like Samuella Becker and Lori Patterson were, starting a business begins as a lifestyle choice. After leaving traditional jobs to gain flexibility, a smaller enterprise may be exactly right-sized for many women to satisfy income and professional needs. That doesn't always mean taking care of family, either. For example, in 1998, Sheryl Keese launched Twisted Limb Paperworks, at the time a pioneering eco-friendly papermaking business based in Bloomington, Indiana. "As one of the first, one-hundred-percent recycled invitation companies in the country, I had the opportunity to really grow if I wanted to. But work/life balance was extremely important to me and my husband," says Keese, adding that the couple don't have children. The right-sized firm provided an outlet for her creativity and passions while offering the freedom to travel and explore hobbies. "I thoroughly enjoyed the business for 15 years," says Keese, "and then sold it to an employee to move on to other things."

Second, research shows women frequently launch as solo founders. "That works against them," says Susan Duffy at Babson. "Men are more likely to partner up and companies started by teams have much more potential to get funding and to grow for a number of reasons." The key factor is the team's diversity of assets, including skillsets, emotional and social capital and bootstrap money from friends and family. Women would do better by partnering with other founders. Even so, when women are ready to scale up, they often cannot secure the funding they need. More than not, venture capitalists still give funds to entrepreneurs who look and sound like they do—that is, hard-charging men. Most investors look for rapid-growth technology startups, lately especially in biotechnology and the life sciences. As we know, women's projects tend to be in other sectors, particularly service firms, which don't scale quickly, if at all. Being left to foot all the bills and support all the funding for expansion often makes women choosier about partners and decision-making.

Third, looking through a wider lens, women may be choosing more—not less—because they're defining success differently. "Women might be willing to take a loss in pay so the needs for more of their parts are met: The mother need, the work need, the need to be a person beyond home or office," says Sharon Chirban, a psychologist and leadership coach practicing in Boston, Massachusetts. Women today are playing multiple roles and exploring a range of territory unimaginable even a generation or two ago. Fitting everything in may mean big enough when it comes to the business. Many women owners also adjust the business to the rhythms of time and family concerns that shape their goals. They know their priorities will shift as businesses, marriages, kids, health, aging relatives, spiritual growth and other outside interests evolve. In other words, that "having it all" clarion call has morphed into a push-comes-to-shove mantra: "I need to make tradeoffs."

"It's a daily struggle between growing my business and being content with where I am—not wanting to put in more time that will take me away from my daughter, my boyfriend, my family and friends," explains Jennifer Krosche, who launched her boutique home-based PR agency in Long Island, New York, after being laid off. "I could definitely grow much larger than I am and look for new opportunities," she says. "But I don't push the envelope the way I should because I'm content—for now." Or, as a Silicon Valley management consultant puts it: "Size is a male obsession, and a less-relevant measure for women's success. Fulfillment may be harder to measure, but it's far more appropriate for women-owned businesses."

Making a difference while turning a profit

The primary purpose of a business, of course, is to make money. That's what separates having a hobby from running a company. You must turn a profit. At the same time, "…women start businesses to be personally challenged and to integrate personal and business goals," sums up the 2012 report from the National Women's Business Council. Their enterprises may grow at a different rate or remain smaller, but women owners also bring new ideas to market to satisfy consumer needs that men ignore or haven't noticed.

For instance, starting in 2007, Romy Taormina, based in Pacific Grove, California, has been producing Psi Bands, acupressure wristbands that alleviate nausea caused by travel sickness, chemotherapy and early pregnancy. She discovered the drug-free wristbands as a mom-to-be suffering from debilitating morning sickness. But bands then on the market were medicinal ugly, gray-green, dreary and uncomfortable. So Taormina and cofounder Carla Falcone (who has since left the company) came up with the idea for Psi Bands: stylishly colored bands that are both fashionable and functional. Business boomed. Psi Bands has gone on to win several small-business awards, rack up enviable and ongoing media coverage, and now is sold nationwide at more than 10,000 US stores, including Amazon, CVS, Target, Toys R Us, REI and Whole Foods.

That impulse to give back or drive change in society hardly limits women to seeing business through pink-tinged lenses. It can also translate into high-charging, high-concept and highly lucrative ideas that scale like an investor's dream, though the climb is accomplished female-style.

"Women approach business life differently," explains New York angel investor Joanne Wilson, who mostly funds women's startups to encourage them to build businesses. To date, she's seeded dozens of women-led companies and also cofounded and chairs New York's annual Women Entrepreneurs Festival. "Women operate differently and think differently," continues Wilson. That includes being more collaborative and more patient than men in the startup phase. "Women are thoughtful and analytical and not interested in failing. They're willing to take another year if necessary to look at what makes sense and to ask for advice. They're not bulls in the china shop."

Wilson also takes on critics who dismiss women owners for so often choosing to build fashion or other woman-facing businesses. Her response: "Then why do men have to keep building technology businesses? You need to build what you know," she declares, mentioning a woman who ended up creating an extremely successful online mortgage business because she couldn't understand the application process when she needed one.

Women start businesses to solve their own problems. That inspires and encourages other women and rewrites the rules about what businesses sell and can do.

Getting a life

Jody Greenstone Miller, cofounder of Business Talent Group (BTG), encapsulates all the foregoing themes: Tracking new and contemporary problems and coming up with forward-looking commercial solutions; turning to entrepreneurship to find better work-family balance; adopting the freelance economy early on; and launching after years of developing impressive skills, experience and contacts.

Started in 2007 and headquartered in Los Angeles, BTG is a pioneering consulting firm that provides C-suite independent professionals for project-based work—"supertemps," as Miller calls them. "By starting your own company, you have much more ability than in an established company to control the culture and make your own choices," says Miller. "You can build the business that works for your style and your particular strengths."

Like thousands of women who launch, when Miller began putting her business idea into action, she was cautioned she'd never make a go of it. Major corporations require fulltime, fully responsible executive management and won't countenance hiring high-level executive talent for project-based work, she was told. Today, in six offices around the country and eyeing overseas expansion, BTG's pool of 4,500 independent consultants and executives (and counting) is in demand by Fortune 1000 companies, private equity firms and large nonprofits. Company growth has been on a tear, with three consecutive years of over 60% growth that's attracted prestigious recognition, including in 2015 being named to the Forbes 100 Most Promising Companies, and ranking in the top fifth (No. 1,209) on the *Inc.* list of the 5,000 fastest-growing privately held companies in America. "Annual revenue is in the double-digit millions," according to Miller, who's in her late fifties.

She readily acknowledges that signing on as a BTG supertemp is an option reserved for upper echelon professionals. "In order for individuals to take advantage of working less than 40 hours a week, they must be able to afford it financially," she says. "It's obviously not a structure that works if you need to work 40 hours a week to support yourself."

Before starting BTG, Miller racked up a blue-chip resume. She was a lawyer at the prestigious Cravath, Swaine & Moore firm in New York, legal counsel to a South Carolina governor, executive at a film documentary division at Time-Life Television, and a fellow and special assistant, respectively, in the White Houses of George H. W. Bush and Bill Clinton. From 2000 – 2007, she worked from her Los Angeles home for a Seattle venture capital firm, where Howard Schultz, now Starbucks CEO, then also worked. From that perch, Miller not only absorbed lessons from hundreds of entrepreneurs but also learned how productive telecommuting could be. She began thinking about her own company. Inspiration hit after she and her husband, Matt Miller, wrote a buzz-generating cover story for *Fortune* magazine in November 2005, called "Get a Life."

The article tracked a budding trend in the top ranks of large corporations. Senior male executives, at last, were becoming as concerned as women long had been about the way 24/7 workweeks drained them of productivity and left no time for family, recharging or other interests. Stated the Millers: "Men are willing to talk about these things in ways that were inconceivable less than ten years ago." The couple reported on some leading-edge corporate initiatives that had been designed to avoid executive burnout and share responsibilities.

Their feature was a call to action for corporations to rethink their cultures, a cause Jody Miller has been championing ever since. Most of the solutions highlighted in the story were variations of installing two or even three fulltime managers with co-equal responsibility for what had always been considered one job. Over time, more companies were acknowledging that such positions had become too challenging and broad for any one executive to master. The Millers argued that the tradition of loading crushing authority and responsibility onto a single executive wasn't effective. If responsibilities were shared, executives would not only gain personal time and greater job satisfaction but also enjoy breathing room and imagination to develop increased strategic vision. The piece included what's become a more familiar scenario: Two working mothers who shared a job. The novelty was in the women's high-level rank and their skill in sharing. Each held the position of vice president at a Boston bank and worked three days a week on an international trading desk. As the Millers described it:

> They didn't divide clients and tasks; whoever was present dealt with whatever came up. They had one set of goals and one performance review, and they operated so seamlessly... that out-of-town colleagues often didn't know there were two of them.... The gratitude factor, too, was huge: having a rare senior job-share doubled their drive to deliver.

Yet when the bank was acquired and the job eliminated, despite their stellar record, the women could find no company willing to risk hiring them as a package. Top recruiters "don't place part-timers," they were told.

That rang the bell for Jody Miller. It dawned on her that dozens of highly skilled professionals who could command top fees would welcome workplace flexibility and telecommuting, especially if they had young kids. She also was ready to strike out on her own. "I looked at buying an existing business but the economics didn't make as much sense and you never can buy exactly what you want," says Miller. "I decided if I was to do it, I had to do it from scratch and get investors." So she did. "I also decided to structure in a way that would give me control over the pace of growth. It was a new category that I expected would need time to evolve."

It took more than a year for Miller to find the right partner to help her build the business. "At the time, I thought I wanted someone on the East

Coast who was a lot like me, grounded in business and management with a lot of contacts so I wouldn't have to travel as much," says Miller, who opted to stay in Los Angeles. "I looked for a long time but couldn't find what I then thought was the right person." Many who might have been a good fit weren't ready to take on lower compensation and a startup's financial risks. People who could manage the risks weren't willing to work as hard as an early-stage company demanded. Eventually, she partnered with cofounder Amelia Warren Tyagi, who was in Los Angeles and had management consulting expertise, especially in the booming health insurance industry. Tyagi had worked with her on some previous projects and Miller was sure they had complementary skills.

Miller's timing was impeccable for a "high-level 1099 marketplace," as she puts it. In the face of the 2008 recession, companies were operating with just-in-time budgets and goals. Managers did not want to commit to pricey fulltime talent. But with minimal risk and no upfront retainer, unlike other management consulting firms, Business Talent Group could deliver topnotch help with issues then confronting companies, such as retooling or launching products, evaluating new or expanded markets, examining pricing or cost reductions and more. Soon, advances in anywhere, anytime mobile technology accelerated everyone's comfort with remote and outsourced work. Miller's business model no longer seemed radical. Smartly, she's been meticulous about vetting BTG's network of experts to ensure a perfect fit for her upscale clients.

"There are huge advantages to being an entrepreneur if you have the right skills and temperament," says Miller today, though she believes most people underestimate just how hard it is, especially because during the startup phase owners think they must do everything perfectly. At first, she was too risk-averse, Miller admitted in a 2014 *New York Times* interview. Responding to a query about management and early "speed bumps," she said, "I had this notion that everyone else knew the answers and I didn't. I felt that the bar for action was high when in reality it's lower. If your bar is set too high for action, you're not going to do very much, particularly if you're an early-stage company. When you look at other businesses, you think, 'Wow, they've got it together.' Then, as you get more sophisticated, you realize that everything's messy, and that even the most successful businesses are always reinventing and are never stable for very long. It's not that the emperor has no clothes, but the emperor has a lot less clothes than you realize."

Opting for both purpose and profit

For many women, often Millennials, growing profits takes a back seat to making a difference. "Women tend to start a lot of socially responsible businesses," says Northeastern professor Jamie Ladge. Of late, that means becoming a "social entrepreneur."

The social entrepreneurship movement, which attracts younger men as well as women, has evolved quickly over the past few decades and is resulting in widening ripple effects. It's a business model based on being transformational rather than transactional. The opportunity to build revenue by offering social benefits drives the business mission. Such companies also embrace "the triple bottom line," a concept and term first coined by a British management consultant named John Elkington in 1994. He urged companies to develop three independent bottom lines measured by three different accounts: the *profit* and loss account; the *people* account, or how socially responsibile the company is; and the *planet* account, or how eco-friendly the firm can be. Unlike entrepreneurs looking to scale up to some billion-dollar payoff, social entrepreneurs focus on the bottom line to fund their companies, lives and the social change they want. Dough is not an end in itself.

Even so, no one has developed an exact or official definition of social entrepreneurship because the movement has grown so fast and attracted such a diverse swarm of activists, thinkers, businesses and researchers. Each group exemplifies its own template of a for-profit business that helps society. The sector's leading academic institution is the Skoll Centre for

Social Entrepreneurship at Oxford University in England, founded by billionaire philanthropist Jeffrey Skoll, eBay's first employee and president who walked away with a fortune when the online auctioneer went public. The Skoll Centre says the "key concepts of social entrepreneurship are innovation, market orientation and systems change." Business magazines are zippier: Back in 2011, *Forbes* defined a social entrepreneur "...as a person who uses business to solve social issues." That's it. Most players, investors and institutions define social entrepreneurship as "doing good by doing well," because company profits are leveraged to drive social benefits or change.

The talk around social entrepreneurship includes the pursuit of an innovative or unconventional model to arrive at a social goal, working to get at the root of big problems. Some call this a "venture" approach, which also surfaces in the nonprofit sector as "venture philanthropy" to define a similar blurring of for-profit and nonprofit models.

Despite early criticism that all its earnest goodie-goodness could never gain traction, the social entrepreneurship model is becoming serious business. Water Aid, an international charity, reports that entrepreneurial improvements that would boost access to safe water in many parts of the developing world, thus avoiding cholera and other diseases, would pump a whopping $480 billion or so into the global economy. Another big-deal example is Bill Gates and his foundation's efforts. For the past few years, the Gates Foundation has been funding and challenging inventors to come up with a cheap and affordable toilet because that alone would revolutionize life and economies altogether in dozens of regions around the world.

But social entrepreneurship encompasses more than values-based business. It boils down to a philosophy for living. Every consumer can become a social entrepreneur by putting her money where her mouth is. That is, using your spending dollars and investments and retirement accounts to work in sync with your values. That's called "impact investing."

For instance, if you buy clothing from an international fashion brand or food from a supermarket chain, you can vote with your wallet to put that company on notice about how you want it to behave or source its ingredients or materials. Or if you invest in technology or manufacturing companies, you can use your shareholder power to insist they treat workers well.

Finally, this blossoming marriage of profit and passions is spurring the rise of the what's dubbed the "Sharing Economy." These are the new peer-to-peer and often controversial kinds of businesses that are flattening industries and skipping right over wholesalers, middle brokers and retailers. Examples include Airbnb, the older CraigsList and Uber. Each of these enterprises has fueled both big bucks and major blowback in the form of unintended consequences and legal challenges.

Even so, dozens of sharing economy models are cropping up, particularly, of course, in the form of mobile apps. While such services surely are remaking social expectations and business models, it remains to be seen how socially engaged the firms will remain. With initial public offerings, valuations of billions of dollars and shareholders on the horizon for the rising players, their brand of "citizen engagement" might not go the distance.

From powering businesses to empowering kids

Other models carry no such ambivalence. The potential for business to change society is what motivated Andrea Lo in 2011 to found Piggybackr, a social entrepreneurship based in San Franciso. Her online crowdfunding platform permits young people, from eight-years-old to college age, to raise money for their teams, projects and causes. "Adults underestimate kids," says Lo, who, at 30, is something of an expert on youngster capabilities.

Despite growing up in Silicon Valley, Lo never thought of becoming an entrepreneur. Oblivious to its high-octane glory, she saw home as simply where she went to high school. At the University of California Berkeley, she enrolled in the Haas School of Business, choosing the corporate consulting track. "I sincerely thought I wanted to go into law, and a consulting training background would offer experience working with big clients in a corporate environment," she says. "I studied white-collar crime, fraud investigation and forensic accounting."

Graduating in 2008, she accepted a long-time offer from a company where she'd done work as an undergrad. A month later, the country slid into financial meltdown. "Lehman Brothers collapsed and it was scary," says Lo. "I watched friends being laid off." Her job was secure because her firm focused on distressed companies. But by 2010, that career no longer beckoned. "I realized corporate America wasn't quite my thing. I was more into being creative and that's not what you do in a financial accounting job," she says. "I was also passionate about making a bigger impact for people like myself and for people younger than me who were just starting to enter college and careers." She was disillusioned, uncertain what to do about that, and began thinking about a startup.

One day, talking to her younger sister, Chelsea, Lo found her sibling at a similar crossroads of being disillusioned, only at the much younger age of 11, and specifically about preserving the planet. "She hated that the rainforest was being cut down and complained about pollution," said Lo. So she encouraged Chelsea to act rather than simply complain. Soon, the youngster had researched options and come back with the name of a nonprofit that worked to save the rainforest and an idea to sell bracelets for $1 each to raise funds for the organization.

Lo thought that was great but suggested bringing the project online and making it bigger. "I'm a business major so that's the way I think," she explains. Together, the sisters developed the fundraising project online and raised over $400. "That's huge for an eleven-year-old," says Lo. "But more than the money, I saw that through the process, Chelsea learned social media and crowdfunding skills and about how to rally people around a cause by telling stories, all of which I consider important 21st-century skills. I also saw how empowered she became after the campaign. I decided I wanted to spread the idea to other people across the nation."

Now she had a startup idea, but still faced a big hurdle. Lo had no technical training and no clue about how to launch an online business. "The media paints entrepreneurs as super-glamorous," says Lo, looking back. "But I have friends who've been working for years and failed multiple times before getting to where they are. People don't realize how much prep work goes into every success story."

She speaks from vivid experience. For about two years, Lo researched her idea while teaching herself how to design a website prototype. She also spent nine months as operations manager at an online community for caregivers. "It's important to have savings and a budget," she says, laughing, "and to eat at home a lot." She devised a cleverly cheap—and analog—stratagem to gain early feedback, using a sheet of construction paper as "the site" and Post-it notes as movable "pages" to interview educators, parents and kids. Through trial and Post-it note error, she discovered what kind of online navigation worked for them and which pages they liked best.

Networking and hard work earned Lo entry into a couple of business accelerators. In 2011, she worked with the Founder Institute, which offers a Female Founder Fellowship, and, in spring 2013, she joined the prestigious 10-week AngelPad program founded by ex-Googler Thomas Korte. Lo was the sole woman in her group. Typically, AngelPad gives its startups $50,000 to $150,000 in seed money. By summer 2012, Lo had hired a fulltime CTO and a fundraising expert for online community outreach.

After countless site iterations—"we basically have an improved iteration every week"—Piggybackr honed its mission. The initial concept was to serve only young kids, but it quickly became apparent that the platform attracted and supported a much wider range of ages. "Every day is still a learning process," says Lo today. "It took two solid years to build a product that was helping our constituents and talking to them in a way that worked. I call it 'product market fit.' We started by thinking we needed to teach people how to fundraise. But we realized that it wasn't so much about putting Internet pages together as about working with people who really didn't know how to crowdfund or tweet. A lot of kids came in and thought they could raise $1 million just by tweeting about it. It's an amazing way to offer experiential learning in a real-life setting because the kids need to set goals, persevere and ask for help. They learn that getting money and capital enables them to do stuff. In addition, we now work with a bunch of different stakeholders, including kids, parents, coaches, mentors and teachers. We have to figure out how to talk to all those people at the same time without alienating people of younger or older age groups."

The mission seems to be working. One campaign was a fund drive launched by the parents of a wheelchair basketball team in Berkeley. "Parents often want to do everything," says Lo. "But giving back to the organization meant a lot to the kids. They created amazing Web pages for their campaign and, in their own words, explained why they cared so much." The parents had never before hit a funding goal. With the kids using Piggybackr, the team raised $5,000 in a month, $1,500 above target.

Lo has also streamlined the business model, charging service fees per donation, credit card fees per transaction and optional monthly fees. All pricing and services are tiered to accommodate individuals, groups and large organizations. On average, Piggybackr users are receiving an average of $90 per donation, which, as Lo says, "sure beats selling candy bars for $1."

"We expect to attract strategic partners and large nonprofits that serve hundreds of thousands of students," she says. In building a sustainable company, Lo developed Piggybackr's exit strategy and plans to sell the company and move on to the next venture. Her advice to startup

to the Global Entrepreneurship Monitor. Meantime, by comparison, contributions of men (that is, everyone who added economic value before women were tracked) have stabilized or slowed. That means the bulk of women's contributions is new and first-time growth, including what they invent, produce, buy and spend to support themselves, their families and their communities. Women therefore will drive the 21ˢᵗ century global economy.

Make no mistake. This tilt toward women is as much about shifting attitudes as it is about recalibrating numbers. You can't measure what's forbidden, unrecognized or nonexistent. Until women joined the ranks of the workforce and launched businesses in sizable numbers, beginning in the West and then rippling around the world, few considered their skills or aptitude worth educating or nurturing. It's not only men who needed to change. "I attended a business conference right after graduate school when it suddenly occurred to me that I had to stop thinking about women as victims and to start seeing them as really powerful players," Elizabeth Vazquez explained upon the release of the book she coauthored in 2013, *Buying For Impact: How to Buy From Women and Change Our World*. Vazquez, CEO of nonprofit WEConnect International, which supports women's entrepreneurship worldwide, continued, "It was a new way of thinking about economic development and the role of women as key economic contributors."

Oddly enough, Chrysler Corporation was first to use the term "womenomics," trademarking it back in 1995 for a national marketing campaign that targeted women's growing purchasing power for cars. Around the same time, several US marketers in traditional male sectors began to realize that female customers were worth their effort. General Motors rolled out the Saturn model in 1990 to compete with the success of small Japanese imports, along with a "no hassle, no haggle" pricing strategy. Both the smaller cars and fixed pricing attracted women. Saturn also made efforts to hire women sales staff. Merrill Lynch, Charles Schwab and Fidelity were among the first to market financial services to women, including such female-friendly lures as life-stage retirement advice and investing seminars. Computer and software marketing, not to mention luxury items, like travel and watches, took much longer but eventually caught up.

The term's more current meaning traces to a themed issue of *The Economist* in 2006, entitled "A guide to womenomics." Sailing on an armada of persuasive statistics, economic forecasts and male gravitas, the London-based business magazine trumpeted: "Women are becoming more important in the global marketplace not just as workers, but also as consumers, entrepreneurs, managers and investors." Ticking off the changes in women's worldwide status and economic influence, the issue covered the massive rise in women workers; the shift from manufacturing to services jobs that are more suited to women; expansion of international trade and supply chains, which is sparking new exports and industries, such as prepared foods, beauty and online retailing; increasing numbers of women earning undergraduate and postgraduate degrees, which is advancing them into top-paying jobs; and so on. "Arguably," concluded the magazine, "women are now the most powerful engine of global growth." Other business media quickly followed suit and upped the ante.

Bankers discover women

Nevertheless, recognition for the She Economy grew out of the critical innovations of a lone woman, and then gained substantial traction because that woman earned the support of investment banker Goldman Sachs. In 1999, Kathy Matsui, who had grown up an immigrant farmer's daughter in rural Salinas, California, was working in Japan as a Goldman research strategist. Japan's then struggling economy faced crippling deflation, including declining population and birth rates and high unemployment. In such conditions, the usual economic tweaks were dismissed as ineffective. Matsui began researching options that could actually boost the economy. That turned out to be women's participation.

Using the term "womenomics" for the first time to highlight women's untapped economic muscle, Matsui showed that as both workforce producers and marketplace consumers, women were the unrecognized resource that could ignite Japan's struggling economy. "It was my personal plea, my attempt to gain recognition for all these talented women in Japan and the role they can play in the country's economic success," Matsui later told *Forbes*. Japan could climb out of economic trouble if women were more educated and actively engaged in business. That would boost the quality of the workforce, increase productivity and expand the number of people working. In turn, women would secure better-paying jobs, increase support for their families and rev up the economy.

Her numbers persuaded Goldman's high-rolling executives and investment bankers. A year or so later, at headquarters in New York, the upper male echelon at the firm took another look at Matsui's research and grew more intrigued: Imagine, women—not men—were the critical factor to turn around an entire economy, even in Japan, where women's rights lagged the West. The firm invested resources to develop womenomics as a global theory. And found it to be sound.

Goldman released the results of that research in 2008, under the headline "Women Hold Up Half the Sky," an ancient Chinese proverb. The report began by acknowledging that the proverb "has long been more aspiration than fact. Around much of the world, women lag men in terms of education, access to healthcare, work, wages and involvement in political institutions." Yes, gender equality shows serious gaps. Sure, gender equality should be a fundamental human right. But the real reason gender equality is worth championing is that it's key to long-term economic growth:

> Bringing more women into the labor force could provide a substantial boost to GDP growth and per capita income. Productivity levels would likely rise as higher competition

for jobs raised the average quality of the overall workforce. In countries with younger populations, greater gender equality is associated with the start of the "demographic transition," which is typically a period of rapid economic growth. Education is key to gender equality.... Over a range of countries... female education has been linked to higher wages; a greater likelihood that women will work outside the home; lower fertility; reduced maternal and child mortality; and better health and education, not only for women, but also for their children.... As education supports economic growth, growth in turn supports further improvements in education and health, creating a virtuous circle that extends the gains to human capital and productivity.

Soon, Goldman began asserting that global gross GDP would be significantly higher if more women were producers and consumers, and especially if nations invested in educating girls. By narrowing the gender pay gap, which typically results from educating girls, per capita global income could climb as much as 10% higher than the firm's then-baseline projections by 2020 and could spike as much as 20% higher by 2030. A few years later, in 2010, *Half the Sky* was the title chosen by *New York Times* columnist Nicholas Kristof and his coauthor wife Sheryl WuDunn for their bestselling call to action to support women's education and economic freedom. Matsui has gone on to become a Goldman vice chair, and continues to develop analysis to help Japan close its gender gap and grow the economy.

Building equity, a woman at a time

Motivated by the research conducted in 2008, and perhaps sensitive to the popular cries of banker greed and foul play during the financial debacle, Goldman Sachs—that bastion of trader testosterone—invested a game-changing $100 million through its foundation in a five-year initiative called 10,000 Women. The program partners with academic institutions and international nongovernmental organizations, or NGOs, to encourage global economic growth by providing business education for women entrepreneurs of up-and-running enterprises (rather than startups) from Beijing to Bangalore and from São Paulo to Oakland.

"This is not where people have generally invested but there really is an open space," said Dina Habib Powell in an interview with me just before the program launched. She was tapped by Goldman to head the foundation and lead the mission while she was serving as deputy secretary in the George W. Bush State Department. Although she loved her job, when the call came, she couldn't walk away. "It's very powerful when Goldman Sachs comes out and says, 'We found our best investment for the future,'" Powell said. "I was sold."

(The foundation also launched a 10,000 Small Businesses program in 2009 to support US ventures, likely again in the face of criticism that enterprises at home could use some help in troubled times, too.)

The impact of the 10,000 Women program, detailed in a progress report by Babson College commissioned by Goldman, is both inspirational and revealing. The bare minimum of thoughtful support for one woman in one business can dramatically change the future for her enterprise, her family and her community. Eighteen months after graduation, nearly 70% of the program's participants had boosted revenues by a whopping 480% average. Nearly six out of 10 (58%) had created new jobs and nine out of 10 (90%) had decided to share their success by mentoring other women.

Testimonials from graduates of the 10,000 Women training put those numbers into focus. Profiles of the graduates (first names only) are featured online and the stories are compelling. In Samfya, Zambia, eighteen-year-old Esnart teamed with other women to launch The Great Ones, an affordable preschool for at-risk kids. Most of the women founders had lost parents as youngsters and struggled to remain in school owing to costs and other factors. Pre-schooling isn't compulsory in Zambia and therefore expensive. "We saw this gap in our community and were eager to set up a preschool for children aged between two and six years old," says Esnart. "If we can enroll vulnerable children in school early, they won't be roaming around on the streets…. It will help prepare them to make something of their lives in the future." The preschool began as a pilot funded by a startup grant of only $350 and a business plan calling for a class of 30. In January 2009, when doors opened, 65 children turned up.

Camfed, an organization that supports women to relieve poverty in Africa, was 10,000 Women's on-the-ground partner, providing business skills and strategy training for the preschool's owners. Since then, the school has received support from the Zambia Ministry of Education and, in addition to parent tuition, received some donations. The Great Ones has become a significant factor in boosting the area's rural economy. Some of the founders are improving their skills by also training at a teacher's college. The women now are eyeing a second school.

Business support in the 10,000 Women program isn't limited to the basics. Training also is designed to bridge gaps in women's operational experience and strengthen access to networks. In Pune, India, for example, Shweta had the technical engineering education needed to start Shweta Engineers Pvt, Ltd, an auto components business that primarily sells crankshafts. But she lacked the financial and management skills to scale her company. "I struggled to remain cost competitive, to access cost-effective capital and to establish a stable platform for profitable growth," says Shweta, in her online profile. After graduating the program, she honed her financial management skills and began to concentrate on increasing profitability by monitoring cash flow and minimizing expenses. She also learned critical negotiation skills and the huge benefits of delegating work. Shweta expects to expand the business to a broader customer base and leverage new technologies to grow.

Global bets on women

Doubling down on its research in 2014, Goldman released an updated report, entitled "Giving credit where it is due: How closing the credit gap for women-owned SMEs can drive global growth," which further emphasized that "investing in women and girls is one of the highest return opportunities available in the developing world." Reiterating the tangible economic benefits of gender equality, this report pointed out that when women have increased bargaining power, their money reshapes communities and the future. "…Households are not only likely to spend more, but also…spend differently. We find that women's spending priorities differ from men's, with women notably more likely to buy goods and services that improve the family's welfare." That includes spending on food, healthcare, financial products and investments as well as education and childcare, "enabling women to work outside the household and allowing girls to go to school instead of caring for younger siblings."

But women-owned SMEs, or small and mid-sized enterprises, in the developing world face serious barriers to entry and challenges in growing any business. "…. Access to finance is typically identified as a critical constraint." Some 70% of women-owned businesses worldwide lack access to financial products and services, including basics like savings accounts, according to World Bank estimates. For women, that adds up to a global credit gap of $285 billion. Acting on its findings, also in 2014, Goldman boosted its support by helping to seed the first-ever global lending program for women SMEs in developing countries: The Women Entrepreneurs Opportunity Facility. The firm pledged to work with the World Bank Group to raise up to $600 million to help women-owned enterprises gain greater access to capital. More recently, during his trip to Africa and appearance at the 2015 Global Entrepreneurship Summit, President Obama announced that the lending facility would also partner with the US government's development finance institution, the Overseas Private Investment Corporation (OPIC), adding up to $100 million financing in new projects.

Dina Powell, now in charge of all of Goldman's impact investing as well as the foundation, and her successor at 10,000 Women, Noa Meyer, have continued to secure the firm's support in expanding the program. To date, it's achieved the goal of reaching 10,000 women business owners, represented by 43 countries, and is moving forward.

"We believe that women, once empowered in every country, including the US, will have a tremendous impact on society, on the economy and on the next generation," Powell told me.

Turning market dials to "female"

When the likes of Goldman Sachs declares womenomics the key to long-term economic growth, it moves markets. That commercial bet has a far more credible and galvanizing effect than any edict from the United Nations or the World Bank, even though both those organizations have pronounced similar conclusions for years. As a result, and after comparable moves and analysis by other investors, today's global policy conversation has switched gears. The argument for supporting women has pivoted from a guilt-inducing moral obligation to a fashion-forward economic advantage. Investing in women's entrepreneurship, largely in emerging economies but in the West as well since the Great Recession, signals that you're in the know. The story of women has turned a corner. It's now all about the money—and the ROI of banking on women.

Evidence for this shift keeps mounting. In 2012, business consultancy Booz & Company (now merged with PwC and rebranded Strategy&) found that "nearly 1 billion women will enter the global economy in the next decade." The study reckons the influx has the potential economic impact of the billion-plus populations of China or India. Therefore Booz has tracked the phenomenon with the "Third Billion Index," issuing report cards for government performances in empowering women in 128 countries. Says the study, "The quantitative evidence in the index reveals a strong correlation between the prosperity of women and a positive impact on the overall national quality of life, including increasing per capita GDP, literacy rates and access to education, and lowering infant mortality." Other studies anoint the same third billion. Research from the McKinsey Global Institute, released in September 2015, reports that if women played an "identical role in labor markets to that of men, as much as $28 trillion, or 26%, could be added to global annual GDP by 2025.

On the prowl for new and expanding markets, international conglomerates are taking note. WEConnect and NGO Vital Voices persuaded a half-dozen giant companies in 2013, including Coca Cola, Exxon Mobile, IBM and Walmart, to award $1.5 billion in contracts by 2018 to 15,000 women-owned businesses outside the US. The women must compete for the contracts, so these can hardly be considered grants. A companion group of large firms and nonprofits will provide training and mentoring. Bill Clinton's family foundation, the Clinton Global Initiative, is on tap to follow how the $1.5 billion is invested and to track outcomes. Putting numbers on success will make it easier for other programs to secure funding. WEConnect has further joined Walmart to create Women Owned, a distinctive retail packaging logo that lets consumers know that those products were produced by women-owned businesses. Women are getting as good as "green."

The technology sector, laggards when it comes to supporting women, is playing catch-up with a range of programs, cosmetic and substantive. Google launched #40 Forward, a million-dollar effort to encourage a mere 40 early-stage enterprises to hire more women, install more flextime to support mothers on staff and to reach out to women founders. Google Developer Groups also forge local partnerships around the world, such as Startup Village in India, which launched in August 2015 to boost women "techmakers." The Dell Women's Entrepreneurial Network actively supports women owners, hosting conferences and events around the world, and has reported spending a sizeable $350 million on women-owned (and certified) businesses in 2014, with increases promised going forward. In June 2015, Intel Capital, an arm of the giant computer processer, set up the Intel Capital Diversity Fund with $125 million to back startups run by women and minorities: "part of a corporate-wide effort to bring more diversity into the notoriously male technology industry." Earlier in the year, Intel CEO Brian Krzanich pledged $300 million over five years to get "full representation" of women and underrepresented minorities in the company's US workforce by 2020.

Booting up "female"

Of course, women could never have gained so much economic ground without the ubiquitous advance of breakthrough and affordable technology. Online resources, along with digital tools and products, have reinvented business worldwide with continuous transformation. However, the latest mobile tools particularly press buttons for smaller and women-led firms—and mobile is moving with the speed of online data. By 2013, the use of mobile Web traffic drew even with desktop and laptop usage for the first time. Some 43% of the worldwide population will use the Internet regularly in 2015, with 32.2% going online via mobile phone, according to eMarketer, a digital market researcher. Developing nations in Africa and Asia, and also in the Mideast and Eastern Europe, are leapfrogging the era of PCs and laptops entirely, ignoring development of expensive and time-consuming wired infrastructure and going straight to mobile networks and smartphones. "The growing mobile Internet user base will drive overall Internet adoption, especially in emerging markets," agrees eMarketer.

Access to smartphones and mobile apps revolutionizes life and options in developing nations. Mobile banking programs, such as one called M-PESA in Kenya, not only allow women owners to process small financial and banking transactions more efficiently but also promote savings, a particular boon for women entrepreneurs who, as we've seen, often lack access to financial services. In India, an NGO organized groups of women to focus on marketing, giving them access to mobile phones

com era in the late '90s. In today's mobile world, communities belong to women as the next iteration of traditional women's associations and clubs—only now with a digital and massive multiplier effect. As an anywhere, anytime resource that lets users share information and seek advice or support, the online community especially attracts the millions of solopreneur women who work at home juggling motherhood and running a business. They're stressed, isolated, often highly credentialed and skilled from former corporate jobs, but lack any air in their schedules to network or develop outreach. That's why virtual communities with timely offerings, relevant tools and an authentic voice can expand so swiftly that serial entrepreneur Jill Salzman, for one, was taken by surprise. The launch of Salzman's now-burgeoning business, The Founding Moms, was an accident.

In 2007, after having her first baby, Salzman was building her second business, Bumble Bells, sterling silver baby anklets with tiny bells that let parents keep track of roving crawlers and toddlers. The jewelry was taking off, especially after pop singer Gwen Stefani clasped a Bumble Bells around her baby's ankle. "I was good at getting press," says Salzman. Also a lawyer, Salzman had earlier started a music management business, Paperwork Media, which she had kept up-and-running. When her second child was born, and she found herself caring for two young children while managing two growing businesses, Salzman figured it'd be a good idea to get together with some other entrepreneur moms who faced similar daily challenges.

She created a group for mom business owners on Meetup, the online networking tool that enables users to create local interest events and groups, posting an invite to meet for coffee. Salzman figured scarcely anyone would show because she lives in Oak Park, just west of Chicago, and at the time, the long-settled area had few young families. But 20 women did. The group began meeting for coffee every month, taking their kids along and sharing business and parenting concerns and victories. "Six months later," says Salzman, "one woman said she hated driving out of Chicago to Oak Park and couldn't we just open downtown. It was a light bulb moment."

Today, Salzman, 37, has systemized the Meetup Mom Exchanges. Founding Moms offers both on and offline resources in some 45 cities and 10 countries for 8,500 members—and counting. "We're more laid back than a lot of the other women's business networking groups," she says. Women pay $10 to attend each meeting, which, says Salzman, are "educational forums and workshops." A volunteer host in each city leads the event, receiving a percentage of the entrance fees. Hosts invite local experts and coaches, such as lawyers or tax accountants, to come talk to the groups. Such pros are usually happy to volunteer because they're addressing potential clients and forging relationships. Hosts also collaborate with groups in other cities, so everyone's up-to-speed and sharing resources.

"The majority of the women are solopreneurs," says Salzman. "They show up in sweats and some bring babies. There's a wide range of ages, from grandmas to new moms. The talk is about how to avoid undervaluing yourself, raising prices, how to deal with running up against bigger brands, about using social media marketing. These are mostly women in the first five, maybe ten years of business. They want to talk about their great idea and have someone take it seriously so they can make some money and get more done. When they hear others are doing that too, there's less fear of going forward. The commonalities come out when you congregate in one room."

For years, Salzman ran The Founding Moms as a hobby. She bootstrapped costs from her other companies, her well-paid speaking circuit and a book she sells. She loved connecting with other mom owners and helping them to grow. In 2011, she sold Bumble Bells, freeing time and resources to focus on The Founding Moms, which kept getting bigger. Salzman decided to monetize. "In hindsight," she says, "I knew in my gut that the thing was huge. I went the Twitter route and it did keep growing. I didn't put a price on it but it was growing quickly, 2,000 members a year." The company now also recruits sponsors for the groups and organizes several conferences each year that charge attendees $400 - $500, while also charging for exhibit booths and event sponsorships.

Over the next few years, Salzman will be ramping up, reconfiguring her online portal with better backend technology, launching a newsletter and brushing up on branding. "Technology makes it an amazing time for women," she says. "Busy moms can have babies and still work alternative hours to bring money into the family."

Taking equity in "female"

A mere decade or so ago, most of the financial services industry was still figuring out whether or not women actually had wallets. Nowadays? Everyone's wide-awake to the lucrative market that women represent. Around the world, women control more than $20 trillion, or nearly a third (27%) of the world's total wealth, according to a global survey by Boston Consulting Group.

In the US, almost half of the country's top wealth holders are now female: that is, about 1 million women each control assets of roughly $2 million or more, with 47% of those older women, 50 – 70 years old.

Since women tend to live longer than men, five years on average, and marry men older than themselves while not remarrying as frequently after a spouse dies, women are in line to control more and more inherited money over the coming decades. That's in addition to the significant income they also earn these days. What's more, we've begun the oft-mentioned giant generational wealth transfer, estimated at $59 trillion starting in 2007 and continuing through 2061 from the World War II and Silent Generations to Boomer, Gen X and Gen Y groups—demographics in which women already wield financial influence. Bottom line: Around the globe, women are accumulating more and more wealth.

That wealth, of course, is accompanied by a sea change in women's education, professional skills and political activism. It's not only male

CEOs and bankers who can see benefits from investing in women's progress and development. Increasingly, affluent women do too. More often than not, their motivation is equal parts social values and profits. A recent column in the *Saudi Gazette*, one of Saudi Arabia's largest newspapers, cautions that the "stereotype of the Arab woman is changing.... With wealth of $40 billion, female Gulf investors are forging a new identity which focuses on financial and social independence." Key to that newfound freedom is that "...the majority of these ultra-wealthy women live in Saudi Arabia, Kuwait, Qatar, Bahrain, Oman and the UAE, where women alone control assets worth $245 billion."

Likewise, the number of women investing in other women, though still relatively small, is rising in the US. Wealthy women philanthropists no longer routinely donate to the arts or the United Way but instead support causes and organizations that help women build lives and thrive, such as Women for Women International, a global nonprofit that aids women survivors of war and conflict.

Most women investors in women-owned startups are angel investors, rather than venture capitalists (VCs). As a rule, angel investors are affluent individuals who like to bet on early-stage enterprises. They offer seed, startup financing in exchange for equity shares, bridging the gap between bootstrapping and formal first- or second-round funding. Angels bank on their ground floor, high-risk seed money to return big rewards, taking bigger risks but with lower investments than later-stage investors. They often work on their own or join private angel networks that pool money, share expertise and divvy the due diligence tasks. The range of individual angel investments can run from $10,000 to $1 million, with typical deals at $25,000 to $100,00. Group or network ventures usually run $250,000 to $750,000 each.

By contrast, VC firms operate as private partnership companies, like private banks or law firms, and men dominate the industry. Usually, VCs don't get involved until second-round funding, if not later, when companies have gained some traction and proven their business model by attracting paying customers. With bigger bets and much more money, VCs also target businesses that will scale big and fast. The payoff and exit strategy is expected within a two-year or so window. That means, nowadays, VCs mostly fund startups in the technology sector, which meet the investment criteria but don't often attract women, either as entrepreneurs or investors. Angels, on the other hand, tend to be hands-on and more connected. They stay close to the CEOs they invest in and are typically more patient, offering coaching, access to expanded networks and entrée to other funders.

Women do diligence

In New York, Angela Lee, in her late 30s, teaches strategy and entrepreneurship at Columbia Business School and is already seasoned by involvements with four startups. In 2012, she launched 37 Angels to encourage women investors and to harness "the untapped capital and experience women can bring to investing." Limited to women investors, who each pay a $2,500 annual fee and commit to investing $25,000 every year, 37 Angels has 50-plus members and, as a network, writes checks for $50,000 to $200,000 to invest in ventures usually raising $500,00 to $2 million. "Half of the women in our network are former or current entrepreneurs and many have backgrounds in law or real estate," says Lee. "That gives us a unique ability to help entrepreneurs." The group also hosts an intense bootcamp—cost $4,500—open to anyone who wants to learn the fundamentals of investing in startups and early-stage companies.

Lee chose the 37 Angels name because when she launched in 2012 only 13% of all angel investors were women and "we want that number to be 50%"—50 minus 13 equals 37. (The needle keeps moving though. More than a quarter—26.1%—of the 316,600 angels nationwide now are women.) Even so, 37 Angels bets on gender-neutral ROI, investing in both male-led and women-led startups. "We invest in amazing companies regardless of the founder's gender," says Lee. "We're trying to remove the asterisk from investing in women. We don't want people to invest in women just because it's the socially responsible thing to do. Men need to be part of this conversation."

In the Bay Area, Cindy Padnos is the founder and managing partner of Illuminate Ventures, and is distinctive on two counts. First, she's one of the rare women venture capitalists with decision-making power. Women partners make up only 6% of US venture capital firms, according to 2014 findings of the Babson College Diana Project. Second, Padnos focuses on cutting-edge and disruptive early-stage technology ventures, mostly cloud computing and SaaS (software as a service), which is also unusual for a woman VC. Established in 2009, Illuminate maintains a consciously gender-neutral profile, with both male and female partners, a robust technology advisory board composed of men and women, and investments in both male- and female-led companies. Which is just how Padnos likes it.

Named one of the most influential women in the industry by both the *New York Times* and *Fast Company*, Padnos is thoughtful and well versed in the challenges women face, both as entrepreneurs and VCs. "Men leverage investments for power and influence and financial reward. They do it aggressively and at much higher levels," she says. "I'd like to see women take that big leap. Frequently women do not choose to take that same path of leadership and power. I just think women don't see it as fun and men do."

Padnos is, however, encouraged by the growth in women angels, which totaled just 5% in 2009 and, as noted, has now reached more than 26%. "I'm optimistic that we're reaching a tipping point for women who have had personal financial success to want to stay in the game by making angel investments."

Abundant evidence shows that when women are involved in a business, performance improves. In research she investigated, called

"High Performance Entrepreneurs: Women in HIgh-Tech," Padnos reported that women-led, venture-backed high tech companies averaged 12% higher annual revenues while using about a third less capital than similar startups run by men. Women-led startups also showed lower failure rates than those steered by male counterparts. Like the beefed-up investments in women around the globe, the argument for hiring more women or minorities in startups is moving well beyond any kind of moral or gender equity issue. It turns out that a diverse team is a clear financial benefit for startups and young businesses because that leads to harnessing and assessing differing ideas, backgrounds, perspectives and experiences. Diversity translates into creating a richer and more robust platform. Plus, when a woman is CEO, more women are hired.

Having senior women in positions of decision-making leads to better performance for established multinational corporations, too. Researcher Catalyst reported a 26% higher return for all companies that had the most women on their boards. Similarly, after looking at international companies with the most women board directors, McKinsey & Company found that operating profits were 56% higher than that of average companies. Other measures, such as return on equity, were also improved with women on the board.

It's not clear why women entrepreneurs often do better, says Padnos. "We don't know the answer historically about why women-led early stage companies tend to generate more revenue with far less capital deployed. It could be because they had less and they just had to figure it out. But it's an uncertain metric. We also don't know why women still tend to raise less capital when they go on to build large successful companies."

She does however tell a story that encapsulates why women can change the equation. "Recently, a tech company was building a mobile product, some software that was targeted at women. The developers showed it to the marketing people," says Padnos. Everyone was excited, except for the one woman on the marketing team. "She looked around the room and said, 'Are you crazy?' And no one understood what her problem was." Turned out, the whiz-bang developers had designed the software to be noticed only when the mobile vibrated. "The woman had to point out that most women don't wear mobiles on their hip but keep them in purses. So it wasn't a product for women."

"There's no question that unintentional gender bias is real and affects all of us," continues Padnos, who's in her mid-fifties. She points to the overwhelming number of white male venture investors compared to decision-making female partners as a factor.

Several studies from Harvard and elsewhere show when two identical business plans and management staff of exactly the same pedigree are evaluated, investors earmark less for women-led firms. That goes for women as well as men investors. "This same issue of gender bias was discovered many years ago in the world of professional musicians," explains Padnos. To remedy the bias, applicants began submitting resumes with no first name and musicians stand behind screens during their auditions. "That approach has contributed significantly to the percentage of women in orchestras, and many more are also now in the first chair," says Padnos. At Illuminate, Padnos and her partners follow a similar practice. All business plans are reviewed by the firm with gender-neutral criteria, "at least for the first screen," she says. "We don't want the issue of gender to be part of any investment decision we make."

The range of groups working on increasing the equity stake in women-led companies now crisscrosses the world, including angel networks like Golden Seeds, crowdfunding platforms like FundAthena and Plum Alley, nonprofits like Ashoka and Astia, and women startup accelerators like veteran Springboard Enterprises (see the Resources section for a full listing). To date, Springboard's portfolio companies, which consist of women-led technology companies, have secured $6.8 billion in financing, along with tens of thousands of new jobs and billions of dollars in ongoing annual revenue. All of these groups are fueling significant funding and higher growth for women's entrepreneurship, which, as we've seen, is being recognized as the most powerful international growth engine.

Says angel investor Holly Lynch at 85-Percent in New York: "We're still at the early stage but VCs are hiring more women to address female startup needs. Over the next few years, we'll be seeing fifty-fifty investments in the startup space."

PART II

Building Business with the Gender SWOT Matrix

There is an enormous untapped investment opportunity for venture capitalists smart enough to look at the numbers and fund women entrepreneurs.

— Candida Brush

Chair, Entrepreneurship Division, Babson College

Lead author, "Women Entrepreneurs 2014: Bridging the Gender Gap in Venture Capital"

The Woman Entrepreneur, Deconstructed

The original SWOT analysis was developed in the 1950s and '60s by business school organizational strategy professors as a tool to teach managing change in companies. Revised and amplified by various experts over time, the SWOT diagrammatic grid has become a popular and widely used evaluation technique for assessing everything from life goals to business plans. The SWOT acronym is self-explanatory, representing a 360-degree analysis consisting of the subject's internal **Strengths** and **Weaknesses** and external **Opportunities** and **Threats** (or **Limitations**).

Accessible and straightforward, the matrix is a useful way to categorize the characteristic traits and practices of female entrepreneurs, including what gives women owners advantages as well as what often calls for examination or improvement.

As an overview of how women tend to steer when they're in the driver's seat, here's a SWOT business model analysis that I created to showcase the Strengths, Weaknesses, Opportunities and Threats of today's women entrepreneurs.

Typically, women entrepreneurs:

Strengths	Weaknesses
Can quickly connect with prospects and stakeholders	Undersell their accomplishments
Multitask skillfully	Won't ask for money directly or ask for too little
Ask relevant questions	Won't ask for help directly or ask for too little too late
Listen and encourage contributions	Won't take regular and rejuvenating breaks/vacations
Strategically assess perilous risks	Don't take time to celebrate victories
Forge strong relationships	Work in the business, not on it
Build consensus	Become overly risk-averse when growing the company
Mold effective teams	Avoid reasonable debt needed for growth
Identify early market opportunities	Wait to receive rather than go out and take it
Bond with vendors and customers	Avoid the spotlight
Nurture online communities	Undervalue the ROI of building networks
Remain open-minded	Resist delegating: prey to Superwoman syndrome
Give generously to charity	Focus on details and lose big-picture strategy
Respect staff and instill loyalty	Hold grudges and take things personally
Capably organize and manage	Lack financial analysis
Run customer-centric operations	Cede control of business tech to IT guys
Take responsibility and are accountable	Set product prices too low
Exhibit greater job satisfaction	Don't monitor cash flow or profit margins
Handle stress well	Don't oversee the financial dashboard of company
Evidence strong communications skills	Don't set up an exit strategy
Empower staff and encourage discussion	Can be indecisive in making strategic decisions

Typically, women entrepreneurs:

Opportunities	Threats/Limitations
Take advantage of social media marketing	Must combat perceptions of incompetence
Leverage new peer-to-peer crowdfunding options	Often need to perform twice as hard at twice the level
Incorporate social entrepreneurship benefits	Limited access to professional networks
Develop cause marketing partnerships	Don't reach out to male or coed networks
Rely on the strength of building diverse teams	Are measured by default male standards
Hire and tap talents of more diverse staffs	Can't find reliable mentors or experienced role models
Adopt new technology early	
Define success in forward-looking ways	Must often reinvent the wheel
Think outside the box of traditional rules	Lack institutional memory for women
Reinvent old-style business models	Encounter bias and must balance assertive and soft
Infuse purpose into products	
Value work-life balance and nurture family life	Must manage sexual come-ons when doing business
Solve problems that men have ignored	Give in too soon in negotiations
Achieve high levels of education	Keep personal life secret or on hold
Identify business problems quickly and accurately	Suffer from not being taken seriously
Envision trends and market niches early	Are overlooked, ignored or rejected by investors
Set up networks/partnerships with women owners	Second-guess decisions or won't let go of mistakes
	Don't trust instincts
	Don't leverage experience of other women

4

Strengths: Women Really Are More Intuitive

"Starting a business is not for the faint of heart," says Penny Sansevieri. "You have to do battle." Like many women her age, Sansevieri became an accidental entrepreneur after a couple of corporate jobs evaporated when she was in her mid-thirties. In 1999, and again in 2000, the two large companies at which she had held marketing positions shut down one after the other. To tide herself over, she took on freelance projects, wrote and marketed a novel, and hired out as a consultant to small publishers.

One client, a print-on-demand business, commissioned her to promote a self-published memoir. "The problem was no one knew how a book like that should be perceived or how to market it," says Sansevieri, looking back. She developed online strategies that got the book noticed. After that success, she figured there was a "gap in the market that needed to be filled."

Today, at 51, Sansevieri is the prescient owner of Author Marketing Experts (AME). Her business has blossomed along with the field of self-publishing. Once relegated to dreary vanity titles and the ego promotions of "thought leaders," self-published fiction and nonfiction print books, audio books and ebooks have gained both quality and respect.

As with other 21st century disruptive business models and technologies, digital publishing tools have gained sophistication and become easy to use, attracting dozens of companies into the space. With self-published outlets, would-be authors avoid the rejections, low advances and minimal royalties currently on offer from commercial book publishers, which release fewer titles every year. Writers by the thousands are instead choosing to pay for a basket of discretionary services that run from writing and editing help to designing covers, printing a finished paperbound or hardcover book and selling it through ecommerce, social media and online channels. Self-publishing costs are affordable, time to market is swift and, if successful—a very big "if"—authors have more control and may net higher sales revenue.

Lulu Self-Publishing, founded in 2002 and an early online provider, boasts nearly two million publications serving authors in 225 countries. Royalties can be substantial—Lulu has claimed some $36 million paid to authors. But big winners are rare, even as some bestseller name brand authors have taken charge of their own titles, for instance through the vertical publish-promote-sell services offered by Amazon. Some standout pay-to-publish work has also been muscling its way into conventional publishing, expanding the field as a talent pool audition for risk-averse establishment houses. Traditional publishers now are purchasing rights to proven self-published titles and re-releasing under their own imprint.

Despite the years of experience, Sansevieri is still learning on the job. "No one teaches you how to start a business," she says. Managing staff has been her biggest challenge. Based in San Diego with an office in New York, Sansevieri's employees work remotely from around the country, including two full timers and up to 20 contractors, depending on the volume of business. "Early on there weren't enough systems for a virtual business," she says. "At that time, when people worked from home, they didn't take it very seriously," she says, adding that remote work is much easier nowadays. "We have pieces in place and managing systems to track progress," she continues, mentioning Basecamp, a remote work project management system. "But even now, people will say anything and I've learned the hard way. They'll turn in work to Basecamp and say it's completed, but it's not." Plus, she acknowledges that the Great Recession has wrought changes. Likely, do-it-yourself digital marketing and social media tools would also cut into her services. "We're offering smaller programs for folks who are not looking to spend as much on marketing. It takes a while for book returns to come back to you."

Sansevieri's best advice: "As a business owner, you need to keep your ear to the railroad to know what's coming. It's hard to run a business and pay attention to everything else going on at the same time. Run a business like it's the first day you're in business. Don't get complacent."

Founder motivations, male and female

Ask women why they started a business and the most frequent responses are a desire for work-life balance, self-fulfillment or job satisfaction, according to research from the US Small Business Administration.

Most of the time, women launch businesses without much hoopla or overall strategy, especially Boomer and Gen X women. After being laid off or experiencing a setback, like Sansevieri, they frequently decide to market a skill honed at previous jobs. Enabled by technology, the expanding virtual workforce and the New Normal adoption of outsourcing, women can make a go of it more easily than in the past. Also like Sansevieri, many women often get an early fix on a niche market or overlooked opportunity because they're tapped for smaller or unusual projects within their field of expertise, and the light bulb begins to burn. Many other women assume free-agent status when corporate jobs become objectionable or unavailable for a range of reasons. They discover an aptitude for being in charge and end up preferring to be their own boss. Another significant cohort turns to self-employment because of its flexibility in caring for kids or relatives. Over time, the interim projects often scale into ongoing and reliable businesses. In contrast, Gen Y women are developing a somewhat different entrepreneurial dynamic, although it's too soon to see how far that will go. Tech-savvy, typically well educated and schooled by the Great

Recession and the Free Agent Nation to always have a Plan B, Gen Y women are launching at younger ages than previous generations.

Whichever the generation, most studies show that men generally start businesses to make money. They typically work longer hours than women owners do. Interestingly, women entrepreneurs are more likely than men to show early positive revenue while male-led companies tend to have more employees than women's firms. Undoubtedly, that's a function of whether the business is something of a lifestyle choice and whether the owner is aggressively trying to grow. Across the board, women run smaller businesses than men do. Lots of explanations for that continue to be advanced. Take your pick. The reason for smaller firms, suggest a range of academicians and pundits, is because women owners suffer from: low confidence; less business experience; smaller startup capital; gender bias in funding; service businesses that don't scale; family responsibilities; fewer role models; a dearth of strategic planning; reluctance to delegate; inability to control the financial dashboard; inadequate pricing; resistance to taking on complementary partners; inattention to profit margins; unrealistic business valuations that discourage investors; and on the hobby horse goes.

In fact, no one has a definitive reason. Might women prefer the fulfillment and intimate control of smaller companies, especially after facing slings and arrows and stress in larger companies? Is it because of choice or gender inequity? Most likely both.

Gender differences matter

Anyone out there still think there's no difference in the way men and women behave in business? Think again. A growing body of credentialed research finds significant differences in the ways women and men not only start, but also manage and operate businesses. For women to fuel success in launching and building a business, it makes sense to look into those sex differences and how sex-based behavior can inform or hamper their goals and performance.

But first, let's set some ground rules about the latest research conclusions because reporting on explicit gender differences tends to raise emotions and eyebrows. Defining or exploring gender differences in no way empowers one sex or belittles the other. That would be like arguing that green is a better color than red. Or vice versa. Just as importantly, no one individual ever is 100% male or female in style or characteristics— we all mix it up. It's a continuum and everyone fits somewhere along the glide path. Nonetheless, ongoing research and studies definitely identify specific traits and behavior as typically male and female. No doubt everyone recognizes at least some of these.

How nature hardwires the sexes

Surprisingly, some of women's key strengths flow from physiological differences, rather than cultural ones. In the past few decades, researchers have uncovered meaningful physiological variations in the brains of men and women. For example, male brains are about 10% larger than female brains, which is a result of managing men's larger body mass and muscles, not increased intelligence. Yet women have significantly more nerve cells in certain areas of the brain. Women also usually have a larger corpus callosum. This thick band of nerve fibers connects the brain's left and right hemispheres, which means the corpus callosum acts like a traffic cop, transferring motor, cognitive and sensory information back and forth between the hemispheres.

The brain variations in the sexes account for differences driven by genetics not sociology. Increased nerve cells and a more nerve-sensitive corpus callosum make women faster at transferring data between the computational and verbal left half of the brain and the intuitive and visual right brain. Women have greater and faster access to both aptitudes. By contrast, men typically are stronger on all left-brain, abstract skills.

In 1999, scientists at Johns Hopkins discovered "striking" differences between men and women in a small area of the left brain called the inferior parietal lobule (IPL). This region, associated with the ability to visualize objects three-dimensionally, gauge speed, estimate time and solve problems in math, was much larger in men. That, said project leader Godfrey Pearlson at the time, is the same part of the brain found to be much larger in Albert Einstein than in most men, not to mention most women. Intriguingly, there was also a "symmetry difference." As part of the cerebral cortex, the IPL is found in both sides of brain, located just above ear-level. Women in the study were found to have slightly larger IPLs on the right side, although not nearly as enlarged as men's left-brain IPL.

These findings put some science behind time-honored sex clichés. For example, much of the time, men really don't need to ask for directions. Their left-brain dominance makes them good at visualizing terrain in a 3D overview. They may not know the exact route, but they have a good notion of the direction that will take them to their destination. Obviously, left-brain dominance also gives then a leg up on math and associated fields, like architecture or physics.

Women, besides being innate multitaskers, truly are more intuitive. That is, they're lightning fast at interpreting nonverbal, contextual cues and then moving that information back and forth between the brain hemispheres, from visual and nonverbal to analytic and verbal and back again. Women's brains simply work faster. The long-running clichés about women's communications skills may well stem from their affinity for noticing nonverbal and emotional cues, including expressions and tone of voice, and for picking up body language that signals when or whether listeners have caught on.

Those brain differences also give women a distinct language advantage, often seen in grade school, where girls tend to do better than boys in learning language. Another noteworthy result is what happens to men and women who suffer a stroke or accident to the left side of the brain. Because men tend to have language only in the dominant left hemisphere and women can use both sides for language, a woman may retain some language from the right side after a stroke. Men are less likely to fully recover.

Unpacking sex hormones

Other sex-based research comes from neuroeconomist Paul Zak, director of the Center for Neuroeconomics Studies at Claremont Graduate University and founder of ZESTxLabs, a Los Angeles market research firm that looks at brain science to determine consumer behavior. Working with a team, Zak has investigated the hormonal basis of decision-making, tracking how people perform after they've been infused with strong doses of male and female hormones, including testosterone, oxytocin and estrogens. His findings: "Women tend to connect better to people and to multitask better. Men tend to be better at a single-minded focus and top-down motivations." Zak also, by the way, found that when he infused people—women as well as men—with high levels of testosterone, everyone became noticeably less generous and wouldn't share resources as readily.

In other ongoing studies, neuroscientist John Coates, a research fellow at the University of Cambridge, is working on the biology of stress and specifically on financial booms and busts, or what happens to the body when we risk making or losing money. Before joining academia, Coates was a financial trader for twelve years. In June 2012, he described his experiences in a *New York Times* interview:

> When I was running a derivatives desk for Deutsche Bank during the dot-com bubble… I began noticing pathologies in this biology. Traders, normally a prudent lot, were becoming overconfident, placing bets of increasing size, with ever worsening risk-reward trade-offs. As profits mounted, traders and investors seemed to feel the bonds of terrestrial

life slip from their shoulders. Assessment of risk was replaced by judgments of certainty—they just knew what was going to happen. Extreme sports seemed like child's play; sex became a competitive activity. They even walked differently. "I can handle anything," their bodies seemed to say. Tom Wolfe nailed this euphoric and delusional behavior when he described the stars of Wall Street as Masters of the Universe.

Such observations led Coates to develop a theory that the atmosphere, overconfidence and rewards of high-risk investment trading fuel higher levels of testosterone in men. That hormone spike, hypothesized Coates, in turn leads to greater and often unjustified risk-taking. Then, as losses and tension mount, the "fight or flight" stress hormone cortisol likely kicked in.

Convinced that someone ought to be looking into the theory, he made the decision—"frequently regretted"—to retire from Wall Street and enroll at Cambridge to spend four years studying endocrinology and neuroscience. After gaining his credentials, he and research colleagues set up an experiment to test his theory. They sampled hormones from 250 high-rolling investment traders in London's financial district, The City. Only three of the traders were women.

Over a couple of weeks, Coates tracked the testosterone levels of the traders and then compared those levels to the traders' profits and losses each day. His theory was borne out. He "discovered that testosterone levels jumped in connection with above-average profits." Further studies found that higher levels of testosterone did indeed lead to geometrically greater risk-taking and that volatile markets and losses triggered stress hormones in the traders. It seems that the physical reactions caused by taking significant financial risks have a great deal in common with physiological responses produced by other risks, such as mountain climbing or facing a physical threat. "Advances in neuroscience and physiology have shown that when we take a risk, we do a lot more than just think about it. We prepare for it physically," he said.

Coates details his time as a trader and the Cambridge experiments in a book called *The Hour Between Dog and Wolf,* from the French *entre chien et loup,* or the twilight hour when danger cannot be discerned because you can't be sure if the animal in front of you is a dog or a wolf. He further examines the role testosterone likely played in the 2008 meltdown in the financial markets, and how the interaction of exuberant risk-taking and spiking male hormones could have been a factor in precipitating the crisis. With women in charge, who have only 10% to 20% of the testosterone found in young men, or with older men on the job, whose testosterone declines as they age, Coates theorized that the meltdown might not have occurred or been less severe because traders would have been more cautious. Among other revelations, his book is a call to action to investment banks to hire more women as traders..

Lately, says Coates, it's become evident that "our physiology shifts risk preferences 'pro-cyclically'" which is becoming an influential factor in his research. In other words, "even though economists assume our risk preferences don't change, we take too much risk in up markets, which morphs a bull market into a bubble and too little in a bear market, which then morphs into a crash," Again, he emphasizes the difference women can make: "Women seem less hormonal in their risk-taking, so could dampen the amplitude of this cycle."

Fighting vs. friending

Most of the biological research focuses on men and extrapolates truths about human reactions based on male responses. Only recently has this practice become something of a scientific donnybrook, with the US National Institutes of Health and other facilities more sensitive now to monitoring women's as well as men's reactions. Clearly, Coates tracked gender-based stress reactions in reaction to testosterone. What about women's hormones?

Back in 2000, Shelley Taylor and Laura Klein, two social psychology professors at the University of California, Los Angeles, stumbled onto an entirely new research field spurred by the jokes they made about how women and men scientists in their lab reacted to trying circumstances. The men disappeared from the lab and holed up elsewhere by themselves until they felt ready to return. The women came into work when they felt stressed. They spent time cleaning the lab and having coffee and bonding with one another. When the two noticed how consistent that behavior was, Taylor and Klein began digging into past research about stress. To everyone's dismay and surprise, they uncovered the fact that 90% of the studies into stress reactions only included males. Few had actually examined women's stress responses. As a result, Taylor and Klein went back to earlier data and also researched women's reactions. Their landmark findings have become the basis of a new field of continuing research.

Turns out the familiar "fight or flight" response to threat or stress, routinely taught to every high school biology student as an instinctive human physiological response, is actually more related to male reaction and not so true for females. The UCLA researchers discovered that oxytocin and other female hormones released during stress situations trigger a response Taylor dubbed "tend and befriend." While men and women both release oxytocin during stress, the female hormone estrogen seems to enhance its effects and the male testosterone works to reduce it. This tend-and-befriend coping mechanism, then, is a female characteristic.

"Animals and people with high levels of oxytocin are calmer, more relaxed, more social and less anxious. In several animal species, oxytocin leads to maternal behavior and to affiliation," Taylor said when the study was published in the *Psychological Review* of the American Psychological Association. "In threatening times, people seek positive social relationships, because such contacts provide protection to maintain one's own safety and that of one's offspring," she wrote. Over the eons of the evolutionary chain, if females had adopted a fight or flight response by either battling or fleeing trouble, they would leave children vulnerable.

What's more, when women do choose tending or befriending behavior under stress, even more oxytocin is released, which further offsets stress and adds to the calming effect. It's a reaction that keeps on giving. Taylor posits that women developed physiological reactions to "tend" children and "befriend" social connections because by building relationships and group bonds, women had a better chance of avoiding danger.

Their study goes on to suggest that women's desire to seek and maintain friendships with other women may be a factor in why they tend to outlive men, reinforcing another common sex stereotype that women are better at relationships and more social than men. They point out that developing social bonds has been shown to lower heart rates, blood pressure and cholesterol as well as to reduce mental and physical illnesses.

Redefining female talents

Evidence of hardwired gender differences may have surfaced only recently, but the sociological and cultural influences that shape gender have been catalogued for decades. As more and more distinct traits owing to nature and nurture are defined as female, it's increasingly clear that the way women intuitively perform—their first and natural choices—isn't particularly valued in large corporations. "The corporate environment is toxic for women because the playing fields are very masculine-infused and women have to prove themselves for the job," says developmental psychologist Birute Regine. "Women are paying a price for that."

Harvard-trained, Regine collaborated in the 1970s and '80s with psychologist Carol Gilligan, then a professor at Harvard, in the controversial now-famous research—some say "infamous"—that first framed girls as relationship builders who invest in caring for others, quite unlike boys. Published as a book, *In a Different Voice*, in 1982, the study pushed the field of psychology to investigate and embrace a specifically female perspective and experience. These days Regine is documenting what she sees as increasing social transformation away from domination and toward collaboration and community. She believes that shift is being fueled by the rise of strong women, whom Regine has dubbed "Iron Butterflies, because they meld a will of iron with the gentle, nurturing touch of a butterfly." Along the way, says Regine, "women are coming to see the limit of what's possible for them in corporate America."

"Women often bring skills to an organization that allow it to be resilient," she explains, citing women's abilities for collaboration, empathy and bridge building. "Women are connectors and connecting people is important in business." But the model for leadership in corporations has always been the warrior hero: the determined lone star who rides in, steers the crisis, works every weekend, and saves the day and the deals. Employees, especially women, are often inundated with pep talk about cooperation and teamwork. Yet putting together people and resources is neither recognized nor rewarded by corporate chiefs. That has led many women to become disillusioned. They buy into the mission and the values of teamwork and perform accordingly, to little notice. Over the last decade especially, many more women are leaving corporate life to create better ways for them to work and live—alternatives that can support female-tilted needs and behavior.

Rewriting the rules

Sarah Walton went through such an exodus. She launched Better Way Moms, an online community and magazine, after she and another working mom got to talking one day about being utterly time-starved and how her son cried every time she left for work. As Walton explains it on her company website, "Suddenly I said (I'm not kidding) 'There has to be a better way.' There is no other way to explain that moment, except to call it a 'brick-to-the-head' moment. If I had been a cartoon, there would have been a light bulb above my head." She launched on Mother's Day 2009 while pregnant with her second child. Her mission is to "start the conversation about women and work, and to challenge women to really look at what their 'Better Way' path looks like." It took two years for revenue to ramp up enough for Walton to quit her corporate job and work fulltime on the Better Way business.

Now 41, Walton spent 15 years in the corporate world, becoming a senior executive who managed hundreds of millions of dollars, mostly at multimedia entertainment companies such as Lifetime TV. About the time she got married and had a son, Walton took an executive position at an online women's community that attracts millions of monthly users. "I was director of products, which meant I touched every aspect of the product and site, from design, UI [user interface], graphics and content to technology development." Walton was also responsible for analyzing the avalanche of daily user data to see what was driving traffic. 'It wasn't what I wanted to do with my career," she says, pointing to the emphasis on technical tasks.

She was putting in long hours when she became pregnant again. "I'd be sitting in meetings with a bunch of men who were telling me what working mothers wanted," says Walton. When she offered other ideas, "the men would say, 'Pregnant women don't care about that,' and all I could say was WHAT? Meantime the company was losing money."

After giving birth to her daughter and while on maternity leave, Walton got an offer from a digital applications provider along with the freedom to create a more flexible work schedule. That not only helped with the family but also gave her some leeway to build a business.

The transition to fulltime stay-at-home mompreneur in 2011 threw up its own set of challenges. "Quitting the job meant losing a lot of security," she says. "My husband owns a family mortgage business and was supportive but I was the breadwinner. It was scary." The couple reconsidered their budget and habits, relying on some savings to tide them over. "We didn't go on vacations. I started dyeing my own hair. I stopped getting my nails done. I stopped shopping altogether." But perhaps the trickiest adjustment was the change in identity. "That was hard," says Walton. "It was an ego blow that I did not see coming."

She was accustomed to high-pressure nonstop work, high-profile appointments, industry recognition and no unscheduled time whatsoever. Suddenly, her days were a lot slower and quieter. "It happens to a lot of women who decide to stay home with the kids," says Walton. "You feel taken advantage of and invisible. I had to clean house. I felt a lot of stress. You feel like the outside world won't see you in the same way. I'd wake up every day and say, 'Really? I'm staying home today?' I was embarrassed and I was stunned at my response." Nevertheless, Walton felt it was the right decision.

She's quick to point to the thousands of women who juggle corporate jobs and kids with no thought of staying home. But she does see more and more women exiting because they're losing time with their children that can't be recaptured. And that's creating a talent drain.

Raiding the gender toolbox

"Male and female minds are different and they work well together," says Walton, who mentored dozens of women as a corporate manager. "Men charge ahead and go straight forward. Women tend to develop creatively and bring more things to the table." In contrast to women, she continues, "guys don't care so much about making good products as much as they care about revenue." Women also have managerial smarts. "If the presentation to the CEO bombs, a male boss will say, 'How could you do this to me?' A female boss will say, 'Are you okay?'" Which is more likely to instill loyalty and lessons learned?

Altogether, says Walton, results get better when male and female traits are combined. "Corporate America is hemorrhaging talent because we're not investing in women or mothers," she says. "We need to talk about it. Women in their twenties who are putting time into careers won't understand what will happen to them when they become moms. We need to get inside corporations and have then understand what they're doing to themselves." Echoing many of today's female entrepreneurs, Walton defines these challenges as social and political issues, not a "woman's problem."

Nowadays, Better Way Moms is growing, earning revenue from advertising, Twitter parties and a line of Better Way to Start the Day tools and products, such as a 90-day notebook designed to help women achieve their goals ($28 each). Walton has also launched an organic skincare line, Love by Sarah Walton. Her founding partner relocated to Italy soon after launch, so the company has expanded to include Better Way to Italy, offering luxury tours for women through Tuscany. "I know that creating my own hours, and being with my children when I want, while bringing in money, is something I'm willing to give up almost anything for," says Walton. "I remind myself of this as I'm up at one in the morning writing articles or working with our developer and designers.

"Women's choices are not just to 'Lean In' or go home. We have hundreds, in fact, thousands, of other ways we can make money and create a life that works for us, and for our families," she says.

How female traits build business

As girls and boys grow up, they're molded by differing sets of social rules and expectations, of course. Gender obviously colors behavior, perception and just about everything else. Typically, girls—and the women they become—are socialized to pay attention to others, to be empathetic, make contact and communicate. Plus, according to research from Claremont Greaduate University neuroeconomist Paul Zak, oxytocin hormone levels are associated with empathy and that biological-behaviorial response is stronger in women than in men.

So women take the time to engage. They listen more willingly. They're more open-minded about sharing authority and information than men tend to be. Women's distinct ways of viewing opportunities and running businesses translate into benefits for starting and stewarding enterprises.

First, by investing more time and interacting, women offen question established procedures or methods and investigate new and different solutions, often improving methods and outcomes. In turn, that empowers their staff and contributors, creating more space for everyone to weigh in and participate. Since technology has rapidly commoditized the speed of production and distribution, competition today is largely about talent rather than how quickly providers can deliver. Whoever has the best team wins. Making contributors feel individually recognized therefore often generates better business. Rewarding staffers also further translates into cost-effective performance and recruiting.

Women's acknowledged social skills have also moved online. Recent innovations in local, mobile and social technologies have accelerated online engagement. For instance, women dominate on Pinterest and Instagram, according to Pew Research. That affinity gives women owners an advantage in the changing landscape of social media marketing and customized customer service.

At Pixo, the technology services provider in Urbana, Illinois, owner Lori Patterson manages a boutique staff in a sector notorious for do-it-now deadlines and cascading deliverables. After some 15 years of deliberately operating with only 18 employees to allow for slow quality growth, Patterson expanded in 2013 to more than 30 staff. She also instituted a training program, both to support the community and to create a pipeline for talent.

Now that about a third of the employees are recent hires, Patterson relies on an hour-long meeting of the entire staff every week to keep all the parts integrated and all the wheels rolling in the right direction. During the meetings, "we do a lot of honing in on culture," she says. Each week, different people are assigned to make presentations about their "aha moment," whatever that might be, and however they choose to demonstrate it. Besides the weekly hour, the entire staff also meets for five minutes every morning, with everyone standing to emphasize the quick in-and-out.

One of Patterson's motivations for the daily get-togethers is to ensure that the newer staffers fully understand the company's culture and feel part of the team. "We've randomly assigned nicknames to everyone so it feels intimate and everyone can get to know one another," she says. But those five minutes are devoted to mission-critical tasks. Each staffer is asked to describe his or her personal stress level. "Are you green, yellow or red?" is the question. Managers can then focus more effectively. "If it's red, we want to know what's going on and what do you need," says Patterson.

Somehow you don't see men monitoring staff stress levels with quite the same level of effectiveness and support.

Managing like a girl

When comparing male and female leadership skills, the dialog is usually framed as men's command-and-control style versus women's team-building or consensus approach. "Women managers tend to have more of a desire to build than a desire to win," says Debra Burrell, a New York psychotherapist who treats couples and trained with John Gray, founder of the Mars Venus Institute and author of the bestselling Mars Venus books. "Women are more willing to explore compromise and to solicit other people's opinions." However, men often think if they ask other people for advice, they'll be perceived as unsure or as an unworthy leader who doesn't have answers, according to Burrell.

Big deal, right? It's hardly a news flash that women typically outperform men at communications and interpersonal skills because those are well-documented female "soft skills." Traditionalists argue that these have little to do with the essential hard tools and analysis required to grow a business. Lately, however, women are also demonstrating higher levels of so-called "hard" or "male" skills as well. Some investigators suggest that many women workers have possessed such skills all along but that male bosses tended to overlook or misperceive them. Others think the cumulative years of experience for women have been broadening their skills. Either way, women entrepreneurs are profiting.

Integrating hard and soft skills

When Anyi Lu looks back at her years in male-dominated industries, first as a chemical engineer for Dupont and then as a field sales agent and marketing manager for Chevron, she says, "I feel like I was always chasing my male colleagues." Then the punch line: "That's because my feet were killing me."

Like most women managers, Lu sacrificed comfort for fashion, donning executive-style pumps and stiletto heels that women can't wait to kick off after a workday. "I was always a step behind the men," says Lu. "I'm sure that made them dismiss me. If I didn't keep up with them physically, it meant I couldn't keep up with them mentally." Eventually, Lu opted to fuse her engineering smarts with her long-time interest in drawing and painting. She created a line of designer footwear that women can actually walk in.

These days, Anyi Lu International creates stylish women's shoes that blend handmade Italian leather craftsmanship with space-age cushioning, support and flexibility—or, as the company's trademark has it, "Couture Comfort." Working out of their home in Tiburon, California, Lu and her business partner husband, David Spatz, debuted 12 shoe styles in 2005, pulling in $450,000 in revenue. By 2010, with shoes retailing for $350 - $500 a pair, sales had hit $6 million. Anyi Lu styles now are found in Neiman Marcus, Nordstrom and Bloomingdale's as well as top-tier nationwide independent retailers. "I do a lot of personal appearances because I like to talk to real customers and hear how they wear the shoes," says Lu. "My fuel is to make a difference in people's lives."

Designing shoes was hardly the career Anyi Lu anticipated. Her family, including grandparents, parents and a younger sister and brother, emigrated from Taiwan when she was 15. They settled in Wilmington, Delaware. When it was time for college, her parents told her to select one of the three "best" careers to study to ensure that she'd be settled in life and could support herself and any children. She was given the choice of doctor, scientist or attorney. "Since I was deathly afraid of blood, I chose engineering."

After graduating from the University of Delaware with a chemical engineering degree at age 20, Lu worked as a Dupont field engineer in Plaquemine, Louisiana outside Baton Rouge. Then her beloved grandfather, who had taught her Chinese calligraphy, became gravely ill. She looked for a job closer to home in order to spend time with him. At 23, she became a Chevron sales agent in the Northeast and Mid-Atlantic regions. Two years later, Chevron relocated her to the Bay Area as a marketing manager. There, Lu met Spatz, then a Chevron executive. When dating turned serious, it was clear one of them had to change jobs. "So I asked him to leave," she says. In 2000, Spatz, some years older than Lu, took early retirement to focus on his sideline real estate business.

She remained at Chevron for another year, but change was inevitable. "I love to draw, paint, create. I was working 60-hour weeks, commuting for hours every day and David was saying, 'Look at your male peers and how they love autos and engineering. Do you?'" He encouraged her to find something she loved. The financial and emotional security of marriage gave Lu the freedom to reboot. She quit and enrolled in design school, unsure of what came next.

The idea of designing high-fashion shoes engineered for comfort—with instep cushioning made of Poron, the foam NASA uses for astronaut seats—came to Lu because of two events. First, she has tiny feet and could never find stylish shoes in size three. "You can only wear kids' Mary Janes for so long," says Lu. "I used to buy size fives that didn't fit." Eventually, she found Arthur Beren, a San Francisco boutique that carries the Taryn Rose brand, which produces small sizes. A chance meeting between Lu and the designer at a shop promotion led to a job at Rose's Los Angeles atelier. "I wanted to know if I could do it," says Lu, explaining her year of learning the business with Rose. "I didn't want to waste my husband's money or forever be the debtor in our marriage," she says.

Next, Lu's sister needed shoes for her upcoming wedding. While she had the perfect pair for the ceremony, those wouldn't do for the reception—they were killer to dance in. So Lu, who was also a competitive ballroom dancer, bought her sister a pair of professional dance shoes. That's when inspiration hit. Lu felt women shouldn't have to choose between style and comfort. "I saw a niche in the marketplace," she says.

After another year of research, design and business trips to Tuscany to find the right factory, Lu was ready to launch. She lucked into a meeting with a Nordstrom buyer at her very first trade show appearance in Las Vegas and has been going full steam ever since, although it took a few years to figure out the volatile international finances of the business. "We never anticipated that the exchange rate would play such a big role because all of our shoes are made in Italy. The euro is a roller coaster. When you set prices for buyers at a trade show, you never know how much it will cost you three or four months later. It could be as much as 20% to 30% more. Now, we buy euro forwarding contracts, which lock in approximate prices, so we know what we can afford."

"I love what I do," says Lu, laughing about the fact that she doesn't have an exit strategy with the company celebrating its tenth anniversary. "I'm not really in it for the fame. I do it for the passion." She advises other women to "Do what you love. If you spend 60 hours a week at something you hate, it's a waste of a life."

Redefining entrepreneurial assets

The key to evaluating women's talents for entrepreneurship lies in looking at what women owners accomplish on their own terms and in their own time, instead of benchmarking their performance by the sole known and available standard: male-led firms. "…Our definition of entrepreneurship is male-normative, and women's potential for entrepreneurship is judged in terms of their resemblance to male entrepreneurs," concurs Tomas Chamorro-Premuzic, professor of business psychology at University

College London and cofounder of Meta, an entrepreneurship consultancy.

In a 2014 *Harvard Business Review* blog entitled, "The Unnatural Selection of Male Entrepreneurs," the professor explains that "this only continues to incentivize behavior that is more impulsive, aggressive, or overconfident." Gender bias, says Chamorro-Premuzic, is at the root of all the handwringing about women's supposed disadvantages in starting and running businesses. Their tendency to be risk-averse, for instance, rather than a drag on success actually protects women from failure by keeping them on guard against problems and threats. "Unsurprisingly," he continues, "higher risk-taking increases the propensity to launch a business, but does not correlate with greater startup success. In fact, conscientious and prudent founders tend to do significantly better."

His list goes on, embracing women's patience, which not only motivates staffs, but supports realistic goal-setting. Finally, as every woman who runs a business seems to say, Chamorro-Premuzic emphasizes the most important reason women are made to be entrepreneurs: "…Startup founders are overwhelmingly happy with their choice: they report higher levels of job satisfaction and a better work-life balance, even when they work more to earn less. …Business ownership is an important avenue through which women can break through the glass ceiling encountered within established organizations…."

Clearly, it's an excellent time for women launch their dream. There's now lots of good company and, at last, a whole continuum of role models of successful women owners who have been there, done that and can offer support and strategic advice.

5

Weaknesses: Beware the Superwoman Syndrome

Passionate, committed and immediately engaging, Lori Cheek began working on her idea for a business in 2008, launched in 2010, and, as she puts it, over the next half-dozen years, made "tons of mistakes, just about every one there is." Her innovative New York-based dating service, called Cheekd (what else?), got her anointed as one of the "Top 10 CEOs to Watch" by American Express OPEN Forum and attracted an admiring media sobriquet: "The Digital Dating Disruptor." Initially, Cheek launched as a subscriber website offering a dating service that combined the intimacy of real-world romance with the mighty reach of the Internet. Then, "after four tumultuous years of building my startup with the wrong partners, lots of bad decisions and some major rookie mistakes," she responded to changing times and reengineered in 2015 as a mobile app. "The newly launched dating app allows users to solve missed connections with a new technology that wasn't available in 2010," she says.

From design to digital dating

A Kentucky native, Cheek earned a graduate degree in architecture from the University of Kentucky, and moved to New York in the late 1990s. Over the next decade, she held high-end design positions in the commercial sector of the business, known as contract furnishings. She helped plan and design offices for such clients as Goldman Sachs Managing Directors as well as standalone spaces for Christian Dior couture boutiques across the country.

The idea for the business surfaced when she was out to dinner with a colleague. As they were leaving the restaurant, he slipped his business card to an attractive woman dining with a group at another table. "He'd written on it, 'Want to have dinner?' I looked back and thought I loved that intriguing moment because he didn't interrupt the woman's dinner." On the one hand, she found the gesture romantic and mysterious. On the other, she couldn't believe he'd just given all his contact information to a perfect stranger. "I had this light bulb go on that wouldn't go off about how to take the business out of that business card and use it for dating," she says. Soon, she gave up architecture and "instead of building structures, began building relationships."

The first iteration of Cheekd leveraged the idea of slipping a captivating come-on card to a romantic prospect. "Ever see an intriguing stranger whether on your morning commute or even in an elevator?" says Cheek. If so she thought we all have three choices. "You could never see them again. You could walk up and say hello. Or you could simply slip them a Cheekd card."

Registering online, original subscribers paid $20 to receive a deck of 50 sleek black Cheekd cards about the size of business cards, and paid $9.95 a month thereafter to keep the cards active. Each card had a unique saying on it, "kind of a pickup line, an icebreaker, and a unique code," says Cheek. Lines were designed to lend a touch of clandestine intrigue about who and what a recipient would find by visiting the website and inputting the code to connect. No one exchanged any personal information to set up the date.

The 50 card options ran the gamut from snarky and funny to romantic and wistful. Choosing one with just the right enticement was key to the appeal. Cheek's favorites: "I'm way cooler than your date." Or, "I just put all my drinks on your tab." Or, for the straightforward approach, "I'm hitting on you." Softer sells included, "My fate is in your hands" or "This leads to someone you should meet." Options included a doggie deck because so many people connect while walking dogs: "You'll like my doggie's style," and "I bark up your tree." As a New York enterprise, there was also a Wall Street version: "Add me to your portfolio" and "All my bank accounts are Swiss." Describing the experience, Cheek says, "It's like online dating, only backwards, because first you meet and, if all goes well, then you connect online."

Passion only goes so far

Cheek spent a year "walking in circles about how I had this idea," talking to anyone and everyone. Branding and the company name came together after a while of trying to figure out what to call the cards. Looking in the mirror one day, and thinking for the umpteenth time how much trouble she had with her name, the idea and the obvious collided. Slipping someone a dating card turned into, "You've been Cheekd."

"I made all these missteps," she says in retrospect. "I was an architect and a designer and I had no idea what I was doing building this business. But I was sure it was a genius idea and I just thought I'd have this website and I'd be a billionaire within a year. I already had my jet planned out, what it was going to look like and everything." Cheek had no notion of how to build a site or create online infrastructure. She didn't have a business plan. She didn't have a strategy. She didn't think to check into any business classes or entrepreneurial workshops. Rather, Cheek had the galvanizing conviction of an idea she believed in, utterly, and some resources that let her focus on it. "In the beginning, I had saved so much money from my career in design that I thought I could just spend for a year, even on marketing."

Some months later, at a party, Cheek met two guys who also thought the idea was genius. "So we met the next morning and started developing a business plan." First came building the website. Self-funded, she outsourced the job to vendors around the world because those costs were lower than in the US, including developers in Bolivia, the Netherlands, New Zealand and London. "We'd have these crazy conversations on conference calls at different hours in different languages that were really difficult to schedule and bring everybody together as a team."

It took a long year to launch, but the site finally went up in 2010. Experienced IT entrepreneurs and developers counsel startups to get a minimal product up and running in no more than three months. Building out just enough to test feedback will reveal if customers want the product and will spend money to own it. Then, with critical customer knowledge and minimal investment, founders can move on to the next iteration to meet market needs. But Cheek got locked into a static and unforgiving cycle.

"I made some serious mistakes in technology by hiring people that just weren't legitimate. For a year my site was pretty broken," she says. Worse, the two partners turned out to be another error. Chosen more by serendipity and their enthusiasm rather than any value they could add, Cheek says, "They both had the same skillset, which was a huge mistake. I needed a tech person and a businessperson."

Shark Tank tunes in

For years, ever since Cheek thought up her business, people kept telling her the company was a perfect candidate for *Shark Tank,* the TV show that famously selects budding entrepreneurs to pitch their ideas and secure funding from a panel of self-made ultra-wealthy business owners. Billionaire Mark Cuban, owner, among other things, of the Dallas Mavericks team, and Kevin O'Leary, the software mogul who sold his business to Mattel for nearly $4 billion, could make or break a startup. In January 2013, when the show was casting Season 5, says Cheek, "one of my big supporters in Dallas, Texas, sent me the link and said, 'Why don't you just apply?'" When she clicked the link, the application looked fairly simple, so she filled it out.

Six months went by until Los Angeles called. It was ABC *Shark Tank* saying they liked her idea and wanted to see a video. "I spent a week making this video and I put everything I had into it because I wanted to tell eight million viewers about my idea." A few months later, Cheek was selected and flown out to Los Angeles. "I think they fly about 200 people out there and less than half of them actually end up airing." Throughout the process, she was asked to complete lengthy applications, most of which she didn't understand. Questions included both business and personal issues, including about the company IP or Internet Protocol address, legal and financial questions, information for background and criminal checks and much more. "I had no idea what I was getting into." Then in September 2013, she flew back out to film the episode. "I don't think it could have gone worse," she says today.

"When I told Mark Cuban that I felt like I could change the population with this business, he rolled his eyes and threw up his arms and said, 'You're delusional, and when somebody is delusional, I'm out.'" After that, the rest of the panel faded. "Mark was the one I had my eye on originally and when he went out, I felt like I had just been stabbed in the stomach." A few minutes later, Kevin O'Leary offered his take. "You need to take your hobby behind a barn and shoot it like a rabid dog." Cheek responded in true Cheekd style, announcing that she wouldn't quit. "I walked off the stage and turned to point at all of them and said, 'You will all see me again.'"

The episode aired in February 2014. Although her final intrepid promise wound up on the cutting-room floor, Cheek still scored a bonanza. Within 48 hours of the broadcast, her website had attracted an unprecedented 100,000 unique visitors and she received thousands of sympathetic emails urging her not to give up. "Nearly 50 of those emails were from interested investors," says Cheek.

What doesn't kill you...

Despite the trials and errors, Cheek, now 40, has consistently poured energy into inspired guerilla marketing. Every day, on New York streets, she drops Cheekd cards into people's purses, backpacks, pockets and briefcases. People will call and ask how a Cheekd card got into their underwear. "That would be me," she responds.

Her flair for promotion, and, of course, the business idea that makes you smile, generates terrific ongoing press for Cheek, including several online videos, TV features and a *New York Times* profile. In a recent Forbes. com interview that recommended her unconventional PR smarts for other entrepreneurs, Cheek explained: "I carry around Fun-Tak (a sticky adhesive) and attach Cheekd promotional cards and now even images of the app to the inside of the subway cars, movie ads on the platforms, the back of bathroom stalls and I even tag noticeable existing street art. I've even slid a few into dating books at Barnes and Noble to see what kind of traffic they'd drive." She also is an astute social media user. "I've built a character for my business and I've built a character on social media. You're telling your story so it's like your virtual diary and if people are interested, they follow you. I've seen a lot of my followers end up purchasing cards and I'll recognize their name from being a Twitter follower."

Rethinking the model

After the *Shark Tank* "blood bath," as Cheek described it, no less determined, she absorbed the criticism and began rethinking her product and business model, in particular, the need to migrate to mobile. There's no question that's where customers are going. Likely, if Cheek had put in place a more stable technology developer and consistent methods for testing customer feedback, she might have identified the remarkable opportunities in mobile apps before the seemingly ill-fated *Shark Tank* appearance. Even so, it's hard to believe just how fast and how far mobile has accelerated.

The debut iPhone sold in June 2007. A mere seven years later, Americans used smartphone and tablet apps more often than computers to access the Internet. In January 2014, the month before Cheek's *Shark Tank* episode aired, mobile devices accounted for 55% of Internet usage in the US while use of the Internet from PCs was only 45%. The migration to mobile from computer access hasn't slowed either, especially with the boom in developer apps and high-speed "phablets," or large-display smartphones. ABI Research reports a whopping 70 billion mobile apps downloaded worldwide in 2013, or 58 billion via smartphones and 14 billion to tablets. Added together, that's 10 apps downloaded for every man, woman and child on the face of the planet.

Dating apps have exploded along with everything else. A February 2015 study from Internet market researcher GlobalWebIndex found that a staggering 90 million people worldwide used location-based dating apps like Momo and Tinder the month before. In the US, 7% of mobile app users, or 3% of all American adults, report using a dating app, according to think tank Pew Research Center. Cheek got the mobile message.

Rebooting to reconnect

"It took a long time to get over that hurdle of having the wrong people on board from the beginning," she says, acknowledging that her weak technology was the main downfall for *Shark Tank*. Correcting her missing links, she sharpened her knowledge of the financials, a part of the business she dislikes and had left to the partners, and recruited an experienced CTO partner. "He's helped to facilitate and finance the new face and technology," she says. That means a sophisticated Bluetooth-enabled app that sends alerts to Cheekd members when compatible matches are available nearby—in real-time. She's jettisoned the catchy black cards. "While the physical cards were a perfect way to break the ice, we found that our users were still quite intimidated to walk up and slip a card to a total stranger. We discovered a mobile solution to make these IRL [in real-life] encounters easier and less intimidating."

The new app, still being tested and tweaked, is gaining traction. But, says Cheek, "I'm thankful I didn't take the Sharks' advice to quit and move on. I feel like I've taken a crash course in building a business, and I have a MBA now. Despite the occasional overwhelming stress, it's been loads of fun. I've gone from 15 years of helping others build their dreams to a life finally dedicated to building my own. It's the most rewarding feeling. I'm at a ramp right now and I'm ready to fly!"

Missteps women make

Clearly, over the past few decades, female entrepreneurs have developed gender-specific business strengths and women's ways of building muscular brands. Unsurprisingly, then, besides the challenges faced by all startups, women also have gender-specific business vulnerabilities. Most of the issues that cause trouble fall under what I call the "Superwoman syndrome." This go-it-alone, perfectionist and largely defensive behavior in women entrepreneurs covers a range of attitudes, choices and consequences that can handicap their businesses. Consider Lori Cheek, whose narrow focus, despite terrific marketing skills and a contagious new idea, drove her to squander topnotch opportunities and resources, as she's the first to acknowledge. Cheek wouldn't or couldn't step back to learn what she needed to know or to evaluate what needed adjustments along the way. Women in business have shown a tendency to wear such blinders.

Overcoming love/hate of money

Foremost among women owners' nearsightedness is a widespread propensity to avoid taking charge of the business dashboard or to deal with finances, as shown in Cheek's tendency. But drafting a business plan isn't just some laborious business school tradition. Besides being a bible for funders and an evolving blueprint for launch and growth, the business plan process is educational, pushing entrepreneurs to construct a persuasive argument—financial and otherwise—for their model and product. Convincingly presenting that plan, becoming fluent in its every detail of pricing and profit, will encourage funders and stakeholders to bet on the business. Being logical and open about calculating the appropriate debt that will increase the odds of succeeding is another essential of being in charge.

"One of the hurdles for women entrepreneurs is that they tend to be risk-averse," says angel investor Joanne Wilson. Women owners prefer to bootstrap and self-fund even when outside funding, such as equity investment or a bank loan, would catapult growth.

"Men grow up with a goal. They have their eyes on the prize," says Laura Fredricks, founder of Expert on the ASK, a coaching and training consultancy. "Women are too random about their goals." An experienced attorney, Fredricks moved from being a deputy attorney general for Pennsylvania into nonprofit fundraising, launching major gifts programs that raised millions of dollars for large organizations, such as Temple and Pace Universities. Recently, she expanded her reach into the for-profit sector, offering coaching lessons to help owners and business professionals successfully "ask" for funding, assets, salary increases or other corporate rewards. Fredricks points to the lack of role models for women to explain their reluctance to discuss money, although like many others, she sees change on the horizon.

One recurrent mistake of women entrepreneurs when talking to funders is "the assumed ask," says Fredricks. That is, when everyone's enjoying the conversation, women assume its genial nature will be enough to drive money. "Women want people to like them, and if everyone's smiling and nodding, women assume money will just happen. Why put that big bad word 'ASK' in there? Women think, 'They know what I want. They see me struggling with my business. They'll do the right thing.'" Not without being engaged in a substantive agenda. Typically, women simply don't get "the ask" out, says Fredricks.

The overriding reason is because "women don't want to hear 'No,'" she continues. "The problem is women feeling as if they're asking for themselves rather than the business." Interestingly, in a 2014 interview, Sen. Kirsten Gillibrand (D - NY) pointed to that exact hurdle when she raised funds for her election campaign: "I was embarrassed to ask people for money," said Gillibrand. "And, at one point something very simple occurred to me—it wasn't about me. It's not about whether I win or lose. It's whether the issues that I'm fighting for, whether we achieve them. And so when you begin to realize the money's not for you, it is so freeing."

Similarly, women entrepreneurs need to learn to separate the personal from the business. If they carefully prepared for presentations by absorbing the details of the business plan and rehearsing potential objections or questions, then women could ask for backing with conviction. "They can say, 'This is what I want, think and deserve because it's a business. It's not about me,'" advises Fredricks.

Comfortable at the bottom

Besides avoiding asking for funding altogether, women often fall into the trap of thinking too small. "Women don't start big enough," says Fredricks. "They say they want to start a coaching business and have, oh, five clients, to begin. I say, 'No, you don't. You want to be international and be at the top. Think big." She suggests women ramp up both their belief and their goals. "You get what you attract. And when it becomes a must, you'll do it."

This start-at-the-bottom attitude poisons the way women organize their funding plans. Their early approach usually taps friends and relatives first, for $25 or $100, instead of the top largest prospects. "Begin with the six- and seven-figure possibilities and then wind your way down," urges Fredricks, "because that sets you up for success. I always hear women saying all they need is a little seed money and that's what they're going after. But when you start that way, you're pushing a boulder uphill. Start at the top and see what you get." Women also often apply for less money from lenders than they want or need, anticipating negative responses.

One woman owner, who's corrected past errors, says: "I've learned not to ask for too little because then bankers don't take me seriously."

Obviously, playing it safe can work both for and against a business owner. But women's tendency to avoid financial risk and substantial loans means they often lack the capital that could grow their businesses into success. As with so many of women owners' other concerns and fears, decisions about taking on debt are colored by their observation and experience. A typical worry is that outside equity partners or investors, usually male, will dictate business priorities and goals or interfere with the alternative ways women prefer to develop the business. They may therefore avoid being in a position of having to fight such battles. In addition, most government and corporate set-asides for women-owned procurement contracts require 51% ownership and that may be driving women's decisions. Finding the right fit and the appropriate financial partner is key, but too many women decide it's easier not to try.

Standing in the shadows

Besides often avoiding risk, women tend to be much more timid and modest about tooting their own horn than men are, and undersell their accomplishments and credentials as a result. For example, a 2015 study by three sociology professors at Stanford, New York and the University of Washington, found that male scholars are much more likely to cite their own work in research and academic papers than are women. Since hiring, tenure, salary and promotions in academia are built on such citations, the researchers speculated that the more modest practices of women might well contribute to the persistent gender gap in faculty hiring and promotions. Suggesting explanations, the study authors noted that men evaluate their own abilities more positively than women, but also, and here's the nub of the issue: "Men face fewer social sanctions for self-promotion."

Going it alone

Women never seem to take a break. Women entrepreneurs think their enterprise won't run at all unless they're around to start and steer the engines. Several factors drive that fear. Whether pushed into it or consciously chosen, women who start a business frequently arrive at that option because of a feeling of not fitting within traditional corporate structures. They are women who had to play by their own rules to get ahead or perform well. As a result, they're unaccustomed to delegating and/or don't trust anyone to perform the way they do. The business becomes very personal, and taking time or resources from work feels impossible.

"Women are relatively new to the professional workforce and those who get to the top tend to work alone, without much teamwork or mentoring," says organizational psychologist Billie Blair at Change Strategists in Los Angeles. "Such women often feel that someone else can't do what they've done." Women also get caught doing double duty. They're continually balancing work and family, weekdays and weekends, while borders between personal and professional keep fluctuating until there's little distinction. That fuels work at a stop-and-go individual pace with customized tasks and schedules that are hard to explain, much less assign, to others.

But women who are continually caught up in the daily whirlwind often lose perspective as well as an up-to-date view of their market or field. Being head down all the time further leads to isolation. Without time to recharge, both business and owner are bound to suffer. At best, doing everything on your own is a recipe for stunted growth. How can anyone build a going concern when the boss is the only one who can get the job done? At worst, it's a path to burnout. Dozens of surveys document that ongoing stress leads to personal health problems and business tunnel vision. As natural multitaskers, women too often put multiple family and business needs ahead of their own health or wellbeing, which means

building blocks of her business. That bodes all manner of problems, from overcharges and missed deadlines to unpleasant surprises and outright disaster. All of it translates into lost dollars, time, energy, resources and maybe even the business.

Learning to speak Tech

Nelly Yusupova is working to change all that. "Women automatically check out when it comes to technology and completely put their trust into their tech person to figure out everything. But I believe technology should be supporting the business, and not the other way around," she says.

A pioneer in women's online development, Yusupova is CTO of Webgrrls International, a networking and mentoring group founded in 1995 for professional women that today has 100 chapters around the world and 30,000 members. She also leads the Webgrrls' largest chapter in New York and is the founder of Digital Woman, her own tech consultancy.

As Yusupova traveled around the country, speaking to startup owners and leading technology workshops, entrepreneurs kept feeding her horror stories. "I felt like a tech doctor," she says. As the rare female techie guru, she thinks people just trusted her with failure stories. "Bootstrap money and years of planning go down the drain when you can't optimize or even understand the tech side of your business," she explains.

After a while, she began hearing common themes in the stories, for instance, the woes of one entrepreneur in the online food space: "A woman I knew called up frantic and desperate, saying she hoped I could help. For the past year, she had paid $60,000 to a developer and hadn't yet seen anything, no product, no coding, nothing. That wasn't even the worst. She had just got off the phone and her developer wanted another $25,000 to finish the project." Listening to the tale, Yusupova heard "so many red flags." She was struck by how easily such mistakes could be avoided or fixed if only entrepreneurs knew how to communicate with developers. "That's when I decided to teach entrepreneurs how to spot the red flags themselves," she says.

Yusupova took three months off to develop TechSpeak, an intensive two-day bootcamp designed to educate nontechnical founders about how to make sure hired IT wizards build the site, software and apps that suit the business. The appropriate startup development process flows from properly using "lean and agile methodologies," she says, referring to a widely adopted entrepreneurial viewpoint. A contemporary and already classic approach, this new methodology grew up over the past few decades to drive technology-based startups. But the process applies to most every business, especially now that technological foundations buoy all business. Generally, the lean and agile notion supplants the traditional command-and-control hierarchy of big companies by putting various sensors in place that will alert managers to key signals from customers and the market. That allows for rapid revisions or reactions. Instead of stockpiling inventory or making decisions in advance that are mere guesses, the company responds to actual customer need and demand.

When applied to startups, the lean and agile concept consists of raising only enough money to sustain the business idea for the six to twelve months the founder needs to test its viability. Over the first three months, developers build only enough of the product that can generate valid customer feedback, say, one to three features. That's dubbed the "minimum viable product" or MVP. Timing depends on the number of developers and the budget, but if that very first MVP stage "takes more than three months to build and launch, you're taking too long and you need to cut out some features," says Yusupova. "You're building more than you need."

"The whole idea behind 'lean,'" she continues, "is to take this big idea and validate it, so you can understand the problem. You're not just saying, 'I think this is a problem for me, so the rest of the world must have it as well.' You need to make sure that's true by talking to customers and getting feedback." It's certainly possible to hit spot-on at the first try but unlikely. "Most of the time, you've either built the wrong solution or targeted the wrong market. Something is off and customers aren't using your product," says Yusupova. That requires regrouping and refining until customers actually want what you're selling.

Success, she and other startup gurus believe, comes from resolving the calculation of vitamins versus painkillers. "Vitamins are a billion-dollar industry and lots of people take them," acknowledges Yusupova. But that's discretionary. "The idea behind customer validation is so you can build a painkiller. That's something people will pay for. As a business startup, you want an idea people will pay money for right away. That means a remedy, something that will fix something."

Knowing which way the weather is blowing

Keep in mind that no entrepreneur can grow a business without making mistakes, and hopefully learning from them. Even so, when markets, models or competition shift, it's up to the entrepreneur to stay up-to-speed on the weather forecast so she puts the wind at her back.

Perhaps that's something Cheek missed in mobile's early potential. She might have been so focused on the website and marketing that when her customers began gravitating to mobile, the change in climate flew under her radar. Had Cheek first built a MVP, she might have saved a lot of time, trouble and *Shark Tank* venom.

6

Opportunities: Adopting New Business Models

Creative and emerging alternatives for financing, marketing, management and technology offer women today flexible and much more affordable platforms to experiment with innovations that will form new kinds of companies and lead to growth. It's no longer costly to get that MVP or minimum viable product up-and-running—particularly if talented friends agree to volunteer time and skills, even from remote locations. Failure to launch has lost its stigma. In fact, trying and tweaking is both expected and a badge of honor.

Younger women especially, ambitious and well-educated, in STEM (science, technology, engineering, mathematics) and other male-dominated fields, are sidestepping old hurdles to explore new terrain. The road ahead for female entrepreneurs is signposting new turns and a broader swath of options for paths to success. Just as the rising She Economy is reconfiguring global expectations and environments, the new byways open to women are slowly and inexorably remapping the landscape of business models and startups.

Re-engineering possible

At 23, Supriya Hobbs personifies these forward-looking trends. A June

2014 graduate of the University of Illinois at Urbana-Champaign with a mechanical engineering degree, Hobbs cofounded a startup during her senior year called Miss Possible: "Dolls to inspire girls across generations." She wants to market doll versions of trailblazing real women in science, and include mobile apps with each toy appropriate to the field for girls age 6 – 10. The mission is to encourage girls to consider careers in science and engineering.

Hobbs and cofounder Janna Eaves, who graduates from Urbana as a materials science engineer at the end of 2015, "thought the dolls would a great way to introduce role models and the apps would give girls hands-on learning about skills. Using the apps would help kids gain confidence about doing things they might not otherwise think they're capable of doing," says Hobbs.

Marie Curie was their choice for the Miss Possible prototype. Curie's singular claim to fame, among her other achievements, is being the only scientist in history to win two Nobel prizes in different fields, one in physics and the other in chemistry. Complete with lab coat wardrobe and coordinating accessories, the Miss Possible childlike Curie doll also comes with a small chemistry kit and playful physics and chemistry apps for activities kids can easily try around the house. Going forward, the cofounders plan to give doll owners free access to online content and app updates while charging users for the apps if they don't want the doll.

Backtracking the gender gap

The business idea was sparked by the women's experiences in studying engineering. "We saw an imbalance looking around in our courses," says Hobbs. Where were all the women? "There weren't many people who looked like us." Obviously, that's also true in engineering classrooms and companies across the country. The field of engineering, points out Hobbs, is fundamentally grounded in solving problems, which led the two students to start looking into the backstory of the gender imbalance.

"They say studying engineering teaches you how to think," says Hobbs. "It's not just about wanting to solve this problem, but also how to take it apart and look at the data and figure out how we actually fix this. What are the various pieces of the problem?"

The pair began talking to peers and professionals to discover what motivated them to study engineering. What came floating back, loud and clear, was the influence of role models. "A lot of people have a strong role model that influences their direction toward engineering," says Hobbs, whose mother back in Yardley, Pennsylvania, is an engineer, too. "A desire to change the world also seems to be a common trend. Once we started thinking about this from a business mindset, we realized that we wanted to reach kids early and make it something that was engaging. That's how we came up with the idea of using toys."

The two spent hundreds of hours leading activities with young girls as volunteers at schools and community organizations, testing their impressions and identifying how to best attract young customers. They also set up listening sessions with parents and grandparents to define what would most influence each user group. Originally, the women planned to launch a virtual world for girls. "But when we did customer interviews with parents," says Hobbs, "we heard, 'I don't want my kid just completely staring at a screen to play. And kids were saying, 'Oh, I use my parents' tablet a lot more than the computer.'" Those findings pushed the founders to create a real-world toy and to integrate their hands-on component as a mobile app instead of an online one.

"It happens that not a lot of people were doing this yet so it ended up being a good differentiator for us," says Hobbs. The value-add attraction of a mobile component certainly sounds like a good bet to help sell dolls, which represents a $2.3 billion business in the US, according to the Toy Industry Association.

Alibaba and the seven producers

Fabricating any startup's product prototype is an utter mindbender: no template; no money; no established design team; no forgiveness for trial and error; no resources; no guidelines to determine when you're on target and when you're heading down the wrong path; no comfort zone or protocol for refining quirks or adjusting glitches—a serious challenge. "We had to recruit people to our team and it's hard to convince anyone this is worth doing, especially when nobody's getting paid," says Hobbs, in characteristic understatement.

To add to the challenges, the founders learned that there are no longer any vinyl mold makers operating in the US. The industry has moved abroad, where it's a lot cheaper and faster. They began researching overseas manufacturers, preparing themselves for a lengthy search and long waits to view model prototypes. Both concerns evaporated after an Internet search led to Alibaba.com, the giant global wholesale ecommerce platform that launched in China in 1999 (and set records after going public in September 2014). Promoting "one stop sourcing," the trade network serves millions of buyers and sellers in 40 commercial categories across more than 190 countries and regions.

Their Alibaba search turned up several third-party vendors that produce custom-made dolls. Working through the list, Hobbs and Eaves vetted firms, checked certifications and identified a Chinese manufacturer. "It was hard to work with people who have the exact opposite hours we do, but it was a positive challenge," she says. It also went fast. Turnaround time for the prototype was only a couple of weeks. The entire process was completed in just a month, and most of that was shipping time to view an intermediate mold and approve a final one.

That left Hobbs and Eaves with a Marie Curie prototype but no money to actually mass-produce the dolls. The next step, therefore, was to launch a crowdfunded campaign, joining the thousands of entrepreneurs who are leveraging the remarkable power of these new multibillion-dollar funding platforms.

Moving the tribe online

The practice of raising small-scale funds and loans from an affinity group or network, such as a tribe, crafts alliance or an extended family, is a centuries-old tradition around the world. In the 1970s, contemporary microfinancing was formally established in the developing world by the hundreds of microcredit initiatives set up by Muhammad Yunus and the Grameen Bank to encourage local economies. Public online platforms began surfacing around 2003, including one called ArtistShare, which reached out to fans of specific artists. But that concept was overly complicated and faded quickly.

To ramp up, crowdfunding needed a critical mass of online users and the coming of ubiquitous broadband technology. Cash-strapped business owners desperate for alternatives during the crippled investment climate of the 2008 financial crisis further fueled its rise. Real success arrived with the debut of Indiegogo, but even that platform had to scramble to make a go of the clumsy new model. Late in 2009, Indiegogo nearly went under until the three cofounders redesigned the site and simplified the campaign sign-up process.

Funding gets democratic

Essentially, crowdfunding lets anyone pitch an idea online, whether a cause, an art project, research, a sports team or a business, and if it draws enough interest, raise money to implement the idea. Asking large numbers of online users—worldwide strangers—to each ante up $25, $50 or more obviously is a much easier sell than persuading an angel to invest hundreds of thousands of dollars. Plus, crowdfunding sidesteps the hands-on involvement of investors, which may or may not be a good thing.

It's hard to overemphasize how radically crowdfunding has changed the startup cosmos and empowered entrepreneurs. Before direct online funding, explains Lee Barken, at San Diego accounting firm Haskell

& White, each hopeful owner had to build a market-ready product that demonstrated scalability and commercial potential before seeking financing. Now, says Barken, even before a product is manufactured or released, "crowdfunding provides market validation and identifies people who actually want to buy your product."

Available in a widening range of flavors, donor options and ROI (see the chart, below), the two main types of crowdfunding are reward-based campaigns or "product pre-sell," and equity investments, or "crowdfunding investing" and "securities-based crowdfunding." The older rewards model, used by Kickstarter and Indiegogo, exchanges perks or products for individual donations, and the campaign can be partially or fully funded for entrepreneurs to receive all the money, depending on the platform and the rules. Either way, every campaign pays a fee to the platform, which varies widely. The newer equity-based model kicked in mid-2015, after changes and approval by the Securities and Exchange Commission to legislation mandated by the 2012 Jumpstart Our Business Startups or JOBS Act. Now, private companies may qualify to sell equity in the firm and raise up to a hefty $50 million from both accredited and non-accredited investors.

CHARACTERISTICS OF DIFFERENT CROWDFUNDING MODELS

Crowd-funding model	Business model	Features	Pros	Cons
Donation	Donation-based	Philanthropic: Funders donate without expecting monetary compensation	No risk	Donors do not acquire security interest. Entrepreneurs have difficulty raising substantial capital
Donation	Reward-based	Funders receive a token gift of appreciation or pre-purchase of a service or product. This model is evolving into a marketplace of its own, with firms raising considerable sums through pre-sales.	Low risk (primarily fulfillment and fraud risk). No real potential for financial return.	Potential return is small. No security is acquired, and there is no accountability mechanism. Most entrepreneurs may have difficulty raising substantial capital without a product with mass appeal to sell.
Investing	Equity-based	Funders receive equity instruments or profit sharing arrangements.	Potential to share in the profitability of the venture. Unlimited potential for financial gain. May attract relatively large numbers of investors.	Potential loss of investment. Equity holders are subordinate to creditors in the event of a bankruptcy. Securities laws related to crowdfund investing may be complex.

Crowd-funding model	Business model	Features	Pros	Cons
Investing	Lending-based	Funders receive a debt instrument that pays a fixed rate of interest and returns principal on a specified schedule.	Pre-determined rate of return agreed upon between lender and borrower. Debt holders are senior to equity holders in case of bankruptcy. Secured status may make it easier for entrepreneurs to raise capital.	May be subordinate to senior creditors. Startups' high-failure rate presents similar risks of loss as an equity investment, but with capped potential returns. Requires a business already generating cash flow. Existing/established, cash flow positive businesses may consider this option because they can offer a more structured exit opportunity than typical equity offerings.
	Royalty-based	Less common than the other models. Funders receive a share in a unit trust, which acquires a royalty interest in the intellectual property of the fundraising company. A percentage of revenue is paid out over a period of time. The payout varies depending on the periodic revenue.	Potential gain is unlimited but the rate of gain is predetermined by the interest rate. Investment presents less risk or return than an equity investment, but more than a debt instrument.	Potential loss of investment. Risk of loss comparable to that of an equity investment, but investment offers lower potential returns than equity. The business could cease paying royalties if it chose to operate without the intellectual property in question. These instruments generally attract smaller pools of investors than other CFI models, so entrepreneurs may find it more difficult to raise capital with this model.

— From "Crowdfunding's Potential for the Developing World," 2013. infoDev, Finance and Private Sector Development Department. Washington, DC: © World Bank.

Feel the peer power

Obviously a boon for all entrepreneurs, crowdsourced funding offers particular benefits for women-led startups, allowing women to find other women and likeminded professionals directly. Women can bypass entire layers of male financial decision makers, lender requirements and middlemen. The small-amount, online ask is also easier for women, who, as we've seen, often shy from asking for big money directly. Overall, women-led firms do well on rewards-based platforms. A survey of more than a thousand Kickstarter campaigns in July 2014 found that women who started projects were more likely to succeed than were men.

Moreover, established male investors have been notoriously disinterested in the kinds of businesses so many women launch: service solopreneur enterprises that don't scale easily or fast. Approval from the crowd may well be ahead of that curve as well. The democratization of online funding is playing out against dramatic and ongoing changes in the services sector. Whether graphic design, career coaching, healthcare support or other fields, women's service businesses are being redefined by the proliferation of inexpensive and powerful digital tools as well as by anywhere, anytime mobile lifestyles. The digital toolbox includes cloud services, virtual, remote-based talent and global 24-hour social media communications. At long last, service businesses can scale more cost-effectively. In the meantime, crowdfunding accelerates such changes by leveraging women's affinities for making online and social connections.

As a result, service businesses may be moving toward a more attractive investor bet. It's a lot cheaper and easier to fine-tune software than it is to re-engineer or invent hardware. Labor-intensive and costly appliances and devices have already turned into commodity buys—one is as good as the other and roughly the same price. For now and the foreseeable future, it's content, differentiated customer services and mobile apps that are key to growth.

By 2011, more than a million campaigns across hundreds of crowdfunding portals had raised over $2 billion. Volume has more than doubled, with the World Bank projecting the industry to hit $5 billion in 2015, and a staggering $90 billion by 2025. Users can now launch campaigns via mobile in minutes. Keep in mind that this all represents new and untapped funds for largely startup and untried ventures—truly a disruptive market.

Crowdfunding has surely come of age.

Mission control for Miss Possible

Hobbs and Eaves launched their Miss Possible crowdfunding campaign on Indiegogo on July 12, 2014. They set a $75,000 goal, calculating that amount would pay for the first production run of 5,000 Marie Curie dolls. They also had to remember to cover the back-end costs of shipping and handling.

Contributor perks ran the gamut from Miss Possible stickers for $5, a first-run Marie Curie doll for $40 (which the contributor could elect to donate to a charity), a Miss Possible birthday party pack of a doll and goody bags for $150 and an Honorary Miss Possible custom-produced doll for $1,000. A grand donation of $10,000 would buy a talk from Hobbs or Eaves to an organization of the contributor's choosing.

The cofounders further selected Indiegogo's all-or-nothing funding option. If they failed to raise the full amount, they'd owe the service fee but would walk away with nothing. Although it was the more risky option, the two figured that if potential contributors thought that less than $75,000 was sufficient, their campaign would seem less urgent and it would dampen enthusiasm. "We didn't anticipate how much work it would take to prepare for the campaign," says Hobbs, who spent months before the launch building all the elements and social networks for the campaign launch. But their work paid off. By August 16, when the fundraising campaign closed, Miss Possible had exceeded its goal, reeling in a total of $85,775. "We were wowed," says Hobbs.

As the campaign got underway, Hobbs took a job as a process engineer at Eli Lilly in Indianapolis while continuing to work with Eaves to develop Miss Possible. She sees today's climate as prime time to create dolls that encourage young girls to think about STEM careers. "The idea of female empowerment is gaining interest and visibility in the public eye and all the mom blogs talk about issues like this and about how the media portrays women," says Hobbs.

Clearly, she's onto something. In August 2015, billionaire CEO Issac Larian of MGA Entertainment, the biggest privately owned toy company in the world, launched a new line called Project MC^2, with four dolls that each represent one of the STEM fields. "I graduated in 1978, and there was only one girl in the class," Larian told online newsmagazine *Business Insider*, citing his civil engineering degree. "And frankly, she was the smartest." Each of MGA dolls comes with a relevant scientific kit meant to spur girls to try experiments at home. No telling if Miss Possible will gain ground before's Larian's dolls do.

Boosting sales with the virtuous circle

Just as social entrepreneurships are bridging the divide between for-profit and nonprofit, a relatively new marketing strategy, called "cause marketing," has been reinventing traditional advertising and brand promotion. American Express first came up with the idea back in 1983. For several months, each time a cardholder charged an item, the company donated a penny toward restoring the Statue of Liberty. The result was a few million dollars to refurbish the Lady, plus glowing press, consumer good will and increased sales for Amex. Cause marketing, also called "purpose marketing," has been growing ever since.

"In the age of social media, 24/7 news cycles and real-time interaction, having a social Purpose in addition to the traditional 4 Ps [price, product, place (or distribution) and promotion] is a way that companies can differentiate themselves and appeal to the hearts of consumers," Carol Cone explained in a *Huffington Post* interview. Founder of Cone Consulting and the field's research leader, Cone has found that, given comparable price and quality, nearly nine out of 10 (89%) of US consumers are likely to switch brands to one associated with a cause.

The competitive advantages of embedding purpose into the purchase of a product have greatly accelerated in recent years, especially because of big popular initiatives, the low-cost of social media megaphones and the heightened awareness of many multinationals trying to offset their image of greed and heartlessness after a string of environment disasters, executive misdeeds and banking scandals. Dozens of such alliances are now underway: Brawny Towels supports the Wounded Warrior Project, which helps injured veterans; global nonprofit CARE partners with hundreds of retailers, from Apple to Staples to Callaway Golf, in a program called We-Care.com that donates a percentage of every shopper's purchase to the nonprofit to support low-income women; Whole Foods, rated by *Fortune* as one of the best companies to work for, supports sustainable food and animal causes. For-profit businesses in North America now spend nearly $21 billion on sponsoring nonprofit causes and that ratchets up to $55 billion worldwide, according to *IEG Sponsorship Report*, a Chicago-based industry newsletter.

Women are particularly influenced by cause marketing, both as consumers and as business owners. "Women are, by far, the strongest believers in the power of supporting causes," finds a survey conducted by the Georgetown University Center for Social Impact Communication. "Eight out of 10 American women believe that supporting causes creates a sense of purpose and meaning in life; and feel everyone can make a difference through their support."

Women also are more apt to start socially responsible businesses than men, and give more to charities than men do, both as individuals and as business owners. More than half of women business owners with companies of more than $1 million in assets give at least $10,000 to charity annually, compared to only 40% of men, reports the Center for Women's Business Research. Little surprise, then, that women-owned enterprises are avid advocates of cause marketing. By linking their brand and marketing to a cause, they can boost customer awareness, drive sales, burnish their reputation, give back to the community and lower marketing costs, all at the same time. Such promotions also drive repeat purchases because consumers feel they're doing the right thing every time they buy the product. Overall, the growing reach of being a responsible business is continuing to grow mindshare and sales—and women are definitely benefitting.

Getting cause and campaign right

Successful cause marketing requires a focus on the *marketing*. It's not charity. The process includes identifying an appropriate cause and spreading the word. To be effective, cause campaigns must be founded on authentic advocacy. There's no mileage in supporting an issue the owner doesn't care about. Customers are bound to catch on, which could make all efforts backfire. Then, too, the cause must align with the company's products. Anyone who runs a dessert bakery should avoid campaigns that talk about obesity or low-fat diets. It's an utter disconnect. Instead, the marketing ought to connect with the overall brand. After that, owners must take a cold, analytic look at the tangible business benefits. "Cause marketing was one of the primary marketing vehicles used to get my company on the map," says Adrienne Lenhoff, who owns Shazaaam! PR agency based outside Detroit. The agency has been providing pro bono services worth millions of dollars since its launch in 2001.

"We've worked with nonprofits ranging from local to regional and national in scope," says Lenhoff, "and we've learned to develop a litmus test for determining which relationships are worth pursuing." Cause marketing works best, she says, when you combine the "right level of the passion or belief in the cause with the right level of passion for the clear benefits to the business bottom line." Her alignment with groups such as research organizations to cure breast cancer, a Detroit urban restoration group, a local university and the Detroit chapter of the National Association of Women Business Owners helped those organizations to raise significant dollars. The partnerships also gave Lenhoff a network of potential clients, a higher profile among executives who might hire her company and an enviable reputation for success. All of that translated into business.

Owners often get lost in the virtue of the cause, but again, cause marketing can only be effective when it's viewed as a marketing effort. "The pitfall for small businesses in cause marketing is not understanding the basics—the equivalent of not knowing how to ask for the order," says Diana Kimbrell, whose cause marketing agency, Kimbrell & Company, is based in Sausalito, California. The partnering nonprofit or organization needs to be held accountable to support its end of the promotional effort. "Calculate how many times your company name and logo will be seen, what kind of information will be placed on their website or social media accounts, how many banners will be seen, what kind of article will be written for the nonprofit's newsletter and how many people it goes to. It's simple math," says Kimbrell.

Most importantly, owners need a signed contract that includes details about how the organization will measure results. Obviously, that needn't mean formal surveys or polls, as these are likely beyond the capacity of a small nonprofit. But owners should see some periodic reports about results. Overall, such campaigns need patience. Cause marketing typically takes time to yield results, which is another reason to choose a cause close to the owner's heart and mind. Once entrepreneurs make a commitment, they need to stick to it.

Participating in community and nonprofit activities is becoming a hallmark of women owners, significantly more so than for male-led companies. That kind of engagement gives women businesses an additional competitive advantage because, increasingly, consumers, stakeholders and even funders now note which brands help and which take the money and run.

Marketing the seal of responsibility

In response to the strengthening traction of social entrepreneurship and corporate citizenship, a nonprofit group called the B Lab has devised something called "B Corp certification." The group awards that designation to companies that apply for and meet B Corp's exacting standards for environmental and social performance as well as for accountability and transparency. As the website puts it: "B Corp is to business what Fair Trade certification is to coffee or USDA Organic certification is to milk." For example, Cabot Creamery, based in Vermont, actively markets itself as a B Corp company, putting the B Corp seal on its butter and other product packaging.

Officially launched in 2009, after a few years of developing its evaluation and application standards, B Lab has now certified nearly 1,400 B Corps in 41 countries and more than 120 industries, says Katie Kerr, the group's communications director. That includes companies like footwear firm Dansko, ecommerce platform Etsy and even Kickstarter, the rewards-based crowdfunding platform. B Lab certified companies cover a range of industries, including banks, food producers and consulting firms, and 40% are minority and women-owned. Nearly half of B Corp companies (46%) offer a generous 26 days of maternity leave for fulltime workers and are more likely than other firms to offer childcare benefits.

Besides the process for a B Corp-certified seal of accountability, B Lab has pioneered a new corporate structure, called the "benefit corporation." Rather than only pursuing profitability, this corporate structure allows owners to align profits with purpose, especially when it comes to exit strategies. Each state controls its own laws for business incorporation and these vary considerably. Forming as a benefit corporation, therefore, depends on whether the state in which the business incorporates has passed legislation that permits benefit corporations. Without such legal structures, owners who want to do the right thing can be hamstrung.

In 2000, for example, the founders of Ben & Jerry's ice cream were forced to sell to an international conglomerate that didn't particularly care about the company's long-established environmental mission. Vermont law then dictated that owners must sell to buyers that have the highest offer for shareholders, no matter what. A decade on, the options for Ben & Jerry's would have changed radically. Vermont became second in the country to allow benefit corporations, after Maryland. Had Ben & Jerry's been structured as a benefit corporation, with a mission of purpose as well as profit, the owners could have held out for a sale to buyers that would agree to uphold the company's practices and values. When California passed its benefit corporation law in 2012, Patagonia, the outdoor apparel company with some $500 million in profits, revised its structure to protect its future as a socially responsible venture.

The movement has grown quickly. To date, 31 states and the District of Columbia—and counting—have passed laws that allow benefit corporation structures, while B Corp continues its legislative advocacy. The easiest time to become a benefit corporation is at startup, before the business has incorporated, assuming it's an option in that state. For business owners, both the benefit corporate structure and B Corp certification provide the brand-building benefits of independent validation that tells customers the company is trustworthy. "We learned in the recession that a focus on short-term financials doesn't work," says communications director Kerr. "Companies now need to share long-term success and a durable bottom line. No mission, no margin."

For female owners, the B Corp opens doors to a community of resources, peers who are doing business with a triple bottom line, and, as Kerr says, "a focus on a full life." An annual gathering every October in Vermont helps to keep the community connected and engaged in shared values and goals. "There's a new generation of entrepreneurs focused on this type of business," says Kerr. "It reflects a cultural trend."

Leading at the bleeding edge

Amanda Kahlow, 39, CEO of San Francisco-based 6Sense, is among the elite few: One of only 3% of startups with a female CEO to be backed by venture capital between 2011 and 2013. She secured $12 million in Series A or first-round funding. Then, in 2015, 6Sense announced second-round Series B funding of $20 million, bringing total investments to $36 million.

Hard driving and focused on little but building her company, Kahlow says, "This is not for everyone. It's brutal. I don't have much of a personal life. 6Sense is my family. My life is my work. I don't think it's realistic to tell women you can have it all. Some women, like Sheryl Sandberg, are fortunate to have the financial resources and support to allow them to have it all, but for most women that's not reality. You need to make choices." 6Sense also is not the first company Kahlow has launched. Like many entrepreneurs on the learning curve to success, she previously started and ran other ventures. And like many women entrepreneurs, she rather backed into the 6Sense concept.

A predictive intelligence engine, and recognized as the emerging leader in the field, 6Sense is part of the fast-moving Big Data market, which tech researcher IDG estimates will grow into a whopping $41.5 billion industry as early as 2018. Designed to drive sales and marketing for business-to-business (B2B) companies, 6Sense takes ranking sales leads to a whole new level. Conventional sales lead scoring done by earlier offerings rank only the likelihood of a purchase by a customer. The innovative 6Sense product analyzes vast amounts of time-sensitive data from a customer's organization, its industry and associated communities to provide detailed information about what business customers want, the stage of their buying cycles, how close they are to purchase, and therefore which new prospects are worth pursuing.

6Sense promises to forecast future buyers with more than 80% accuracy. Similar predictive services typically focus only on a company's known contacts making inquiries and "profiles" of appropriate customers—that is, the bottom of the sales cycle or "funnel," as it's called. Kahlow says that represents only about 10% of prospects. In contrast, 6Sense intelligence comes up with more exact predictions for what a client or prospect company or contact will buy, when they will buy it and how much they will buy—all pretty nifty data if you're a business marketing to Fortune 1000 customers. In a trade publication interview, Kahlow explained it this way: "Amazon knows what you want to purchase before you even know you want to buy it, and that's what we're doing for sales."

Growing up entrepreneurial

From one perspective, Amanda Kahlow's background logically led to piloting a pioneer high-tech company. Viewed from another, it's a wonder she navigated the choppy waters altogether. Her parents divorced when she was two and she, her mom and two older brothers "moved all the time," living in some 22 houses in Virginia, Washington DC, Maryland and Colorado before she turned 18.

"My mom was a secretary to Averell Harriman, worked for Winston Churchill, Jr., and was an operative for the CIA based in Copenhagen," says Kahlow. She left that behind to look after Kahlow and her two brothers, skipping from job to job and city to city. "She never made more than $19,000 a year while raising us, but I didn't feel poor," says Kahlow. "My family ate block cheese, frozen peas and powdered milk but we never lived without. I don't know that I recognized how little we had because Mom always gave us incredible love and belief in ourselves."

Kahlow saw all the changes as an adventure, with new rooms, schools and teachers to reward each move. "My brothers hated all the moves and inconsistency, but I always got excited," she says. "It was an opportunity to make new friends. I think that's why I thrive in new environments." Adjusting to all those moves likely allows her to quickly establish personal connections and business relationships.

Kahlow's father, who lives in Virginia, was the techy one. Kahlow and her brothers visited often. "He would always ask what was going on in our lives. He made me feel special and smart, even when I wasn't excelling."

He started a few companies, mostly software. "When I was seven, I'd go to his office and play with the huge software tapes on big movie reels. I saw how things get created and how you build things and got my first taste of business."

After college, with a degree in journalism and marketing, and after briefly working on a startup with her father, Kahlow headed for San Francisco, drawn by an earlier visit she'd made with a college boyfriend. It was in 1999. "I sat on the steps of a Jones Street building stoop, looked up at the big houses on the hill, and thought, 'One day I'll live there,'" says Kahlow. And of course, now she does.

Identifying the sixth sense

In 2010, Kahlow was assisting Cisco in an effort to overhaul the sales process for some of its products. By then, she'd been running CI Insights, her first real launch, for several years. A precursor to 6Sense, CI used Web analytics to generate new business for B2B clients. Kahlow was presenting her findings when a marketing executive interrupted. According to an interview with *TechCrunch,* an online industry magazine, she remembers the next few minutes this way:

> Suddenly one of them dramatically stopped the conversation, looked at me and said, "Amanda do you know what you are doing here?" I responded, "No, what?" And he said, "You know [what] our customers are going to buy before they even know they are going to buy." The room moved to discussion about sending customers a PO [purchase order] before the rep calls the customer. This was the moment I knew we had something game-changing. I knew I no longer could be a modest services business and that I needed to build a scalable repeatable product. I knew there was a door open in front of me and I was going to walk through it.

She was raising money and trying to figure out how to migrate her services model into a technology product when she met the founders of a tech venture called GrepData, which had recently been through the Y Combinator program, one of Silicon Valley's most prestigious startup incubators. Kahlow had an innovative business model in search of a product. The founders of GrepData—Viral Bajaria, Premal Shah and Dustin Chang—had a Big Data analytics platform in search of users. It was a match made in tech heaven. Kahlow has since brought on the trio as cofounders, with Bajaria as CTO, and has ramped up staff to about 35, with about a third women. For now, customers are multiplying, mostly among IT firms, including Cisco, Dell and CBS Interactive. Kahlow foresees the platform expanding to hospitality, manufacturing, healthcare and financial services.

Being the female in the room

Kahlow has a push/pull attitude about being a woman leader in the extremely male-driven sector of high technology startups. She'd rather not nod to gender at all, preferring to focus on personality, work ethic, ambition and determination as the fuel for her success. "I'm a strong woman and I haven't had an issue. I was always taken seriously. Perception for women is because we think we ought to conform. We internalize the bias and if we don't value ourselves, no one else will."

All undeniably true. On the other hand, Kahlow is well aware that she and her company are unusual. She's also begun thinking harder about the role she can play in helping more women get to the top. Choosing the term beloved by entrepreneurs to announce a shift in their model, Kahlow says she "pivoted a few years before the funding and made a conscious decision that it was now okay to look and act feminine."

The realization came during a lunch with a friend who works as a "happiness director," coaching clients on authenticity, among other things. Kahlow was "in a white dress all dolled up," and the conversation shifted to how she wouldn't be taken seriously if she dressed like that for meetings and work. "My friend said I wasn't being my true self by 'acting masculine,' and she was right. I can't win by not being who I am. If I can do that in this market, then I can be the role model for girls and women to be loving and kind as well as strong and have conviction. It's a fine balance."

She adds that while her masculine side is important for business, she also wears pink and red nail polish. "I want women to know that they can do it if that's what they want."

Despite daily pressures, the 24/7 schedule and no time or space for dating though she'd like to be married and have kids, Kahlow says she's never been happier. "I have a company and a culture all driving toward the same vision. Every step is a lesson. I'm at inner peace and loving it. I relish my life every day."

7

Threats: Why a Woman Can't Be a Man

Top to bottom, the default ways of doing business are male. However sweeping and simplistic that may sound, it is reality, and accounts for the bulk of perils and restrictions routinely encountered by women entrepreneurs. Male styles of leadership, organization and business performance inform and influence an extraordinary range of workplace expectations and daily perceptions. That goes for everyone, from funders to staff, customers to suppliers, business schools to media and entire industries that have yet to sincerely embrace top-down change to ensure diversity.

As a result, male-defined benchmarks and attitudes are what women must buy into. They grow up groomed to meet and internalize definitions, standards and marks of success that men have shaped over time. These are called "social" and "corporate" standards, with no thought given to its male foundation. Yet none of the prevailing standards note, much less integrate, women's ways of thinking or working.

For sure, the gross gender bias practices that, to varying degrees, characterized the 20th century have dwindled, at least in developed nations, although dozens of exceptions indeed prove the rule here. Some activists label the last century as the one that secured civil rights, while the

21ˢᵗ century is slated to be all about the rights of women. Perhaps. But if so, think how many years of history and unrest in the 20ᵗʰ century had to unfold before rights for people of color took on any urgency. And those battles endure.

Consider that laws for women's rights have been on the books for nearly a century when it comes to voting and a half-century for mandating equal pay. Yet here we are: A scant minority of women in Congress, 19% in the House and only 20% in the Senate; less than 5% women CEOs in the Fortune 500; 80 cents for women to the male $1 on the job; and legions of women cracking their heads and hearts on glass ceilings. What's the hitch here? What's taking so long?

Men will be boys

Decisions and behavior are certainly more nuanced nowadays. Policies have been modified. Efforts have been made. Insensitive language is frequently unintentional or simply careless habit. A few years back, Heidi Roizen, a high-profile partner at Silicon Valley venture capital firm Draper Fisher Jurvetson and formerly a successful entrepreneur, posted a blog entry about her earlier stint at a different firm. Virtually every senior woman in business in every field has a similar tale to tell.

At the former firm, all the male partners and Roizen, the lone woman, were gathered around a big table in the conference room. The investment firm was riding out an economic downturn and the partners had to decide which of the ventures they'd backed should be cut loose. Each was fighting for the deals he, and she, managed.

After a dozen such bids, one of the guys, posted Roizen, "…pushed back from the table, stood up, and said, 'This is bullshit. Each one of us is just sitting here with his dick in his hand asking for more money without truly justifying it.'" Dead silence as everyone looked to Roizen to react. She said, "This is making me very uncomfortable. Because I don't even have a dick to hold." The instant reply: "Well if you need a dick to hold you can borrow mine anytime." That, says Roizen, broke the tension and everyone laughed.

Sex and the entrepreneur

Nine out of 10 times, it's male clients, lenders and investors to whom women entrepreneurs must pitch. Approval by those men is critical for business. It's therefore always a calculated decision for women about how or whether to put the brakes on such behavior.

When male colleagues or clients edge into improper territory, "I typically prevent them from making a bad decision instead of shaming them or embarrassing them," says Ashley Swartz, founder and CEO of Furious Corp., an enterprise solution based in New York and Israel that manages inventory and planning for video and TV publishers. "I'm the one who takes the responsibility by putting on my big-girl pants and dealing with it. Your path to resolving such behavior has a lot to do with the kind of woman you are and your personality. I don't think there's any right answer. But it does affect your business."

For about a decade, with a background in finance, Swartz worked in electronics, components manufacture and technology media, running the interactive TV practice for ad agency Digitas, developing a global Samsung Web portal and moving around Europe, Asia and Central America before returning to New York. Struck by how few women were represented in the field of advertising technology, especially in her arena of media, TV 2.0, online video and digital automation—that is, media convergence—she founded Furious-Minds in 2012, which evolved into Furious Corp. in 2015.

"For the first time in my career, I was in the right place at the right time," says Swartz, in her early forties. "There were a bunch of small companies, typically venture-backed, that had taken a lot of money to build an advertising revenue-based business model, pitching to me on the agency side of the business. But they knew nothing about the industry."

She also began investigating industry leadership positions and likewise found a lack of women. "I found it interesting that as a woman, although I had consciously and objectively created value, it never resulted in board or advisory invitations." That's despite the fact that advertising agencies sell to media companies, which usually consist of lots of senior women. "So I left and started Furious. I wanted to make a greater impact and I thought a meaningful way to do that as an individual was to create jobs." She has three others on her team, a cofounder and CTO, based in Caesarea, Israel, a VP of product, and a senior engagement manager. "It's a blessing to work with people you love," she says. Having secured $1.1 million in funding from both angel and institutional investors, Swartz is now raising the Seed B second round.

She's learned that it takes time and practice to react confidently when you're the only woman at the table or in the room. "There are many occasions in my career where I've remained quiet and I've allowed myself to accept or tolerate bad behavior from men." These days, she's calmer, less prone to outrage and more direct. "When I was younger, I was a bull in the china shop and I ran into a lot of brick walls and I made a lot of mistakes and I was very prickly." She's come to realize that delivery matters if you want to get across your message. Otherwise, it "reinforces the fact that women can't play nice and be in the workplace with a bunch of boys."

Why is it not a surprise that such situations tend to happen on the road, when men are out of their office and away from home territory? "I was at an industry retreat where I had been invited to speak and the host and I were having a drink and we'd been talking all night," remembers Swartz. "He led a sales region in the Midwest and he had a younger client, probably ten years younger than I was, who got quite intoxicated. That guy ended up literally striking me across my face, in jest, thinking it was funny. The sales manager host, sitting beside me, and other men in the area just sat there and did nothing. I looked over at the sales manager and I said, 'You know, I respect you and I'm your guest so I'm not going to beat his ass, for lack of a better term, but I am going to remind you of this as you raise your daughters. Because this is stuff we deal with every day.' We'd been talking about his daughters all night. So that was a poignant and salient moment that he got and he's not going to forget it."

Women who run their own shows these days are adjusting expectations. "It's generational and it's about sorority," says Swartz. "It's different than the generation that was there to mentor me. They believed you had to forego gender and take on masculine roles and masculine objectives to succeed. They expected every woman working beneath them to work the same way. They'd give directions about flying the plane, but they didn't actually teach you how to fly."

"I'm further along in my career and it's now my job to run air cover for younger women," continues Swartz, who believes that's what all women in leadership positions, especially those in technology such as Yahoo! CEO Marissa Mayer and Facebook COO Sheryl Sandberg ought to be doing. "It's our responsibility to create runway and to give the next generation the keys to the plane—to teach them," Swartz concludes.

Girls just can't impress the boys

Cultural biases and conventions simply don't put "woman" and "entrepreneur" in the same space. That archetype remains tethered to the hunter male, a relentless warrior who vanquishes any and all unbelievers. Women continue to be seen by funders, and really the public at large, as newbies or juniors-in-training.

Those widespread perceptions portray women as unable to risk or withstand the pressures, no matter how much evidence has mounted to the contrary. As a direct result of such perceptions, most women entrepreneurs do not attract the moneymen, as we've noted. About 75% of the country's 316,600 angel investors are men, according to the Center for Venture Research. That jumps to a shocking 95% male for decision-making partners at venture capital firms, according to PitchBook, an industry researcher.

On average, in raising funds during the first year of a startup's operation, men "raised about 80% more capital than women did," reports the Kauffman Foundation. Women's blocked access to funding clearly caps their prospects, even when they run the tech ventures most attractive to investors. Certainly, more women owners ought to step up to take on greater risk, responsibility and ownership of business financials, including asking for funds, as Laura Fredricks emphasizes in the "Weaknesses" chapter. (The section on "Money" that follows further describes specific ways women entrepreneurs frequently shy from appropriate levels of risk.) But while it's true that women often resist debt and equity partners, it's equally true that women's funding requests and qualifications continue to face gender bias, which is restricting the potential of women-led ventures. "When women do want to scale up, they don't get the funding they need, from both a venture capital standpoint and a banking standpoint," says Northeastern management professor Jamie Ladge.

Early in 2014, Ladge and her team researched nationwide bank funding for men- and women-owned firms, choosing companies that were similarly sized and had all operated for similar lengths of time. The researchers also controlled for profitability and the amount of time and personal capital owners committed to the business. "Not surprisingly," says Ladge, "we found that women received less money even when they could show all the same measures of success as the men-owned firms." Ladge interprets the results with the care of a researcher: "We attribute that to the possibility that gender sends a signal that might obliterate any signals the positive business might send. We gathered that what's driving these inequities for women are deeply entrenched stereotypes."

Established loan channels continue to ignore the needs of female owners, as Ladge's survey shows. Nationwide, according to an August 2014 report from Sen. Maria Cantwell (D - WA), chair of the Senate committee on small business and entrepreneurship, "Only 4% of the total dollar value of all small business loans goes to women entrepreneurs." As for loans from the Small Business Administration, which are specifically designed to support women and minorities, only 13% of SBA loans went to women in fiscal 2013. In Chair Cantwell's home state of Washington, women received only 11%.

Although overt bias has quieted, says Ladge, there are implicit biases as well as those long-established stereotypes that do kick in. For women in particular, the public and lenders tend to think, "'Oh women go into starting their business as a lifestyle choice,'" says Ladge, meaning women don't really need capital. "I've heard this called 'the cupcake stigma.'"

Coping with "the cupcake stigma"

Lack of funding for women entrepreneurs, then, is directly owing to gender bias. Business models for women entrepreneurs have not gained sufficient traction or respect, particularly from funders. As a result, instead of any real effort to pinpoint or erode funder prejudices, the failure of women to raise capital continues to be blamed on the women themselves, on the types of businesses women typically choose and on the characteristic (read: unacceptable) ways they start and grow them. One recent example of how such bias is perpetuated offers a chilling model of how doors close for women entrepreneurs.

A 2014 Harvard Business School study of nearly 100 randomly selected founder pitches in three different competitions identified, "a profound and consistent gender gap in entrepreneur persuasiveness. Investors prefer pitches presented by male entrepreneurs compared with pitches made by female entrepreneurs, even when the content of the pitch is the same… Attractive males were particularly persuasive…." Whether or not good-looking women fared better than unattractive ones didn't surface in the study's conclusions.

In their report, the researchers work hard to account for investor disinterest in women presenters. Citing women-founded enterprises such as Mary Kay, Estée Lauder, Martha Stewart and billionaires Sara Blakely at Spanx and Tory Burch, the study notes that women entrepreneurs pursue ventures that "focus on the female consumer, such as fashion, cosmetics and cooking," whereas men start a wider range of businesses. Ipso presto: It's that characteristically narrow female business focus that limits women's appeal to backers, concludes the study.

Here, then, is the full-dress parade of tired perceptions and default male stereotypes masquerading as academic rationale. The researchers implicitly blame women for the investor bias they first document and then blindly share and broadcast in their conclusion. Where to start? First, how can spectacular successes like Sara Blakely and icon Estée Lauder possibly be invoked as examples of "narrow" choices for launching a business? Next, the researchers somehow suggest that to truly deserve funding women ought to be starting the kinds of "wider" businesses men prefer. Third, the idea that a business model that relies on female customers has inherent deficits is laughable. Women now account for some 80% of all purchases in the US, including cars and computers. Women also represent 51% of the population. They are hardly a niche market, a minority demographic or even a homogeneous consumer target for which revenue might dry up. And if "narrow" markets are the issue, what about the continued deal flow to boutique ventures in male-dominated gaming technology and sports? Last, men are as engaged in cooking as women these days and comprise significant audiences for cable TV food networks and online outlets. Food businesses and content hasn't been a gendered subject for years. If all that isn't enough, for anyone paying attention, it turns out women today actually *are* starting a wider range of businesses than ever before.

Boris Wertz, a well-regarded tech entrepreneur, angel investor with a 40-company portfolio and founder of Version One Ventures, a micro VC firm based in Vancouver, Canada, posted a blog not long ago, writing, "In the past, female CEOs were largely limited to those areas where they have a distinct advantage over their male counterparts (i.e. selling primarily to a female audience). But today we're seeing women building companies across all sectors and areas."

Entrepreneurs who get pregnant

Bias against women who seek funding is real and ongoing. Of the nearly 7,000 businesses funded by venture capital from 2011 – 2013, 85% had nary a woman on the executive team. Only 3% of the VC-funded ventures had a woman CEO. Conventional equity funding models clearly are ignoring or misinterpreting what women bring to the table. "Women approach business and life differently than men do," agrees angel investor Joanne Wilson. "Women operate and think differently." An ongoing frustration, she says, is that "men can't separate women's business lives from their personal ones."

Recently, Wilson attended a prospective funding meeting with a young woman CEO of a company she backs. "We were pitching to a man I know well," says Wilson, "and he said to the young woman, 'You're so beautiful. Why are you doing this?' He literally said that." Wilson requested the man to step aside. In private, she asked how he'd feel if his son were pitching to her and she mentioned "how handsome he was and kept looking at his ass."

The funder was abashed. "I don't think men realize what's coming out of their mouth," says Wilson. "He said, "I never realized what I was doing.'"

Another New York investor wouldn't consider one of Wilson's woman-led firms because he "didn't want to invest in people who are pregnant," she says. "These old-school men think women can't have children and run a business." Understandably, women in startups also assume there's no place for having kids in entrepreneurship. Not long ago, a startup CEO called Wilson in a panic, asking for advice because she was pregnant. "What do I say to everyone?" the CEO asked. Wilson suggested she tell everyone how excited and joyful she was because she was going to have a baby. "There's no need to justify being pregnant. Men don't do that," she says. "They don't put their personal lives on hold."

Is she, should she, does she?

Men in power are often uneasy when women don't stick to traditional gender roles or behaviors. "When a man pushes for a higher salary, he's viewed no differently by hiring managers, but when a woman negotiates for a higher salary, she's viewed as pushy and the hiring manager—whether a man or a woman—won't want to work with her," pointed out Victoria Budson, director of the Women and Public Policy Program at Harvard University's Kennedy School of Government, at a 2012 conference on gender intelligence. All women in business must deal with stereotypical attitudes to greater or lesser degrees, and that puts more pressure on women who run companies. Instead of being able to simply get down to business, women must skirt the direct approach and manage men's expectations for sex roles and business practices.

Managing male perceptions

When young Australian founder Nikki Durkin was desperately seeking bridge financing to keep her Manhattan-based 99dresses ecommerce startup afloat in 2014, she said, "I'd be invited to cocktail parties full of VCs where I'd don my painful sky-high heels because I'd split tested heels versus flats, and for some reason a 5-foot 11-inch woman in seven-inch heels commands more talking time and attention from investors than one in the comfy flat booties I wear to work. Apparently height gives you presence. Once or twice I'd have an investor asking if I knew what an angel was, or if I also modeled because of my height, or some other unintentionally patronizing comment that I doubt any guy would be subjected to. I learned to take it all in my high-heeled stride."

On the flip side, many more women today are founding enterprises that defy the girl clichés. Beth Borges has a passion for brewing mead, the time-honored alcoholic beverage made from the fermented sugars in honey. It began as a hobby, and after earning her MBA, Borges developed her mead-making skills into a craft brewing company. As founder and brewer of House Bear Brewing in Amesbury, Massachusetts, she and her partner produce half-a-dozen varieties of gluten-free meads flavored with ingredients such as apples, strawberry-basil, chocolate pepper, blueberries and lemonade. Five new flavors will be released soon.

"Craft beer drinkers are also mead buyers," explains Borges. Sales of craft beer or microbrews increased almost 18% in 2014, to nearly $20 billion of the $106 billion US beer market, reports the Brewers Association. So Borges has high hopes for her mead. To date, there are only 200 or so mead makers and producers scattered across the US but sales jumped 130% from 2012 to 2013, showing much stronger growth than beer and wine, according to the American Mead Makers Association. Average annual sales for a mead maker also climbed from $48,600 in 2012 to $112,000 in 2013. At the first anniversary of being on the shelves, House Bear Brewing is available in nearly 60 regional locations, with the local Whole Foods and other spots on the horizon. The founders hold well-attended mead tastings, have won several gold medal competitions and are discussing alliances with bigger producers.

Yet invariably, when she and business partner Carl Hirschfeld go on sales calls or attend business meetings, Borges, in her forties, gets taken for his spouse or the company marketer. "People don't realize that I'm the brewer, too," she says. "I started as the brewer in our friendship and introduced him to brewing. I did a lot of research before deciding to open the meadery and knew I wanted Carl as my partner. But I had to convince him there was market traction. Once I did, we have worked hand-in-hand on recipes, names, ideas for graphics, packaging, marketing and other tasks. We both brew. We both bottle and label. We make most decisions together."

When the partners face challenges, says Borges, "he looks at our budget, resources, schedule or something else and sees the constraints. He generally takes the safer route. He often asks 'Why?' and I often ask, 'Why not?' and wonder what could possibly hold us back." Borges isn't sure that represents a male-female divide. "But my male colleagues have often said that they start with no because it doesn't commit them to anything. With my partner, I often have to summarize the benefits and brainstorm ways something can be done. Once he sees the different ways we can approach it, his mind opens up to the possibilities." As an example, she points to her partner's idea for lemonade-style mead. "I wouldn't have thought of that. But I realized it was a great idea, and I perfected the recipe. That's how we work together." Borges also spent years as a landscape gardener, which has accustomed her to manual work. "People are always surprised by how much heavy lifting I can do. When I landscaped, I didn't do little jobs and I've gotten used to it." Echoing 99dresses' Durkin, Borges says "I take it in stride."

Clearing the hurdles of bias

To date, the majority of women owners have not developed the critical business and social networks that lead to being in front of the right people with the right venture pitch. Women entrepreneurs also tend to lack models and mentors to tap for encouragement or guidance when developing the business plans, elevator speeches and honed presentations expected by both angels and venture capitalists. That's a key reason why crowdfunding is attracting so many women startups, as the "Opportunities" chapter reports. But successful crowdfinance campaigns rely on populist messages and accessible consumer business models. Campaigns also demand huge commitments of time, effort and robust social media platforms. That doesn't suit lots of women-led startups. For most ventures, crowdfunded or not, it's business intersections and social introductions that develop the necessary relationships for funding opportunities.

It doesn't help that most women owners run not only businesses, but also households and families. There's scant air in their schedules to build outside networks or associations that might nibble away at the stereotypes and perceptions. Being invisible and lacking connections continues to cause serious challenges for women. It may take a village to raise a CEO, but someone's still got to get dinner on the table and the kids to school.

In response to such circumstances, and slowly over the past half-dozen years, a broad and scattered confederation of public and private organizations has been building to encourage women's entrepreneurial instincts, efforts and future. As barriers to launch fall and the number of women owners rise, the potential that they represent is rattling traditional hurdles. Groups large and small, for-profit and nonprofit are moving to support female-focused channels, engaged by economic interest and the global She economy. Marketers anticipate new and repeat customers. Government agencies expect the new ranks of women entrepreneurs to help sputtering economies, creating jobs and tax revenue. Increasingly, public agencies have been developing women-specific programs to help women-led enterprises to launch and scale.

Getting certified as a woman-owned company

The most established and wide-ranging of the programs is becoming certified as a woman-owned and operated company by an accredited third party in order to qualify for special opportunities. Such options developed as response and acknowledgment that women and minorities faced years of discrimination and must continue to overcome greater obstacles when government and corporate contracts are awarded. Becoming woman-certified puts the owner in position to bid for big long-term contracts that have been earmarked for women-owned firms by large corporations or by local, state and federal government agencies. The programs are designed to open up old-boy networks and make the contract bidding and approval processes more transparent and equitable.

There are several types of certification granted by private organizations as well as public agencies. Choosing one depends on what kind of contracts owners want to pursue. At the federal level, recent legislative changes, passed in the National Defense Authorization Act of 2013, raise the ceiling on federal contract set-asides for eligible women-owned ventures. The Small Business Administration has not managed to reach its mandated 5% contract quota for women in awarding some $400 billion in federal contracts. The new law is expected to help reach that goal. On the other hand, municipal government certification, such as by the city of San Diego or New York, is usually best to target community and regional vendors. Municipal small business initiatives may also reach out to women who need training and funding. For instance, New York City Small Business Services recently set up a private-public initiative, called Women Entrepreneurs NYC, to provide more than $425,000 over the next few years to help 5,000 women in underserved communities launch businesses. Private nationwide certification by such nonprofit associations as the Women's Business Enterprise National Council is more appropriate for owners who bid on business from large corporations.

Each certifying group has its own forms and rules, with no universal application, which makes the process labor-intensive and time-consuming. But many owners find certification helpful. "It has opened doors with large corporations. We think it has helped us locally and regionally," says Elaine Lyerly, whose Charlotte, North Carolina, marketing agency became certified in 2004.

Expanding alternatives for funding women

"I'm bullish on the development of alternative sources of capital for women entrepreneurs," says Carla Harris, a managing director at Morgan Stanley and current chair of the National Women's Business Council (NWBC), the high-level government advisory group. "We didn't always have angel investors to talk about for women who often lack access to VC funding networks or VC funders, who generally aren't women. Now there are more opportunities," she says. Overall, angel investment in women-led companies remains low, but it has been increasing and lately, even setting records. About a fifth (19%) of the roughly 71,000 ventures that secured angel funding in 2013 went to women CEOs, according to the Center for Venture Research.

As the economy continues to improve and accessible online lenders streamline the application process, women-led firms are seeing a benefit. For example, a 2014 study from small business lending portal Biz2Credit reported a 12% uptick in loan approval rates for women-owned businesses over 2013, with total 15% approvals, although male-owned firms still received nearly 22% approvals, up 19% over the previous year. Other forward-looking options include new and nimble microlenders that are harnessing technology to analyze risks and applicants, making loans less dependent on traditional credit scores. Older banking channels are also retooling to meet new needs, including the nation's 7,000-plus community banks that have long been a primary source of small business lending, accounting for nearly 60% of all loans to small businesses, according to the Independent Community Bankers of America. Nonprofit credit unions also usually offer better rates than commercial bankers.

Tory Burch gives back

Like Madam C. J. Walker before them, women entrepreneurs at the top are buying into the "lifting-as-we-climb" philosophy. Fashion mogul Tory Burch, for instance, established a foundation in 2009 with the mission of supporting US women entrepreneurs and their families. Her foundation partnered with Community Development Financial Institutions (CDFIs), specialized financial institutions certified by the US Treasury to work in market niches that traditional institutions usually avoid. The alliance provides affordable microloans of $500 to $50,000 as well as education, networking and mentoring for women. In 2014, Burch expanded those efforts by teaming with Bank of America, which kicked in $10 million, to develop the Elizabeth Street Capital spinoff, offering low-cost capital for women-owned businesses in about a dozen cities across the country.

"When I started my company, it was clear that there was a big need to help women in particular," Burch told *The Charlotte Observer* when the program was announced. "…The entrepreneurs I'm meeting are often having two jobs, they're single mothers. They're incredible business people." Overall, in 2013, Bank of America reportedly granted close to $11 billion in small-business loans. Women and the Elizabeth Street alliance clearly will be good for business. Burch's success and deep resources have buoyed her effort, but every community nationwide now boasts women who are giving back in similar ways.

Hatching your baby biz

Heightened interest from lenders, marketers and government agencies has spurred increased attention to entrepreneurship education. In 2007, a survey of about 1,200 community colleges in the US found that almost seven out of 10 (66%) offered at least one course in entrepreneurship. The field has since exploded for several reasons. Corporate jobs have shrunk, free agent status has become more viable and attractive, the new American Dream lives in Silicon Valley and entrepreneurship has expanded into for-profit/nonprofit hybrids that work for social change and social good. In the New Normal, Millennials are attracted to starting businesses for those reasons and more.

A multiplying breed of venture hatcheries—incubators and accelerators—of all sizes and shapes has kept pace with expanding interest. As of 2012, there were more than 1,250 incubators in the US, up from a scant 12 in 1980, according to the National Business Incubation Association (NBIA). Such support systems give investors and entrepreneurs access to coaching and mentoring, speeding the on-ramp to launch and profitability.

Technically, the difference between an accelerator and an incubator is telegraphed by the name. In exchange for low levels of equity, mostly single digits, an accelerator will invite a high-potential startup applicant into its facility, providing digital tools, peer collaboration, funders and, most of all, hands-on strategic blueprints. Leveraging these "accelerated" tools, the startup is expected to rev up to launch within a few months. On the other hand, incubators with similar offerings have a longer hatching period, sometimes a few years. Accordingly, they usually require a greater share of equity. However, practically speaking, every lab operates along a continuum of time, money and equity dictated by its own rules and expectations. It pays to thoroughly screen any potential launch lab. The selection process can be rigorous, since facilities want to ensure that their limited resources are efficiently harnessed.

Predictably, like the venture capitalists whose money mostly backs these facilities, venture labs favor quickly scalable technology startups. In a now-familiar story, that means male-led enterprises. "A gender split of four men to every one woman is common in accelerators, as is an unquestioned—and likely unintentional—masculine-normed culture," says Susan Duffy at Babson's Center for Women's Entrepreneurial Leadership, who figured that a woman-focused lab might work to change the climate. "In our area of Boston and across the country, we said there's a lot of potential value from very smart and highly committed ready-to-go women entrepreneurs being left on the table," she says. That motivated Babson to establish its woman-focused accelerator in September 2014, the Women Innovating Now or WIN Lab.

Choosing female-friendly

"I knew since the age of two that I wanted to go into the beauty business," says Brittany Lo, who graduated from Babson in June 2014. "In the second grade I wrote in my journal that I wanted to have a beauty company." However, it was one thing to imagine owning a cosmetics company when she grew up. It was quite another to figure out how to actually do it.

Support for a business launch was the key reason Lo accepted an invitation to join the debut batch of 15 undergrad participants in the WIN Lab during her senior year. "I knew it was going to be a big time commitment, as most of these accelerators are. But wanting my own company is ultimately why I chose Babson, so when I heard about this accelerator, it made sense for me," says Lo. "We met every Friday for three hours and they brought in different professionals, mostly women. It was really great."

At the time, Lo's vision was a retail beauty bar for women that opened early enough for clients to be made up for work and stayed open late to accommodate women's evening professional and social events. Walk-ins would get a $50 half-hour makeover or $30 makeup for eyes and lips. Lo focused on women's crammed schedules and pampering, such as complementary cocktails and desserts.

Why do women need a special version of an accelerator? For one thing, as Duffy points out, what other accelerator would have accepted an enterprise based on makeup bars? "When we start early, we can suggest thinking bigger. We can say, 'Yeah, a beauty bar is a great idea but a chain or a franchise or global domination of beauty bars is a lot better.'" Another reason is women's different style of work, even though, "core curriculum and competencies required to run a business are gender-neutral," says Duffy. "At WIN, we are getting at the same outcomes by offering a way for women to collaborate with each other. The process is different, but that doesn't mean easier or any less rigorous than what would go on in a male-dominated environment."

She explains the differences as a shift in tone and approach. "Instead of saying on day one we're going to make you stand up there and shout about your business, and we're going to cut you down and Shark Tank you until you're ready to just scream, we say, 'All right. Let's get together and as peers who really want to push our boundaries, let's talk about what's right and what's wrong with this business and what you're committed to do to fix it in a process of collaboration and support.'"

For Brittany Lo, the WIN Lab indeed gave her a launch pad, as well as access to an angel investor within the Babson network. "The first half was discovering who you are," she says. " I learned about my strengths, my weaknesses, how to build a strong team based on those weaknesses and how to move forward." Lo also wrote her business plan while going through the program. "I wanted to attach some service to a product and I went in with only a vague idea of how to execute that." She worked on the plan throughout the year. "The advisors really helped me hone in on what the rollout would be." Besides WIN, Lo joined another coed accelerator group at the same time. There was a marked difference between them. "I found the questions that were asked in the mixed gender group were all focused on funding and financing. In the woman's accelerator, there was no barrier and no one was trying to impress anyone. It allowed the program to go in different directions. It was more fun."

Since graduating, with $110,000 in angel funding, Lo has revised her plan, adjusting to market conditions. Originally expecting to open pilot boutique bars in spas and gyms, she's instead launched Beautini, a Manhattan-based on-demand beauty service, with makeup stylists traveling directly to clients. Her client focus is brides and bridal parties, and there's always some bubbly to celebrate the occasion. Challenges include the many competitors popping up, especially in New York City. "But by honing in on the wedding niche market, and focusing on building a brand rather than a company that wants to grow and be bought out, we've been able to grow steadily," says Lo. And then adds: "Maintaining a routine and going to the office like many of my peers in corporate has allowed me to stay focused, be treated like everyone else with a job and to separate my work life from personal life. That's huge in terms of staying mentally healthy through this tough journey."

Most experts and coaches brought in to guide entrepreneurs at accelerators are male with expertise in high growth and high-tech sectors. The WIN model pursues a different perspective. "We want the participants to see women role models, women experts, women coaches and women CEOs that have launched big, bold businesses so the young women can look to them and say, 'Well if she can do it, I can do it,'" says Duffy. In time, the goal is to be coed. "When there are models of venture acceleration that meet more people's needs and offer a wider platform for early-stage entrepreneurship, we won't need a gender model," she sums up.

Advancing women promotes profits

Increasingly, high-level sources show that when women work in the business, it's good for the bottom line. That's true for women who are founders and executives in startups, as well as when women have senior authority at large companies. Dozens of studies now have documented that teams with diversity are better at solving problems, driving innovation and improving the revenue. Companies that include women who steer simply do better.

"We see that a company's odds for success... increase with more female executives at the VP and director levels," reports a 2012 Dow Jones VentureSource study called "Women at the Wheel." What's more, "for startups with five or more females, 61% were successful and only 39% failed." Other research corroborates those findings. A 2013 SBA report called "Venture Capital, Social Capital, and the Funding of Women-Led Businesses," found, unsurprisingly, that most VC firm investments are filtered though the partners' familiar social networks, and so don't include women. Yet when "venture capital firms do invest in women-led businesses, they generally improve their bottom line," concluded the report.

"As investors look for new opportunities, and as we focus on ways to grow our economy, we should look to women entrepreneurs for a good share of new growth," announced Winslow Sargeant, SBA chief counsel for advocacy, in the study report. "Policies that encourage venture capital networks to be more inclusive will create the environment for new high-growth innovative businesses," he said. Similarly, Carla Harris at the NWBC has found that "companies started by women or led by women are producing good returns. Data says that companies with diversity in the [executive] C suite tend to do better and there's a trickle-down effect for entrepreneurs."

At the same time, women have begun to build bigger businesses, though that's been largely overlooked and unrecognized, according to research from American Express OPEN and Womenable, a for-profit advocacy group. In "Growing Under the Radar," released in 2013, researchers were surprised to find that over the past decade, there's been a whopping 57% spike in the number of female-owned firms with $10 million or more in revenues. That's a growth rate roughly 50% higher than for all $10 million-revenue firms. Between 2002 and 2012, the number of $1 million-plus women-owned firms is also up handily, nearly 31%. While such percentages are impressive, the actual numbers remain small.

Even so, it's the first time research has spotlighted higher-earning female companies, mostly, according to American Express, because no one had bothered to crunch the numbers that way before. One of the challenges is likely because women-led firms stop being counted as soon as the owner takes on male partners and no longer owns 51% of the firm, even if the partner simply is an investor and has no day-to-day involvement.

Squandering women's resources

The impact of systemic underfunding and undervaluing of women's businesses constitutes an ongoing threat not only to women entrepreneurs but, of course, also to national and global economies. We're losing an extraordinary depth of talent and potential. If we did a better job of backing women's businesses, we would develop skills, inspire the next generation and spark more innovation. "We have a country full of educated and experienced women churning out innovative high-potential companies only to be choked off from the capital required to catalyze growth," Susan Duffy has said. "It's time to write a new chapter in the startup story where investors, entrepreneurs and the economy benefit from a broader, more inclusive ideal of entrepreneurial success."

PART III

USING GENDER TOOLS TO GROW

Ask not, "What difference does gender make?" but rather, "How can gender make a difference?"

— *"Rethinking Management: What's Gender Got to Do with It"*

Center for Gender in Organizations

Simmons School of Management

8

Power: Consent and Compromise vs. Command and Control

__Her way__: Growing up, girls tend to establish relationships.

__His way__: Boys usually vie for leadership.

Like many of today's teenagers, at age 14, Ava Anderson grew concerned about the effects of toxic chemicals on people and the planet. But instead of growing out of it, she began to engage.

Her concern was sparked by news of detectible levels of many harmful chemicals found in the bloodstream of teens in a study conducted by nonprofit Environmental Working Group. "I immediately began researching," says Anderson. She couldn't believe the products she used could be bad for her health. "But I couldn't have been more wrong," she says. "The shampoo and lotions and hand sanitizers and everything I was using each were loaded with carcinogens and mutagens and hormone-disrupting chemicals." Mutagens change genetic material, usually DNA, and are also likely to be carcinogens. Anderson decided to switch to products labeled "organic" or "natural," no matter the extra cost. But further research revealed that such brands were more about marketing than health.

Soon, Anderson launched a blog to share all the information she had uncovered. With true teen zeal, she began discarding all such products around the house, not only the ones she used but her mother's and grandmother's as well. Then came the dawning realization: She had no recommendation for replacements. "The more I learned, the more disturbed I became and I knew I had to do something about it. There were no full lines of products I trusted to use or to recommend to family and friends," says Anderson.

After a year of more research, with help from friends and family, she identified a facility that would work with her and meet her requirements for ingredients. In December 2009, at age 15 and a sophomore in high school, she launched Ava Anderson Non Toxic, starting with six skincare products.

The teen CEO

Now a 21-year-old college grad, Anderson is running her expanding line of truly all-natural products, about 90 so far in 17 categories, including home, baby, men, kids, face, skin, body, pets and more. She's also winning young entrepreneurship awards, attracting media attention, blogging for *Huffington Post* and appearing on women's leadership panels. Outgrowing its base in Anderson's hometown of East Providence, Rhode Island, the company recently moved to a facility six times bigger in nearby Warren.

Early on, the young CEO had lots of steering help, from her cofounder mom, entrepreneur Kim Anderson, an interior designer and former retail executive, and her father Frohman Anderson, an experienced direct sales executive. The family also tapped executives from Princess House, a direct-selling home goods company. Likewise organized on the direct selling model, like the Avon company, Ava Anderson Non Toxic depends on independent sales agents or "consultants" who each buy a $99 startup kit and then earn commissions by selling products directly to consumers at "avaHOURS," or events they host, similar to the Avon model. To date, Anderson Non Toxic has attracted an impressive 11,000 consultants across the country and is reeling in double-digit millions in annual revenue.

The company lives—or fails—by nurturing relationships with the field agents, which includes working to build their networks, training them to market the products and offering incentives to boost their sales. "The sky is the limit!" says Anderson about prospects for growth. "We want to become as big as possible, as quickly as possible, so our Ava consultants can share this important health message with every family in this country. We believe we reached about one million American families in 2013, and we're hoping to double or triple that."

Currently working with a half-dozen or so outsourced manufacturers, as well as manufacturing in-house, the company has grown to about 40 employees, with most working in shipping and about a dozen senior staff. "We brought distribution in-house after about a year because we wanted to have more control over how the package arrived to the customer," says Anderson.

The women all-stars

Profit isn't her driving motivation. "This has never been about money, and instead is about creating chemical policy change in this country," says Anderson. "The rewards are knowing that hundreds of thousands of people now are using safe products and are not exposing themselves to toxic chemicals, while less is going down the drain to harm the environment and water supply."

"Unfortunately," she continues, "in this country just because a product is sold on a shelf doesn't make it safe. There are only 11 ingredients banned in the US but over 1,300 banned in the European Union." The result is that "your favorite lip balm or deodorant and even sunscreen gets reformulated to sell in other countries but those harmful chemicals stay in products for us." In 2013, Anderson twice traveled to Washington DC to support a bill introduced by Rep. Janice Schakowsky (D - Ill), The Safe Cosmetics and Personal Care Products Act of 2013, which would have given the US Food and Drug Administration authority to monitor personal care products. But that bill died in the 113th Congress. Instead, Anderson is betting on parents. "Nothing creates change faster than angry moms and dads demanding better for their families."

Equally rewarding for the activist founder is "hearing the stories from our consultants of how this business opportunity has changed their lives. For $99 anyone can become her own boss, and educate others about this message while making an income doing so." Part of the company's commitment is in emphasizing the potential of commissions for the women sales force, which are set toward the higher end of the average for the direct selling industry: 30% to 50% of sales revenue plus bonuses from the sales of any team the consultant recruits on her own.

"Hearing from single moms who would have otherwise had to file for bankruptcy and are now able to send their child to private school, or to put on that home addition they always dreamed about is beyond moving," says Anderson. "Even the little things really make a difference in someone's life. I remember one consultant who was just over the moon that on her date night for the month with her husband she was able to whip out her wallet and pay."

The mother-daughter executive team, the all-women sales force and the woman-focused mission and products all make a difference in management decisions, especially when it comes to maintaining relationships with consultants and customers, says Anderson. Because her mom owned retail shops in their small town, she learned that "reputation is everything and you have to make the customer happy no matter what, even if it costs you. A happy customer could tell five friends but an unhappy one could tell 50. We have a few men on our executive team, and I think sometimes men can be more numbers-driven, which, of course, is important in any business. Maybe it's because my mom and I are more in touch with the field and our customers through Facebook forums, training calls and other channels that we might see the value in sending an unhappy customer a few products to make it up to them. Someone looking at cash flow who hadn't seen the disgruntled customer's email doesn't see the necessity in spending a few dollars."

"I just love that we're a mom and daughter team on a mission," she says.

Leading with gender

Look around any workplace and gender characteristics are immediately recognizable. As women gain higher profile as business owners and executives, such gender differences in leadership roles increasingly play out. The sexes impose authority with noticeable differences.

"Men tend to use transactional styles of leadership whereby they exchange rewards for results and lead through power and control," agrees Kimberly Eddleston, professor of entrepreneurship and innovation at Northeastern University in Boston. By contrast, "women are more relationship-focused. They tend to use more democratic and participative leadership styles." Women are often more collaborative, which can help the business. Sharing power and information encourages teamwork, brainstorming and greater contributions, which leverages talent and resources.

Each sex might benefit by taking a cue from the other. "If a man tones down his command-and-control management style, he can gain deeper trust, greater initiative and, perhaps most importantly, a climate that facilitates thinking out of the box," says Eddleston. "That's because men's transactional tradition usually causes staff and stakeholders to worry more about making mistakes than about how to grow sales or profits." The goal here is to delegate outcomes rather than monitor tasks. Women, however, notes Eddleston, "need to be careful not to spend too much time on relationship matters at the expense of business issues." All too often, women who rely on relationships to motivate are uncomfortable imposing exacting performance standards. By moving past that tendency, women can gain greater efficiencies.

Women see around business corners

Recent investigations into such differences point out that while each gender's style can be effective, "female" lately has the edge—or, alternatively, women's traits today are coming into stronger focus. Obviously, no individual embodies all the many characteristics we call "female" or "male." With that understood, researchers are finding, sometimes to their surprise, that women's ways of leading are more relevant for 21st century business success.

In *The Female Vision: Women's Real Power at Work*, coauthors Sally Helgesen and Julie Johnson researched a variety of companies and women, looking into job satisfaction among other issues. They deconstructed three components that define women's distinctive ways of seeing and performing: Women have the "capacity for broad spectrum and radar-like notice; …the tendency to analyze information in a broader social context; and…women have an emphasis on intrinsic satisfaction rather than abstract measures of achievement." (No doubt, some of these abilities flow from the genetic characteristics of women's brains as described in the "Strengths" chapter.)

The result is that women account for a significant widening of business horizons with more opportunities than occurs when only men have influence. When women have power in an organization, they provide value by surfacing and maintaining relationships as well as by early forecasting of market shifts and conflicts. As Ava Anderson figured out, those abilities are particularly effective in today's hyper-connected global marketplace where service and strategy are increasingly sacrificed in the race to scale fast or beat the competition. "The female vision," say Helgesen and Johnson, informs the business bottom line by leveraging creativity, insights and the increasingly important ability to inspire diverse talent and teams.

Measuring women leaders

Other studies built on science and metrics reach similar conclusions. Jack Zenger and Joseph Folkman, based in Orem, Utah, run a leadership development company that trains executives to be "extraordinary leaders" by leveraging people's strengths, rather than relying on traditional methods that attempt to correct their weaknesses. The award-winning program is based on "16 competencies that our 30 years of research shows are most important to overall leadership effectiveness," according to their marketing.

Summarizing the findings of a 2011 survey, the two coaches put "some hard numbers into the mix" of who's better at leading, men or women, writing on a blog post of the *Harvard Business Review*. Their survey queried more than 7,000 leaders at public and private organizations, corralling data from 360-degree performance reviews to track the perspectives of peers, bosses and direct-report staff. Questions included "how good a leader is at taking the initiative, developing others, inspiring and motivating, and pursuing their own development."

To no one's surprise, Zenger and Folkman found most leaders are still men, or, 64% male generally and an overwhelming 78% at the upper levels. Also no shock, women leaders excelled "at 'nurturing' competencies, such as developing others and building relationships, and many might put exhibiting integrity and engaging in self-development in that category as well." Then the kicker: "But the women's advantages were not at all confined to traditional women's strengths. In fact at every level, more women were rated by their peers, their bosses, their direct reports, and their other associates as better overall leaders than their male counterparts—and the higher the level, the wider that gap grows."

Mirroring Zenger and Folkman's results, executive recruiter Korn Ferry found that, "with the exception of confidence, women generally score higher than men in all dimensions of leadership style, such as comfort with ambiguity and being socially attuned." In a survey released in September 2014 that analyzed thousands of worldwide leaders, measuring outcomes in the areas of competencies, motivators, leadership styles and experiences, Korn Ferry reported that women "also scored higher in most of the skills and competencies deemed necessary for senior leadership success, such as employee engagement, customer satisfaction and building talent."

The most sweeping pronouncement of the ascendancy of women's leadership traits comes from John Gerzema and Michael D'Antonio, authors of *The Athena Doctrine: How Women (and the Men Who Think Like Them) Will Rule the Future.* The authors surveyed 64,000 people in 18 nations and found that by a wide margin a majority believes the world would be better off if "men thought more like women." That is, their respondents overwhelmingly chose leadership traits that are conventionally considered "female." Gerzema and D'Antonio then looked at businesses, nonprofits and governments worldwide to see how they operate and, according to the authors, the best-run organizations subscribed to this "Athena Doctrine."

It would seem women often manage better than men.

Women's leadership disconnect

If women have the managerial edge nowadays, why are so few in positions of power? On average, women currently make up less than 20% of boards at S&P 500 companies, according to Institutional Shareholder Services, a consultancy that provides worldwide corporate governance solutions. As noted, less than 5% of Fortune 500 CEOs are women.

For at least a decade now, the same rationales have been trotted out to explain the scarcity of women at the top ranks of corporations: Women don't step up. Women don't ask. Women don't get in queue for big-job pipelines. Women won't sign up for profit and loss positions. Women lack confidence. Women won't travel enough. It just goes on. Such rationales always end in calling for women to change, implying that until and unless women rectify all the things they get wrong, the scant numbers for their leadership won't budge. That Korn Ferry study is a case in point.

Despite its findings from thousands of respondents that women manage better than men, the report makes no mention of the need for top-down institutional changes or even greater diversity efforts to propel more women leaders. On the contrary. Korn Ferry's recommendations to remedy the lack of senior women focus on how women ought to amend their behavior in order to ascend:

"Women need to seek out and say 'yes' to experiences that stretch their skills and organizations need to provide women with opportunities to accept those challenges earlier in their careers."

Yet we've seen, from studies by Catalyst and others, that even when women "do all the right things," they still don't advance. Part of this dance, of course, is the famous—or infamous—"face time." That is, the need for staff to stick around afterhours and at professional events to build relationships with bosses and demonstrate their commitment to job, company and career. But more often than not, women need to zoom home to care for family or aging relatives. That lowers their executive profile, even when their performance is at peak levels. When women do put in requisite face time, they're often cut out of the loop as bosses invite out "the guys" while pointedly leaving the women behind. That behavior isn't limited to large corporations, either.

Cocktails take on new meaning

In the hard-driving tech sector, as elsewhere these days, "work follows you home and it's your social life. I've worked in those environments in the past," says BuzzFeed product design manager Sabrina Majeed. "You feel like you're missing out on your career or not getting ahead if you're not out having drinks or dinner. It might be your only chance to talk to the founder that day. I'm young and single and don't have children or other responsibilities so I always felt like I am capable of doing those things." As it turned out, her male colleagues at the time didn't quite agree.

"What's really frustrating is when you want to do those things but you're excluded anyway because you're a woman," says Majeed. "Or, because the male founders only want to take out the male engineers for drinks and, basically, go pick up women. So you're just not invited or given the opportunity." On several occasions, when she was out with male coworkers, "they all got text messages from our male boss asking them to go meet up with him later that night." Except for her.

"I try to push forward," says Majeed, who's in her mid-20s. "We're told that women have to be proactive and make your own opportunities, so I've tried throwing my own parties and invitations. I've tried to take the initiative, like, 'Can I grab coffee with you?' to be one-on-one with my boss. But that only goes so far," she says. "I've definitely tried but it's a pattern and the effort is never reciprocated and the treatment is never equal. It just gets exhausting and you move on to greener pastures."

What makes a successful woman leader?

"Women who are too tough are labeled 'aggressive' or 'abrasive,' while overly feminine women are labeled 'too soft,'" according to executive leadership coach Anna Marie Valerio, author of *Developing Women Leaders: A Guide for Men and Women in Organizations*. "In this damned-if-she-does and damned-if-she-doesn't double bind, leadership becomes more complex for women…. Women must walk a narrower path and are given less leeway in the range of leadership behaviors they are allowed to display."

Men are accustomed to running the show and promotion always is a subjective call about whether the candidate is "ready." Generally speaking (not every woman and not all the time), when women are vying for a promotion, they sidestep opportunities to get ahead by publicly beating or destroying a competing manager; I win, he loses. All that does for a woman manager is create a resentful enemy at her back who badmouths her and wants revenge. Then again, as Valerio says, women must take care to avoid looking too aggressive. More typically, women who win would rather leave behind an ally. Then, working strategically, women create opportunities to lead the team or coworker across the finish line; I win, he wins. It's not about being nice or thoughtful or afraid of competition or too anxious to please. It's how efficient women play to win.

Needless to say, men don't understand this. Nor do male managers feel confident about women subordinates who avoid chances to crush rivals. No guts, no glory, no promotion, thank you very much. Most of all, male managers do not reward female-style management because they see it as weak. Women have to prove that their way of managing works, repeatedly.

"The throneless mentality"

Does putting a woman in charge really make a difference? It depends on the woman and the arena, of course, but more and more often, the answer is yes.

"Corporate America has major challenges," says CEO Lori Gold Patterson at Pixo Technologies in Urbana. "Leaders assume they know everything instead of taking responsibility for recognizing what they don't. Men are less likely to think they don't know everything. Women are less likely to think they do."

Patterson believes the culture of big corporations is a large part of the problem because subordinates are dedicated to fulfilling whatever the leader says to do while protecting him from learning about any critical roadblocks they encounter en route. As a result of that belief, she manages her 32-employee technology firm with a philosophy she calls the "throneless mentality." That is, no one person has royal privilege and no one is king, least of all the owner.

She learned that lesson early, in the mid-1990s, when she signed on at age 30 as a computer programmer working at the Urbana facility of a Chicago-based global foodservice company. "I'd been with the company for five months," says Patterson. Management was then heavily invested in a big computerized project to install a new CRM or customer relationship management system. In short order, Patterson found that the project was fully on the way to failure. All the consultants working on the project were in India. "I pulled the consultants from India together, asked a bunch of questions and, together, we came up with a strategy to turn it around for success." She brought the strategy to the CTO and her plan was embraced and implemented. "It was all way above my level, which was part of my saving grace. I just had to present it," says Patterson.

Then, in 1995, a few days after Patterson gave birth to her first baby, the CTO called. "The VP of the company was looking for an internal change manager to reengineer processes because the systems were losing money," she says. "They needed someone internal who could take on the issues and binders and recommendations and implement." Based on her CRM strategy, the CTO had recommended her for the job. Was she interested?

Absolutely, she was. "I was a computer programmer with a mind that couldn't stop thinking about business operations," says Patterson. The opportunity also had the potential to be a career game changer. Then again, she had a brand-new infant. "I said, 'I'm thrilled that you see me in this light but I've just given birth. Can I do this interview by phone?'"

No, the VP had told the CTO he wanted a face-to-face. "So can we do this in two or three weeks?" asked Patterson. No, they needed to make a decision that week. If Patterson was interested, she had to make the three-hour drive to Chicago the next day. Make that six hours, round trip.

"My husband and I talked and he thought it was crazy but was willing to go ahead and make the drive with a five-day-old baby," she says. He had a caveat. Unsure of whether he could care for the newborn, he wanted her to agree that if he needed her help with the baby while she was interviewing, he'd call her cellphone and she'd immediately leave the building. She agreed. The next challenge was proper interview attire. Says Patterson, "What does a woman wear for a job interview five days after giving birth?"

"I put some parts together and it was all wrong and cumbersome, but I got to the interview," she says. "And sure enough the phone rings. You could hear the baby screaming through phone." She immediately stood up, saying, "I'm sorry I have to go. I have a brand-new baby five days old outside."

To which the VP immediately replied, "My god, why didn't we do this interview by phone?"

Patterson, of course, was too sharp to throw the CTO under the bus, but the lesson took hold. "The CTO was told that the VP wanted the interview in person, so he didn't question it," she says. "But if the VP had all the information he needed, he would have done the interview by phone."

Patterson did get the job, and months later, that lesson came in handy. The company was rigidly divided into brains and manpower. While top management and engineers worked at Chicago headquarters, 400 or so manufacturing staff were based in Urbana, where Patterson was working as the change agent. The VP, to whom she now reported, had never even been to Urbana. "When I burrowed into the real problem, I found that Urbana management, down to the secretaries, didn't trust the executive management in Highland Park," says Patterson. "They felt no one cared about them. Yet big changes were needed and even though I had been put there, they didn't trust that I really had the power to do anything."

She realized that the top brass had to visit to turn things around. "The VP had to come and get in front of management and have a real dialog. They needed to see that I was bringing the attention and the resources of the company to bear." So she called the VP and asked him to travel to Urbana the following week. His response on the phone, says Patterson was: "If I knew I had to do this job, I would have done it myself. Did I hire the right person for this job?" She hung up and began "beating myself up," upset that she'd made a mistake and that he was right and she should have figured it out for herself. For a half-hour Patterson thought about calling back and telling the VP exactly what was needed to emphasize that she was the right person for the job.

And then caught herself. "Instead of taking him at his word, I decided he didn't have enough information." She rang back to say: "You did hire the right person and she says she needs you down here this day." And the VP said, sure, he'd be there.

Running her own company now, Patterson makes sure to question what she's told and to add to what she knows. "You shouldn't assume you have all the information you need to make decisions. You have to find out whether your vantage point is correct."

Advice from real-life leaders

Many breakthrough women entrepreneurs, age 60-plus, are still at the top of their game and leading impressively successful enterprises that have racked up countless awards for best practices. Yet these women had very few role models to mirror success for them on the way up and have done it by themselves and on their own terms. Two such women have advice about leadership for up-and-comers. Each has figured out, not once but repeatedly, how to propel her business forward, making the tough calls and leap-of-faith decisions that expanding businesses demand. Since experience is the best teacher, their real-life examples offer touchstones for younger women entrepreneurs and hopefuls.

After taking over from her father in 1993, Ann Drake transformed the family warehousing business into DSC Logistics, a multimillion-dollar, high-tech supply chain company with 2,800 employees headquartered in Des Plaines, Illinois. Now chairman and CEO, Drake's focus has been on integrating supply chain solutions and leveraging the power of collaborative partnerships. She also actively promotes diverse talent to groom as leaders. "To be a leader, you need tenacity and positive energy. You also need to seek advice from mentors, male and female, in a formal program or from someone you approach on a semi-regular basis. Becoming knowledgeable about your industry helps to make you a leader. You need to take charge of the organization and be the chief spokesperson, getting involved in training and setting an example. HR can't do everything."

Gloria Bohan launched her walk-in travel agency in 1972 with one employee. Today, with more than 500 staff and a billion-dollar business, Omega World Travel, based in Fairfax, Virginia, is one of the country's largest travel management firms. Bohan was first in the field to integrate computer reservation systems and was also an early adopter of 24/7 customer service.

To keep employees motivated, says Bohan, "we give people responsibility. Good people want responsibility. My setup has a lot of offices and the travel industry is extremely competitive. I need creative thinkers in the field to build the business and keep the entrepreneurial spirit alive. So I give people the freedom to be creative. I also find that people want to sit down and talk. If you're more open with people and tell them you trust them, it makes them feel more a part of the company. When they don't have to make assumptions, it avoids a lot of the crazy grapevine gossip."

Rethinking leadership

Many advocates of gender equity in the workplace believe all the fuss about which sex is the better leader and whose style is more effective pulls the rug out from under the real goal. "This tug-of-war...leads us to conclude that we are asking the wrong questions because we're stuck in a frame that we need to move out of," say professors at the Center for Gender in Organizations in Boston. Since research emphatically proves that women leaders and workplace gender equity is both a business benefit and a competitive advantage, it's more important to talk about the strategic value of women's roles than who's better at what skill. When organizations have trouble advancing or attracting women, CGO suggests, it's not a "women problem" but rather a more general problem. Like the canary dying in the mine, it's a signal that something toxic is being released in the work environment that is affecting everyone.

But until women entered organizations in large numbers, the problem was something that workers adapted to unquestioningly as a constraint of the work-a-day world, regardless of the costs to themselves or to the organization. "Of course you have to work eighty hours a week—that's being committed!" or "Of course you have to travel five days a week—how else can we meet the clients' needs?" or "Of course you need to act like a bully—it's the only way to make it in this profession." These are cultural assumptions, and by questioning them and changing work practices to reflect a different set of assumptions, we not only make organizations more equitable, we often enhance their effectiveness as well.

The strength of women entrepreneurs and the rising tide of women starting and running their own businesses are molding a new mode of leader and, just perhaps, models for how larger and more established businesses can lead teams into the winner's circle. The best route to leadership, not to mention smart and effective management, is for women to jump off corporate ladders and launch now.

9

Communications: Questions vs. Solutions

**Her way:** Women delve into all the details, ask questions and verify.

**His way:** Men want only enough information to get the big picture.

Men tend to view language as a tool for problem solving while women see it as a means of empathy. "Men grow up in a world in which a conversation is often a contest, either to achieve the upper hand or to prevent other people from pushing them around. For women, however, talking is often a way to exchange confirmation and support." That's the key difference in how men and women interact in conversation, as defined in _You Just Don't Understand,_ the bestseller by Deborah Tannen, Georgetown University linguistics professor and the godmother of the study of gender-based communications. She distills this difference into conflicting sex-based agendas: Men pursue status. Women seek support.

To prove her point, Tannen tells a story about herself and her husband. When they had jobs in different cities, she says, people often made comments like, "That must be rough," and "How do you stand it?" Tannen accepted their sympathy and sometimes reinforced it, by saying things like, "The worst part is having to pack and unpack all the time." But her husband was irritated by such comments. He'd respond by explaining that their situation offered unique advantages. As academics, they had long weekends and breaks and summer vacations together.

Tannen agreed with him but couldn't understand why he bothered to say it. When she asked, he explained that the comments implied that theirs wasn't a real marriage. He assumed people were really saying, "I am superior to you because my wife and I have avoided your misfortune." Until then, said Tannen, it hadn't occurred to her that conversations included elements of one-upmanship. She concluded, "I now see that my husband was simply approaching the world as many men do: as a place where people try to achieve and maintain status. I, on the other hand, was approaching the world as many women do: as a network of connections seeking support and consensus."

Speaking in gendered tongues

Today, with three out of 10 American enterprises owned by women, and with women launching businesses at roughly twice the rate of men (plus the women who make up nearly half the workforce), such gender crosstalk has migrated from social interactions to the workplace. There simply aren't models or conventions for how women should or could behave once they're in charge. Amid the confusion and frequent irritation, few consider gender characteristics the reason for misunderstandings.

Yet many tangled conversations directly stem from the sexes' distinctly different communicating styles. Men and women request action and advice in divergent ways. Their verbal responses and conversational pace are different. The sexes make workplace demands differently. They define and communicate project needs and performance expectations in disparate ways. Resulting tensions particularly arise over issues involving power, advocacy and managing the troops.

People are individuals first and collections of cultural and genetic traits after that, as noted in describing the sex-based biological research in the "Strengths" chapter. But now that male and female characteristics have been documented by years of research, it's evident that gender disparities also play out in scrambled communications snafus. By and large, disconnects spring from the sexes' *styles* of talking, rather than the substance of business conversations. Most of the time, men and women in business communicate similar data or information. But it's the manner and ways in which information is expressed that throws up roadblocks. In turn, mistaken or lopsided assumptions can fuel a cascade of misunderstandings. The result is miscues, mix-ups, lots of that crosstalk and, in due time, probably business missteps.

Women owners must obviously understand how men in business talk— and vice versa—to communicate goals and operational needs to both sexes all along the business chain, including male and female customers, vendors, partners, staff, investors and more. Closing the tangible gender communications gap can not only help individual owners but also boost efficiencies for sales and customer service.

Mr. + Ms. Talk

Like the support-status divide highlighted by Tannen, there are definite themes that surface when communication between the sexes goes off the rails. For instance, in the research conducted by leadership development firm Zenger Folkman, the trainers found that "while men excel in the technical and strategic arenas, women clearly have the advantage in the extremely important areas of people relationships and communication. They also surpass their male counterparts in driving for results. This we know is counterintuitive to many men."

The everyday scenarios that follow offer models for examples of these themes. They offer food for thought and cause to pause to assess how to interact with the opposite sex in business dealings.

Scenario 1: Power Plays

Women tend to ask lots of questions before beginning any project. They usually want to hear and understand the rationale for the work and, if possible, some context and history of how and why and what's needed and how everything fits in before starting work. Men simply dive in and get to it.

The resulting assumptions each sex therefore make about the other are far from accurate and often end in misinterpretation. If women were competent and understood what was needed, they wouldn't ask so many questions and continually move backward, reason men. They'd just get to work. Men view asking questions as a sign of weakness. It irritates them. But in fact, women typically verify and validate data before starting tasks. Generally, they rely on what they learn to improve or reinvent performance. The reverse setup is since men don't like to ask for directions or background, they don't. Yet women assume that if men don't ask questions, they must know enough to get the job done without direction. Frequently, that's far from the case.

For women bosses, it's a good idea to check that men have enough knowledge to complete a task well. Women leaders ought to monitor the work in the early phases or offer help without waiting for men to ask, because they usually won't. Men ought to pause and listen to the questions women are asking. That additional time and attention can pay off in adding value or insights. Even so, women need to be mindful that asking lots of questions frequently translates as incompetence, insecurity or passivity.

Angel investor Joanne Wilson relates a story about getting exasperated after calling around to high-profile men and women to ask them to act as mentors for a Techstars New York series, a seed-investment accelerator for startups with programs around the country. "All the men I asked to be mentors said, 'Here's my name,' and that was it," says Wilson. "All the women asked, 'How many hours would it be? What's expected? What money is involved? How much time will it take? What's involved besides showing up?'" In the end, says Wilson, "that's how women miss out on opportunities. When the door opens, they should just walk in and not spend so much time thinking about it." She puts all the questions down to women's perfectionist nature: "If women are going to do something, they want to make sure they do it right."

Scenario 2: Picture Imperfect

Each sex underscores emotional impact with noticeable differences when offering narratives for motivation or sales. They connect different dots for listeners and team members. Women frequently illustrate points or offer examples based on home life or relationships. Men gravitate to metaphors about playing fields, winning and losing, conflict and battle to emphasize points or buttress arguments. Dialogue can hit a dead end. Women often do not follow the full-court-press, touchdown images. Or, they may walk away convinced that the male speaker isn't interested in their buy-in, otherwise the story wouldn't be so male-focused. Similarly, men tune out women's relationship narratives. Those examples hold little persuasion for them.

Sherron Bienvenu, a communications consultant and co-author of *Straight Talk: Oral Communication for Career Success,* hit just such a conversational wall during a sales pitch. After a male client had completed a series of coaching sessions, she told him that follow-up training would be the "icing on the cake" for his presentation skills. "I envisioned icing as the finishing touch that completes the project and makes it most presentable to the receiver," says Bienvenue. "But his perception of icing was the sweet, unnecessary, junky stuff that you scrape off to get to the cake." Needless to say, she didn't sell any more training.

The solution isn't simply to gender-reverse images when talking to the opposite sex. Instead, while taking into account an audience's knowledge and interests, relying on gender-neutral images works best. That might include metaphors or anecdotes from nature, the movies, pop culture, weather and so on. Or, if culinary or sports images are important, make sure to provide explanations. Don't leave it up to the listener's conjecture.

Scenario 3: Devil in the Details

Women like to hear and tell tales. They relate stories that include tension, ordeals, errors, tangents and motivations for all the moves, including left and right turns and re-turnings. Women like to explain how and why you will arrive at the destination. Most of the time, women's interest in details is for one of three reasons: first, to show concern; second, to vicariously participate in the experience, event or journey; and third, as in asking questions, to verify their assumptions. Men, of course, prefer to get to bottom and finish lines as soon as possible, so the route is inconsequential. They collect only enough data and details needed to make a decision or understand the big-picture message. Everything else is jettisoned as unnecessary or trivial. As a result, each sex becomes too impatient to hear out the other, or sometimes, to even hear each other at all. Women frequently consider men's brusque, get-to-the-point approach arrogant or rude. In turn, men often find women's longer-winded storytelling ditsy or boring.

Each sex can find advantages in adopting some of each other's tactics. If men took the time and effort to more fully explain their thinking, they might avoid jumping to conclusions or acting on incomplete data. They'd also likely forge greater consensus with more loyal and lucrative relationships. On the women's side, no question, it'd be a boon for women to move to the bottom line more quickly and efficiently. That could help a team or project to move forward more efficiently and maintain better focus.

Scenario 4: Emotional Exchanges

Typically, most of us bring into the workplace some version of the sexual dynamics we have at home. We also usually gravitate to office confidants, mentors or employees who most resemble the intimates in our personal lives, especially significant others and spouses. For same-sex couples, the dynamic may shift, but, as with heterosexual couples, one partner likely is more dominant. The result can be subtle and tricky gender miscommunications that people are loath to examine. Nevertheless, struggles in business frequently are quieter reflections of the same conflicts that arise at home, perhaps including disagreements about who's right and who's wrong, disputes about money, who feels overlooked or unappreciated or powerless and so on. At work, this plays out by men saying, "Women take everything personally." Women's version is, "He always needs to be right."

When engaged in a professional standoff or if a workplace colleague doesn't feel recognized or understood, it's smart to take a break to think it through, even though it's hard to be honest about blurring business and homelife reactions. It's possible that personal issues are being imported into the business environment.

Scenario 5: Decision Drivers

Generally, women are more comfortable talking about their feelings while men usually prefer to dwell on the facts and skip the emotions. The result is perhaps the most frequent and extended kind of communications trouble. When a woman shows her feelings, a man typically believes she's unprofessional. When an unmistakable emotional situation arises, and a man doesn't react, a woman figures he's dishonest or cold. The message for both sexes is that every instance of communication includes both components, the intellectual and the emotional. Nothing is totally one or the other. No matter what the topic or issue or content, there are both feelings and facts in every conversation, to varying degrees. Misunderstandings and ruffled feathers result from ignoring either of the two dimensions. That's not to suggest that every interaction is or should be fifty-fifty. But conversations can radically improve if men and women would just own up to the other's perspective.

For example, a man might say: "I know this is a difficult conversation for you. It's difficult for me, too." That way, he's validating the emotions in play. A woman might dial down emotional intensity by analyzing the problem, perhaps talking about how the issue breaks down into components, saying, for instance, "I think there are three pieces to the issues we've been discussing." She then ticks off those issues, one by one. That moment of analytic reflection on her part can move the conversation toward a more thoughtful mode while his acknowledgement of the emotional component will make her feel more engaged or connected.

The digital divide in gender communications

While women have had to adapt to male-speak as they entered and moved up in the workforce, the Internet, of course, has been the great equalizer. Women speak its language faster and more often then do men. Perhaps it's all in those details women like so much. Then, too, the Web is designed for smart shoppers, whether the goal is for retail, information, dating, vacations, finding high school buds or what have you. Offline, women have long been the nation's buyers-in-chief. Those skills and interests have intuitively migrated to online interactions. Men? Not so much, except in niche arenas, such as video gaming, and even that's changing. As shopping on the Internet evolved from techie toys in the 1990s, to consumer-based search services through the mid-2000s, to the current multichannel powerhouses and mobile apps, it was only a matter of time before women flexed their economic muscle online as well.

Women now account for nearly $6 out of every $10 (58%) spent online, according to "Women on the Web," a June 2010 comScore global report. "Our research helps illustrate just how massive an opportunity exists for marketing to women and the advantage of developing technology and products that speak to their needs and improve their lives," said Linda Abraham, comScore's chief marketing officer, when the report was released.

Recent innovations in local, mobile and social technologies have accelerated women's online engagement, particularly in social networking activities. In turn, women's enthusiastic adoption of social media and growing online spending bolster the rise of female-friendly portals and mobile apps, including social shopping sites and channels that specifically target women's needs and compressed schedules.

As women have strengthened their online presence, marketing has evolved to boost sales and better serve them. Echoing the differences in men and women's offline conversations, women use different vocabulary and methods for online talk and search. "Women are more likely to use long-tail keywords when searching for an item whereas men will just type in one or two words," says Teran Dale, a pay-per-click marketing expert. Plus, in email marketing, female-focused subject lines and text generate much higher CTRs (clickthrough rates) than generic messaging.

Speaking women's online language

An early adopter in harnessing the power of women online, Z. Kelly Queijo develops navigation, language, user utility and mobile platforms that specifically target women. In 2009, she launched Smart College Visit, an online portal based in the tech hub of Blacksburg, Virginia, to help parents and students navigate the fraught and daunting challenge of searching for the right college. "I thought I'd be doing a pretty good service for the college-bound audience," she says. "It was a way to present information in a consistent format to make it easy for parents and their teens to get the information they need to visit campus."

In developing the SCV site, all the analytics showed that "moms were really the primary audience," says Queijo. "Other data shows that in mom and dad households, it's typically moms who help children navigate the college admissions process. And we know that moms plan 70% of all family travel." In response, Queijo launched the site and the business to attract mothers, and that directly informed the utility and efficiency of her offerings.

_____

At Queijo's first college admissions job at Virginia Tech back in the '90s, before the Web or mobile, she was asked to rewrite the campus visit planner. "I needed to make it friendlier and to get the information in front of people who would visit the campus," she remembers. "The whole concept of the importance of the campus visit was ingrained in me from my very first day on the job." After leaving Virginia Tech, she worked as a consultant for several other academic institutions. "It was always the same goal," she says. "Everybody wants more people to visit campus." As technology moved into the college recruitment market, Queijo did too, directing Internet sales, software and Web-based services for outreach and admissions officers.

There's nothing like being positioned at the crossroads of change. As an admissions officer, Queijo became the expert at developing marketing communications that target families with college-bound teens. Her early experience in college admissions software and online services allowed her to integrate that marketing know-how with the drill-down chops of a technology developer. Fusing these skills turned Queijo into a pioneering digital marketer in the college visit and admissions space.

Her early adopter advantage continues to help in an arena where robust and time-sensitive content continually changes and expands. "As technology improved, keeping up-to-date has actually became easier to coordinate," says Queijo, mentioning geo-tagging longitude and latitude data. The site offers detailed regional travel information, including airports and driving routes, lodging and restaurants as well as local sights for each college. "The challenge of getting the other type of data, such as events on campus and the actual schedule of campus visits, that's a work in progress. As we work with colleges individually, we try to include that info and we invite schools to update that content on the site. There's no charge for them to do that."

Today, the award-winning SCV site has reinvented the market of college visits, alleviating the exhaustion and frustration families used to face while elevating the adventure of the experience. Revenue comes from online advertising and by marketing business services, such as developing native apps for a college in addition to SCV-branded mobile apps. As Queijo continues to develop SCV's multimedia platform, its female-centric sensibility influences how her mobile apps communicate. "I like the ability to get information when you need it," says Queijo. "Specific apps, such as shopping advisors for what to buy, from cars to technology to houses, appeal to women. I want to give them access to information that will help them to make a good decision. That's the value of a mobile app." So long as SCV's content and services stay up-to-speed with the times and the tools, the company has the enviable benefit of a built-in renewing customer base.

Learning to talk to moneymen

Securing capital, as noted earlier, is perhaps the greatest hurdle for women-led firms, for a range of reasons, not least, the male funder indifference to women's businesses. Studies cited in the "Threats" chapter and other sections demonstrate that women don't get across their pitch messages or ideas as often or as well as men do. Another recent in-depth investigation conducted by Babson College, "Women Entrepreneurs 2014: Bridging the Gender Gap in Venture Capital," came to similar conclusions but puts the responsibility on the investment industry: "Our study raises new questions regarding women entrepreneurs' access to venture capital. While recognizing its unique and targeted purpose, the equity model that exists in the United States does not seem to be a particularly good fit for many entrepreneurs, especially for women," wrote Candida Brush, project leader and chair of Babson's Entrepreneurship Division. Yes, most startups don't get funded, but women-led businesses least of all.

With so much of the pitch process beyond an entrepreneur's control, and with such diminished odds for women, it pays to zero in on elements that can be influenced. The dance of funder access and interaction has its special rituals, rhythm, vocabulary and conventions. Yet too many women don't or won't invest in learning how best to talk to moneymen.

Starting the pitch

Preparing for an investor pitch starts much earlier than many understand, well before drafting any kind of presentation. For Holly Lynch, the pitch process begins with learning how to sharpen the startup idea by collaborating with other entrepreneurs and advisors. That goes a long way toward refining the idea and, in turn, the pitch. Lynch, whose New York-based brand strategy firm, 85-Percent, works with clients such as Dove, IBM and Volvo, also is a member of 37 Angels, the all-women angel investor network. She focuses on investing in and mentoring women-led startups.

"In 2009, when I got involved with startups in New York, I noticed women have a different approach," says Lynch. "When guys start companies they want to talk about their brilliant idea to anyone who might help. Talking to some outside advisor would be awesome and men don't hesitate. Women may have a great idea, but they're concerned about finding the right person to talk to. They have a fundamental fear about talking about it too early." Women think they'll jinx their chances by talking too openly or too soon, says Lynch. "It's a matter of confidence."

Women tend to be more secretive about their business, especially with groups that may be competitive or judgmental. That often relates to other parts of women's lives as well. "Women also won't talk about job opportunities or new relationships too early in case they fail," says Lynch. But with any startup model, she believes, "the sooner you talk about it and the sooner you know about other ideas, the better. It's essential to find great people to talk to about your idea early on so you can close gaps, get the right advisors and put it out there. Women worry that someone will walk into their space, but there's always another idea that already exists. You're not going to be first to market."

Ready for the pitch speech

After honing the idea and model, the next critical phase is to craft a crisply persuasive elevator or pitch speech. According to Pace University's entrepreneurship program, this is "an extremely concise presentation of an entrepreneur's idea, business model, marketing strategy, competitive analysis, and financial plan, which is delivered to potential investors." Originally, the elevator speech was so-named because entrepreneurs, desperate to get in front of funders, would lie in wait for potential investors in building lobbies and follow them into elevators during the short ride to hold them captive for a quick passionate pitch. Such all-or-nothing minutes are more formalized nowadays.

More art than science, the contemporary elevator speech is a coming-attractions tease with just the right calibrated mix of talking points, market data and emotional detail to pique investor interest. The goal is simple: Earn more time with an interested investor. "All you're trying to do, whether it's a three-minute pitch or a six- or eight-minute presentation is to whet the appetite for a follow-up and get an in-person meeting," says Somak Chattopadhyay, founder and managing partner of Armory Square Ventures, an early stage venture capital fund in New York, and a longtime judge of the Pace University pitch contest.

The most important factor is the overall story, he says, or, the genesis of the opportunity. Chattopadhyay also points to three critical arenas that must be quickly and clearly explained: (1) the management team and how their qualifications suit the opportunity; (2) how the startup idea fits into its competitive landscape; (3) how the idea will scale. "This is where most companies don't make it to the next step," says Chattopadhyay. "It might be a $1 billion healthcare market but if you're selling software only used by receptionists at certain types of medical practices, that's another story." Founders should specify the percentage of their startup that will be captured in large markets. Last, Chattopadhyay advises an explanation of why the opportunity will work and why industry competition or other startups haven't been successful.

Joining a pitch contest

These days, pitch contests in which entrepreneurs can sharpen their presenting skills and ideas are popping up everywhere as VC and other groups encourage startups and try to cast a wider, more egalitarian net. Competition hosts run the gamut from nonprofits and accelerators, to networking groups, academic institutions, investment firms and more. Typically, contest organizers audition applicants' business plans and presentations and then select a specified number to show up, PowerPoint slides at the ready, and deliver. Judging panels are usually the most prestigious and credentialed entrepreneurs and investment professionals that the host can corral, whether known locally or nationally. Winners generally receive some seed money, all-important VC attention and real-time practice in selling their startup idea.

When Brittany Lo was going through the Babson WIN accelerator program and developing her makeup bar business plan, advisors offered her the opportunity to compete in several pitch competitions around the Boston area. "That was in addition to the $20,000 in funding from Babson's own competition," says Lo. WIN advisors as well as the contests, she says, "helped me gauge different aspects of the plan."

That support is increasing for women, helping to develop the kinds of networking groups that men have traditionally tapped. Holly Lynch, for instance, hosts "salon sessions" to bring women together in a safe community to present ideas. The meetings don't cover actual pitches but rather provide a comfortable setting for women to ask for help, present ideas, network and get advice from relevant people and women's advocacy groups. "The goal is to get women to eventually work with the right people," says Lynch—like pitch dress rehearsals. Springboard Enterprises, which focuses on women technology startups, is among the biggest and oldest of the dozens of groups and bootcamps around the country that today help coach women founders and offer access to interested investors (see the "Ways and Means" section to find a listing).

Bridging the gender crosstalk

We're now experiencing the first generation of widespread success for women-owned businesses. That means the been-there/done-that parts of the calculation for women entrepreneurs is not nearly as deep or wide as they are for men. As much as male advisors may be invested in women's success and sincerely motivated to support women-led companies, male advice isn't always relevant or appropriate. Men's—or anyone's—lessons can only go so far. Women must trust their own instincts and experience to define who they are and how they can work best because their goals, challenges and choices do not mirror much that's gone before. As a result, women may need to discard the constraints of traditional "best practice" conventions.

"Men in business can learn from women that critical to the bottom line is how people are treated and that care is a power word and power action," says psychologist Birute Regine. "Women in business can learn from men that dreaming big is good but everything doesn't have to be perfect in order to move forward on your dream."

10

Money: Passion and Independence
vs. Risk and Rewards

Her way: Women often put purpose, passion and staying in control ahead of financial gain.

His way: You have to take a real flyer to gain big rewards.

"On my fiftieth birthday, with my adult son and adult daughter looking on, I joined their names in a symbiotogram that I designed and had it tattooed on the inside of my left wrist. I was all in then and I'm all in now," declares Cathi Locati, a micropigmentation or medical tattoo artist. A symbiotogram is a unique design that reads as one word when right side up and another word when upside down, and is thus a fitting symbol for Locati's intricate skills and interwoven experiences. Formerly a portrait painter, art gallery director, Kinkos account manager and Miss Montana USA beauty queen, Locati says, "I am your quintessential career changer."

Based just north of New York City in Tarrytown, Locati calls herself an Areola Architect and, in 2011, launched cathi.ink, a service for medical micropigmentation after mastectomies. This kind of medical nipple tattoo is usually the last phase of reconstruction for breast cancer survivors, both women and men. Drawn on flat skin and the "blank canvas" of a reconstructed breast, the three-dimensional-looking areola micropigmentation is designed to give nipple tattoos the appearance of depth. Locati likes to invoke the art of Michelangelo to explain how flat designs can look as if they have realistic dimension. The procedure lets women regain natural-looking breasts in a significantly less invasive way than the additional surgery needed after reconstruction to restore the nipple area. Increasingly, women who undergo mastectomies as well as those who've had lumpectomies, implants and breast reductions or enlargement are choosing micropigmentation over more reconstructive surgery. As more women learn about micropigmentation options and request the service, facilities and hospitals from Atlanta to Denver and from Miami to UCLA's division of plastic surgery have begun offering medical nipple tattoos.

A Maryland tattoo artist named Vinnie Myers, who previously had been an army medic, was first to experiment with the practice. In 2002, a Baltimore plastic surgeon called Myers to ask if he could try to create nipple tattoos for breast reconstruction patients. Myers rose to the challenge so successfully that word began to spread. Today, while still maintaining his Maryland studio, Myers spends time in New Orleans working with the prestigious Center for Restorative Breast Surgery, which performs the kind of sophisticated reconstructions that actress Angelina Jolie had after her elective double mastectomy.

Clearly, a medical micropigmentation practitioner is hardly what young girls dream about becoming when they grow up. Nor is it the business Locati envisioned during the three decades she devoted to fine art and portrait painting. But while it's understandably seldom talked about, and still little known, the service intimately touches countless hearts and lives. As the testimonial from one Locati client put it:

The emotions I feel right now have taken me by surprise. Being my breast cancer was 5 years ago, I had accepted that my nipple was as good as it was going to get which I have reluctantly accepted. I am so very grateful to you and cannot express the words I feel right now. You have made me whole again; something I thought could never happen during my lifetime. I have tears rolling down my face…. as I let go of everything that has happened. You have rolled back time for me and brought me to a place when I didn't even know that cancer existed…. Thank you, thank you, thank you for… this very needed step in the healing process.

Finding a calling after failure

Born in the state of Washington, Locati was raised in Montana and lived in Utah before moving to the New York area several years back. She was running her own art gallery, working as the career services director at a local medical training school and exhibiting her paintings in Europe and New York when the economy melted down in 2008. She wound up depending on unemployment benefits. "I started asking myself some really tough questions because for the first time in my life I had no job options and I had just sold my house in Utah," says Locati. "Challenging myself like I never had before, and believing in my artistic abilities, my past experience and education, I transferred my skill from canvas to skin. I did it for my ladies!" Locati aims to become both evangelist and leader for the growing modern medical micropigmentation field. "I am dedicating the rest of my life to helping as many survivors feel whole and sexy again as I possibly can."

As a survivor of cervical cancer as well as having experienced breast reduction surgery, Locati is quick to bond with women who come to see her. "With medical micropigmentation, less is more," she says. "My artistic background gives me a high confidence level and I use my own minimalist technique. I have invented new services never done before because my mind is always asking the question, 'How can I make the experience the very best for the survivor?'"

Passionate about her work, Locati also wants to educate cancer survivors about the restorative options for medical micropigmentaton as early in their diagnosis as possible. "I want to establish quality standards so that great results are a given and not an accident. My success comes from educating survivors, surgeons and other practitioners about proper areola application. I believe that more surgery is not the way to fix the 'white problem,' and that surgery should stop being the only recommended solution after mastectomy." Under current regulations, surgeons and nurses are allowed to perform nipple micropigmentation services without any training or experience. No doubt, Locati says, medical pros are well intentioned but the results can be dreadful. She also wants to educate women about the federal Women's Health and Cancer Rights Act of 1998, which mandates health insurance coverage for medical tattoo services. "This is wonderful news for breast cancer survivors to know," says Locati. "As an out-of-network provider, I work hard with my patients to get them reimbursed by their insurance company, and we do get reimbursements."

Learning growth lessons

Incorporated in New York in 2015, cathi.ink has been growing slowly, with obvious challenges in getting out the word about medical micropigmentation options. Most clients arrive via word of mouth, so Locati is developing key affiliations with regional doctors, hospitals, breast health centers and plastic surgeons who will recommend her service. Building those relationships is also a step-by-step process. Her recently retooled website, cathi.ink, is the prime marketing starting point for the recommending medical pros, providing detailed background and information about her service. That's freed up a lot of the phone time she spent talking to doctors and potential clients. "I can now concentrate on performing procedures," she says

To raise profile, Locati is reaching out to business groups, winning awards—the *Westchester Business Journal* "Women making an impact"—and attracting media attention. In May 2014, the *New York Daily News* covered Locati's medical micropigmentation procedure for actress and dancer Tatyana Kot, 38, in video and photographs after her double mastectomy. Upon seeing the results, Kot said, "I got my sexy back."

Profit in transforming lives

While entering pitch contests and negotiating with a few equity investors to secure funding, Locati hasn't retreated from her "all in" declaration at launch. She's selling the artwork she produced over the years to fund the business. "After thirty years of establishing my value and credentials as a fine artist, I am selling all of my artwork at fire-sale prices to pay for more areola procedures for survivors who can't afford it," she says. "The list is long of thousands of survivors standing by with white breasts who are desperate for my services," she says, citing statistics of 31,000 breast cancer survivors in the New York, New Jersey and Connecticut tri-state area alone. "And the numbers are growing."

At the end of each day, Locati defines success by the number of women she's helped. "I am the lucky one when the magic happens each and every time I see the tears of joy and join the survivor in the happy dance. Two different women inside the same body come to see me—the hopeful one trying her best to be brave who walks in with head hung a little low and nothing but white and memories and scars and the happy one who dances out with sexy gorgeous areolas and nipples in full living color."

Doing business unusual

Casting women as the socially responsible gender is a long-cherished cliché, dating back at least to eighteenth-century Lady Bountiful and, indeed, carrying into modern times. Women donate more to charity than men do, even though they often have lower incomes, according to research from the Center on Philanthropy at Indiana University.

Women also make corporations more generous. When women are in senior positions and on corporate boards at Fortune 500 companies, annual philanthropy contributions go up, markedly, according to a 2011 study by Harvard Business School professor Christopher Marquis and Matthew Lee, a doctoral candidate. Subsequent analysis of that study, with Marquis partnering with women's business researcher Catalyst, added some dramatic numbers to his initial findings. When three or more women were on the corporate board, philanthropic initiatives spiked. The average annual contribution from companies without any female directors was just under $1 million. Boards with three or more women members averaged a whopping $27 million in annual donations. All companies with women on the board gave more to charities but, remarkably, each additional woman accounted for about $2.3 million more per year to the corporate philanthropic efforts.

In reporting these findings, Marquis neutrally notes that no one really knows whether having a woman CEO at a Fortune 500 company would make an even greater difference in giving than simply having women board members. So few women are at the helm that it would not be statistically valid to measure, Marquis explained. We can, of course, speculate.

An older study that focused on women business owners and charitable contributions, conducted back in 1999 by the Center for Women's Business Research (now part of the US Chamber of Commerce Foundation), found that more than half of women owners with companies of more than $1 million in assets give at least $10,000 to charity annually, compared to only 40% of male counterparts.

Starting businesses that generate social change

It's much easier to identify and measure women at large corporations than it is to find and corral women entrepreneurs to survey, as the lack of updates since that 1999 study telegraphs. Most experts assume that women's natural affinity for social responsibility translates into the kinds of businesses they launch, especially as interest in social entrepreneurship climbs. But such assumptions lacked hard data until recently. Now, a study released in 2012 reports: "Data reveals men most likely start businesses for the money, women for social value."

Diana Hechevarria, then a doctoral candidate at the University of Cincinnati's business school, along with three colleagues, investigated 10,000 individuals at economic, social and environmental types of startups in 52 countries, based on the 2009 "Global Entrepreneurship Monitor," the annual review of worldwide entrepreneurial activity. Announcing their findings, published in *Global Women's Entrepreneurship Research: Diverse Settings, Questions and Approaches*, the researchers said, "When it comes to starting a business, women are more likely than men to consider individual responsibility and use business as a vehicle for social and environmental change." By the numbers, women were 1.17 times more likely than men to create social ventures than economic ventures, and 1.23 times more likely to pursue environmental ventures than economic-focused ventures. "Traditionally, men have always been more active in startups, but that's because we typically have studied economic, social and environmental startups all together," said Hechevarria, when the results were released.

One more time, if experts don't specifically look for women, they tend not to find them. Perhaps, speculates Hechevarria, governments and international policy groups will begin encouraging social ventures as a way of supporting women, closing the global entrepreneur gender gap and growing local economies.

Besides socially responsible missions, women entrepreneurs also work harder at sustainable business practices than men do. An October 2014 study by Cox Conserves, a national sustainability program run by Cox Communications and Media, looked at how male-led and female-led firms manage supplies, energy and recycling. Researchers found that 70%

of the women and only 62% of the men were committed to increasing the level of their sustainable activities.

Social consciousness and the gender gap

Of course, the very existence of today's millions of women-led companies fuels ongoing social change simply because women didn't used to be in charge at all. The old women's movement slogan to inspire young girls and provoke more equitable policies—"You have to see it to be it"— keeps resonating. Nevertheless, questions remain: Are socially conscious companies more in tune with women's business acumen? Certainly, most of the women entrepreneurs profiled in these pages manage businesses with social values front and center, even the cutting-edge tech firms. At 6Sense in San Francisco, for example, Amanda Kahlow is 24/7 dedicated to scaling her Big Data startup, and has attracted $36 million in VC investments in validation of her idea and skills. But Kahlow also is a committed advisor to Girl Rising, an organization that works for global education of girls, and openly talks about her staff as family. "Emotional connections drive the business," she says. "In the morning, when I walk in, I'll tell them I love them." Somehow that doesn't fit the profile of similarly hard-charging male CEOs. "One of the greatest lessons in life is the more you give out the more you get back," says Kahlow. "It's no coincidence that the year I chose to give freely with no expectations of return to Girl Rising was the same year my company 6Sense was funded."

Can women fuel both change and the economy? Can they transform the nature of business and make the triple bottom line a more common goal? Most of all, will socially conscious ventures work to bridge the many gender gaps, in equality, in finances, in politics?

As of now, the jury's out. Currently, the difficulty faced by socially relevant firms, which are so often operated by women, is the widespread perception that such businesses are "boutique" or "indulgent"—read: can't scale and won't make money. That's despite the millions of dollars in intellectual and financial capital that game changers like Google Dot Org, the Clinton Global Initiative University, the Gates Foundation and others are investing in social for-profit ventures worldwide. Time will tell.

Taking charge as well as responsibility

Besides the socially conscious choice, women entrepreneurs share other tendencies that often lower expectations for their success. Women owners typically opt for control over growth, security over risk and a preference to stay out of the ring and the limelight. "Women tend to value security to a greater degree than men do," says Debra Burrell, a certified Mars Venus psychotherapist in New York. "They're more risk-averse and often wait for 'permission' before they venture into unknown territory. Women are conditioned to wait to receive, rather than to go out and take it." They prefer the sure-and-steady approach.

For all the reasons reported earlier, women like to bootstrap financing to start their companies while men are either more able or more willing to raise external funds, whether by debt or equity capital. That outside financing allows male-owned companies to grow faster and bigger than the firms women pilot. Three years after startup, and although the numbers are ticking up, still only 20% of female-owned firms in the US earn more than $100,000 in revenue. By contrast, 33% of male-owned firms do. The gap widens for larger companies. As a result, the millions of women-owned firms have less economic impact than their numbers would suggest. "With nearly half of the workforce and more than half of our college students now being women, their lag in building high-growth firms has become a major economic deficit," says Kauffman's 2011 "Overcoming the Gender Gap: Women Entrepreneurs as Economic Drivers." "The nation has fewer jobs—and less strength in emerging industries—than it could if women's entrepreneurship were on par with men's. Women capable of starting growth companies may well be our greatest underutilized economic resource."

Support organizations and programs for women need to shift focus to helping them build companies rather than just starting them, advises the report. "What it takes to succeed in business is not necessarily the same as what it takes to succeed in *starting* a business. While women have made great strides in breaking through the proverbial 'glass ceiling' to advance to high rank within corporations, few have made similar strides in breaking out laterally—through what might be called the 'glass walls'—to start their own high-growth firms."

Pushing boundaries for women-led startups

Proposed remedies to build women's skills at scaling run the gamut, but typically come down to two main components: improving access to capital and boosting women's belief in themselves. Private and public actors are working on both. Global consultancy Ernst & Young runs the "Entrepreneurial Winning Women Program," a national competition that connects a select group of high-potential women entrepreneurs with handpicked advisors, customized mentoring and resources. The federal National Women's Business Council has introduced long-term goals and initiatives to increase women's access to capital and markets and boost job creation and growth. Perhaps most interestingly, the Council also recommends revamping the tools by which women businesses are measured.

Currently, conclusions about how women business owners launch, grow and manage businesses are based on government and private data that only look at businesses majority-owned by women. That is, 51% or more. Women CEOs with 50% or more male equity funders or operating partners are not counted. The NWBC suggests expanding that horizon to include "women-led" as well as "women-owned" because the prevailing practice "ignores the economic impact, possibly up to $1 trillion, of women who own less than 51% of their businesses." Imagine, for instance, that a venture capital firm makes a big bet on a woman's future success by investing funds that account for 50% of the firm's equity. Immediately, even though the same women who founded the firm still runs it, that business falls off the women-owned radar. The company abruptly turns male-owned and ceases to represent women founder success. Similarly, if a woman-led firm takes on an equal male operating partner, the company becomes male-owned. Half equals men. Majority equals women. It's that simple—and wrongheaded. Measuring women-led businesses would dramatically influence perceptions of women's entrepreneurial achievements, which would change on-the-ground realities. "In business, if you cannot measure it, it is not real," argues the NWBC.

Although women continue to significantly lag behind men in growing their companies, the climate is incrementally changing. High-earning women-owned companies remain a small percentage (3%) but that still translates into a quarter-million or so businesses. At the top, within the women-owned group that reels in over $1 million in revenue, 35% earn more than $5 million, 2% generate more than $50 million, and several boast revenues over $1 billion. Looking ahead, NWBC chair Carla Harris anticipates continued improvement as women become more experienced and boldly take more risks: "I'm excited by the advent of accelerators and incubators for women startups," says Harris.

Let's also remember that economists don't measure the value of women's childcare, home or family work, so substantial economic impact is buried by conventional metrics. Then there's the other perspective on women entrepreneurs' relationship to growth. Like Cathi Locati, it may simply be more important to make a difference than to make a ton of money. Nonetheless, if social ventures had lots more money, the differences they make would be that much significant. The learning curve for women to climb is to think big as well as social. The more income they generate, the greater the transformation women could bring to the table and to the market.

Making friends with money

For many women, discomfort with money still runs deep. "Women will talk about anything but money," declares Laura Fredricks at Expert on the ASK. Women owners often need to work on changing internal attitudes and habits before they can take charge of business financials. Frequently, women need to pay closer attention to their breakeven cash flow and the revenue thresholds that will turn a profit. And, like most newbie owners, women typically overspend at the outset, buying more furnishings, technology or office supplies than they really need. New owners don't realize that few customers pay promptly. Even when sales are immediate, cash can be tight.

Other common missteps are misjudgments in pricing. Talk to experienced entrepreneurs, male and female, and there's always a backstory or two about pricing wrong turns and course corrections. Pricing products is always hard to nail, even with bigger businesses, but it's particularly tough at the beginning with little experience or sales to go on. If you ask a child to choose between 12 rhinestones and one diamond, she'll go for the rhinestones every time. Startup owners are like that. They fall for the fallacy of quantity over quality, figuring that although the prices are rock bottom, more sales will bridge the gap. It definitely doesn't work that way.

Succeeding into failure

Sarah Shaw learned that lesson the hardest way possible. A serial entrepreneur, she currently runs Entreprenette, a coaching service based in Durango, Colorado, that helps women take products from concept to reality. Before that, Shaw lived in Los Angeles, working as a film and TV costume designer. In 1998, she created a line of handbags that quickly attracted celebrity buyers, among them Jennifer Aniston, Cameron Diaz, Katie Holmes and Gwyneth Paltrow. Soon enough, Shaw's handbags were being sold in some 1,200 boutiques and department stores nationwide, racking up terrific press and celeb sightings in *InStyle, Oprah, Lucky* and more.

"My biggest mistake when I started my handbag company was not understanding costing," says Shaw, looking back. "I came from the movie world where money was no object. So long as you stayed within the budget they gave you, everything was fine." Playing with her own money was a giant reality check.

Although the bags were racking up retail sales, Shaw had underpriced them, never calculating the profit margin she'd need to continue production. "Coming from the film business made me financially savvy about covering my monthly overhead," she says. But she slipped up by not anticipating a host of "hidden costs," particularly in the manufacturing process. "I didn't understand all the costs that go into the raw materials." For example, although she relied on local Los Angeles manufacturers to produce the handbags, she brought in parts from suppliers elsewhere. "I had gold feet for the bottom and magnetic snaps that I brought in from New York. I'd see a snap and say, oh, it's only 65 cents. But I didn't take the cost of freight charges into consideration to get it to me." Those ancillary costs crept up on Shaw. "It led to the immediate downfall of my company. I had no one to turn to when I started," she says. "If I'd had a guide even in a couple of areas, especially costing and pricing, I would have gone beyond five years and passed the $1 million mark."

The moral of the tale, however, is entrepreneurial education and grit. Shaw went on to launch a second lifestyle and home goods business, including a closet organizer that she patented called Handy Hold All. She also launched an ecommerce site called SimplySarah.com that reeled in million-dollar sales.

Women on the margins

When working with clients of her third business, Entreprenette coaching, Shaw often uncovers the same pricing mistakes she made. "For the women who have already created a product and come to me for sales and marketing consultation, 99.9% have mispriced their products," she says.

"The process is about more than just knowing the real costs of goods on the products being sold. You must also know what kind of margins to use going from costs to wholesale and then wholesale to retail."

"A lot of people tend to just double their prices from costs to wholesale, but that doesn't work," continues Shaw. "I work closely with people in fashion, lifestyle and baby products who sell their products in boutiques, department stores and sometimes big-box stores. You have to take different margins of markup into account, including overhead, sales rep commissions and distributors. You may not be doing all those things today, but you want to make sure you're doing everything accordingly so there's room for growth. The profit margin for the future needs to be built into the original price."

Guidelines for setting prices are also helped by research or conversations with a firm's best prospects to get answers to some straightforward questions, such as: What price makes this product so expensive that you won't buy it? What price makes it seem worthwhile? What makes it a good deal? What price would make you walk away? What price makes it look cheap or makes you suspicious about quality? What added benefits or features would make you buy it? If those were added, how much more would you pay?

Turning a profit takes more than booming sales. Owners need to be careful that they're not selling diamonds for the price of a rhinestone.

Losing is critical to winning

Unlike Shaw, too many women haven't learned to cut their losses and move on. They haven't realized that to profit from a business risk or an investment in a new product or market means sometimes you lose the bet. When a financial decision goes south, men blame it on the economic climate, competition, markets or bad advisors. Women blame the loss on themselves. Men also assume they'll figure out how to make up the loss. Women pine, feeling it's been lost forever.

"It's interesting to me how few women that have had great personal financial success set aside capital to play around with as a way to build relationships and leverage their leadership," says VC Cindy Padnos at Illuminate Partners in Oakland. That holds true, she says, for high net worth women who have both inherited and earned their wealth. "I believe women still are more risk-averse than men when it comes to their personal investments. They frequently abdicate financial decisions, other than those regarding philanthropy." Similarly, says Padnos, "I'm puzzled that women who get to a point in their lives where they have a solid nest egg seem to use little of it for fun or to vocally promote the causes or projects they believe in. I'd like to see women understand the tradeoff they are making by frequently staying behind the scenes or being anonymous participants versus leveraging their financial position as role models and providing an incentive for other people to support what they believe in." Women don't take that path as often as men do.

As an example, Padnos points to men's behavior at charity auctions compared to women. "Guys will wave the paddle one after another, sometimes just to be competitive or gain recognition, which builds support from others in the audience." Men also know how to reach out to one another to reinforce each other's favored causes, she says. "It's quid pro quo and they have no issue whatsoever in being expected to do the same in return." Women-only events have a different flavor. "Women prefer not to be asked to support things that aren't their own cause and they don't want to be competitive with each other," says Padnos. Women have trouble saying no and avoid situations where requests for contributions or investments might come up. They don't often say yes and gain that buy-in or favor for the future, as men like to do.

"When I ask why women don't feel more comfortable making their own investment decisions," says Padnos, "they frequently say they've never done it before. Some say they are concerned about having to replace the money if they lost it and don't want to risk the financial freedom that has allowed them to leave a challenging work environment behind."

Defining next-gen ventures

For younger women, the gamble of entrepreneurship is coming easier. "The younger generation has a bigger risk appetite," agrees NWBC's Carla Harris. "Part of that is coming from a generation that had parents who provided a lot for them, including opportunities to take risks. Millennials and younger women who come from that environment were raised to take some risks."

Undoubtedly, Gen Y's growing-up experiences inform their entrepreneurial interest. Born roughly between 1980 and 2000, these are the 70 million-plus offspring of both Boomer and Gen X parents, or about a quarter of all Americans. They are the first generation to be totally wired and then totally wireless. Every generation, of course, is shaped by the distinctive cultural and geopolitical events of its time. But Gen Y was weaned on some of the nastiest and most transforming national and global traumas. That list includes the O.J. Simpson trial and Monica Lewinsky scandal, the horrendous precedent of the 1999 Columbine school shootings and the debut of mean-spirited partisan politics after the presidential election that failed to anoint a winner. All *before* 9/11.

When the 2008 international financial crisis is added to the mix, it's easy to understand why so many younger women and men are choosing to steward their own fate rather than trust to corporate advancement. Gen Y generally gravitates to work at smaller firms "that allow for more flexibility, an opportunity to embrace their entrepreneurial ambitions and the opportunity to use social networks at work without strict corporate guidelines," reports a 2012 study conducted by researcher Millennial Branding and PayScale, a provider of on-demand compensation software. The report "confirms that Gen Y is an entrepreneurial group, highly versed in social media, and prefers freedom and flexibility over big corporate policies," said Millennial Branding founder Dan Schawbel when the report was released.

Interest in entrepreneurship now starts much younger than in previous modern generations. Four in 10 youth, ages 8 – 24, of both sexes want to launch their own firms mostly to "use their skills and abilities or to build something for their future..." corroborates the Kauffman Foundation 2010 "YouthPulse" study. Here again, younger women were more interested in nonprofit work while men preferred commercial opportunities.

Ripple effects of the Great Recession

Thousands of young adults across the country, often regrouping owing to the economic climate, are harnessing ideas and the latest technology to start viable enterprises. Chante Goodwin began working part-time at a computer repair shop at age 15, and soon signed up dozens of her own clients. She launched her technology services provider firm Your Way IT Solutions in the Washington DC area when she was a first-year college student. Goodwin credits nonprofit Network for Teaching Entrepreneurship (NFTE), which encourages young people from low-income communities to convert street smarts into business intelligence, for helping her launch, including with classes on how to draft and present a business plan. Says Goodwin, now a CEO in her mid-twenties, "We have a well-defined and proven 10-step business process. We rely on it to solve issues while ensuring customer satisfaction."

Younger entrepreneurs also are reworking older business models to suit the times and their sensibilities. Natalie MacNeil, 30, leveraged her experience traveling the globe as a young ambassador for Canada to launch She Takes on the World, a business built on inspiring and educating young women to become successful entrepreneurs. In addition to workshops, video tutorials and books, MacNeil debuted the Conquer Club in 2015, an "implementation incubator" that offers women entrepreneurs 12-month support with live calls and mentoring.

As a kid, MacNeil always wanted to start a business. "But at first I was discouraged by those closest to me, who are now my supporters. My teachers always suggested I become a lawyer." It was that lack of a support system and community that inspired her to start her company. Having racked up awards, including an Emmy for Outstanding Digital Program for an online documentary she worked on and being listed four years in a row as a Forbes Top 100 Websites for Women, MacNeil is confident that "the new contingent workforce is now the norm. We're never going back to the way it was. This is the future."

She has widespread agreement for that. More than a third (34%) of the US workforce now is freelance, or 53 million workers, according to a 2014 survey from the Freelancer's Union and Upwork. Women account for much of that. These "women-owned self-employed enterprises are making significant contributions to our nation's economy and are a harbinger of what the workforce of the future may increasingly look like," predicts "Women-Owned Businesses," a 2013 overview from the Center for Women in Business (CWB). Foreseeing an expanding 1099 economy, so-called for the federal income tax form filed by freelancers, the CWB, like many women's business groups, advocates programs that will boost growth for women-led firms. "As successful solo enterprises led by women grow into employer firms, understanding their character and impact will… help more women scale up their businesses and ultimately serve national and international markets in unique and groundbreaking ways."

MacNeil wants to work on the leading edge of such changes and "empower young people to become entrepreneurs who can learn to use the tools at their fingertips. It's a different kind of economy today and self-employment is more secure than getting a corporate job." Her advice to young women: "Surround yourself with the best and the brightest people you can find. Connect with others who have been in the trenches to learn what you should be doing, what to give up and what would help the most."

11

Sales: Pull vs. Push

__Her way:__ Listen and mirror feelings until you understand the problem.

__His way:__ Offer solutions and present products.

Back in the early 1980s, after graduating from beautician school, Carolyn Gable worked as a waitress at the then-revolving restaurant atop the O'Hare Hyatt at the Chicago airport. She liked watching the women travelers, who were just getting into business big time back then. "They used to come in carrying briefcases and wearing those power suits with big shoulder pads," recalls Gable. "And I thought, 'I can do that.'"

She was right on the money. Today, Gable is President and CEO of New Age Transportation, Distribution & Warehousing, a $30 million freight transport business based in Lake Zurich, Illinois, that she founded in her home in 1989. New Age manages traffic and distribution for manufacturers and producers too busy creating products to also worry about moving their wares to market. On any given day, the company has hundreds of contracts with air and trucking carriers around the country, sometimes storing freight loads in its 85,000-square-foot warehouse that houses corporate headquarters. "I didn't have any supporting family or education," says Gable, who has won numerous awards for outstanding customer service and best practices over the quarter-century she's operated. "If I can do it," she says, "anyone can."

Walking through the door of opportunity

Gable got started by refusing to take no for an answer, a trait most entrepreneurs will recognize. She decided that she was meant for sales despite her lack of experience, training or encouragement.

When the Hyatt restaurant was damaged by a storm and closed for repairs for a few months, Gable registered at an employment agency to look for interim work. A few days later, she lucked into an interview at a trucking company in Elk Grove that had trouble retaining employees because of the long commute from downtown Chicago to its offices. The recruiter cautioned Gable to avoid any mention of sales. This was an inside service position, no more. She got the job. But she kept waiting tables at the Hyatt after it reopened, just in case, working 70 hours a week. She also launched a persistent campaign with her trucker boss to give her a chance to sell. When he finally gave in, she proved to be pretty good at it. "It's all about the relationships," she says, "whether you're selling widgets, food or freight."

Gable's luck, and eye for an opening, stayed true. Soon afterward, when her trucking employer went out of business, Gable was called to interview for a position with Carolina Freight, one of the nation's leading carriers. It seems some of Carolina's customers had seen Gable in action and mentioned her abilities to the manager. "It was the opportunity of a lifetime," says Gable. With Carolina's reputation and training to capitalize on, she soon turned into a top producer. By that time, in her twenties, she had also gotten married.

Characteristically, Gable's next moves were to take on more risky challenges. In the mid-'80s, the freight industry was roiled by consolidation. Gable, who by then had two kids and a fresh divorce, jumped to a startup, and then to a larger regional carrier. In 1986, she remarried. "That probably prompted me to go out on my own," she says. "I wanted more kids and it gave me a bit of a safety net."

She began working out of her home basement as a commissioned rep for several trucking companies. By 1989, when she realized her commissions were lost because her hard-won customers were placing orders directly with the truckers instead of calling her to place them, Gable decided to set up shop for herself. The business took off. "It was unbelievable," she says. "I was billing over $100,000 a month. I hired three employees and they'd arrive at 7:30 in the morning. I'd still be in pajamas." She rented an 800-square-foot office in nearby Schaumburg. "It was a beautiful corner office with many windows, full of light," she says. That turned out to be a prescient move.

Rethinking the model

In 1992, her largest client consolidated all its freight business with one carrier and no longer needed her placement services. "Overnight," says Gable, "I lost 40% of my commissions." She saw more change coming to the industry and went to work on a new business model. "Most carriers had contracts with clients that charged a standard 5% to 7% of their revenues on all accounts," says Gable. Instead, she calculated that by brokering, customizing and tracking freight services, she could offer innovative discounts and still provide top customer service. "I decided to become a broker and take over billing," says Gable. The handsome office turned out to be just the ticket to impress new clients. "I stopped working on commission and that beautiful office made me look legitimate. I got the pricing I asked for." Before divorcing again, Gable had five more kids, for a total of seven—with a spread of 24 years between the oldest and youngest. In 2000, she landed a lucrative contract to distribute Time Warner's cable TV equipment, just about doubling her revenues. "That opened the door to the cable industry," says Gable. She then signed up Cox and Charter, too.

She credits her success to a passion for selling, and to never taking any deal, any customer or any account for granted. "Selling really is about building relationships. Everyone with a big title is still a person. Whoever it is will enjoy it when I ask about his daughter. Share your life. Get to know clients as people. Relationships put you over the top."

Like most successful female owners, Gable has set up formal ways to give back. Motivated by her own experiences as a single mother, she's established two foundations for what's called "the working poor." The first foundation supports children of single parents and her subsequent one, an extension, focuses on the needs of the single parents themselves. In 2011, Gable was invited to join the Fetzer Institute's Advisory Council on Business Professions, a nonprofit that develops networks and practices that encourage love and forgiveness at work, such as providing jobs to the disabled, donating a percentage of sales to provide books worldwide and to "operating a business under core values of love, forgiveness and compassion." Advising business owners to have a personal life— "I'm a mother first. The business can be gone tomorrow"—Gable has documented her journey in a book, unsurprisingly entitled *Everything I Know as a CEO I Learned as a Waitress.*

What women have that men do not

Nailing a sale is more an election than a contest. Top salespeople don't beat the competition. They earn the customer's vote. Male or female, every salesperson needs proper training and practice to become successful. Yet it turns out, whether owing to nature or nurture, women frequently demonstrate the skills and aptitude that win more customer votes than men do. Women are most often credited with superior "soft skills," meaning they empathize, mirror and express feelings more readily than do men, and that encourages bonding and communication. "Women business owners are skilled at building relationships that are caring and based on really listening and responding," agrees Kathleen Burns Kingsbury at KBK Wealth Connection in Waitsfield, Vermont, a coaching service that advises financial services pros how to better communicate with clients, especially high net worth women.

Those are useful traits for the traditional 90 – 10 sales rule: A prospect should do 90% of the talking, with a salesperson weighing in only about 10% of time, mostly to ask questions about the prospect's needs and goals. No doubt, women's sharper listening skills come in handy for sales. But it takes more than listening to close deals. "Women are more open to coaching than men are," explains Los Angeles sales trainer Sam Manfer, who has led dozens of sales coaching seminars, and adds that women are inclined to learn and ask questions. "Women find out what the customer's problems are and that sets the stage for them to sell better," he says. In contrast, men tend to push information, preferring to provide answers rather than ask questions. That often leads men to deliver solutions without fully grasping the problem or understanding exactly what prospects want.

Typically, women more than men choose to pitch the "benefits" rather than the "features" of products and services they sell. That echoes sex differences often tracked in personal investing. Women usually invest in the stock market to earn funds for life goals, the *benefit* of retirement or their kids' college tuition. Men invest with the idea of scoring, the *feature* of making money that's unattached to any other objective. But selling features—that is, the mere facts of what's being peddled, such as "Navy or Black," "Antilock Brakes" or "Broadband"—isn't what convinces customers to purchase. They'd rather learn about what they gain from buying, such as saving time or more convenience or both. When marketing benefits, the emotional transaction counts as much as the financial one, and women typically score higher in such situations. That's another way of saying that women earn more customer votes.

What women do that customers want

On-the-ground surveys and in-the-field observations back up the fact that women have a specific knack for selling. From 1994 – 2006, at the Real Learning Company (now BTS Group), founder Richard Hodge and program expert Lou Schachter developed tools and training programs to improve sales and management skills. Summing up their experiences and insights, the pair coauthored a book, *The Mind of the Customer,* which included research they conducted to identify what corporate decision makers look for in sales professionals. They wanted to know which attributes in salespeople most persuade buyers to seal a deal. The coauthors talked to purchasing decision makers at Fortune 500 companies, including Real Learning's clients at the time, such as American Express, Bristol-Meyers Squibb, Toyota, UPS and more. Among the 25 attributes that emerged, says Hodge, "six had the highest priority for decision makers." Women are strongly identified with most of those top six. According to Hodge, these include accountability; honesty and integrity; timeliness; partnership/cooperation; problem solving; and understanding the customer's business. "Women tend to work so both sides win," notes Hodge. "The ability to draw on a large network of contacts to solve issues and concerns is important."

Earlier studies, conducted by Nigel Piercy and Nikala Lane, business professors at Warwick University outside Birmingham, England, along with David Cravens, a professor at Texas Christian University, suggest that women also do better than men at leading sales units because women managers motivate sales staff by building relationships rather than financial incentives. "Females display higher levels of 'behavior control' in how they manage rather than relying on commissions and bonus to motivate their team," concludes the study. In addition, "female sales managers do more coaching and support activities in managing their units and they appear to do it better than male managers." The researchers go out of their way to dispel any implicit gender stereotypes in their findings. "These differences do not reflect the traditional assumption that female executives are naturally 'nurturers and carers.' The evidence is they are just as demanding and critical as male managers. The differences seem to be in the ways in which they manage their salespeople."

What women need to work on

Some issues in selling do trip up women, however, and these are areas where men tend to outperform women. Predictably, as we've seen in other arenas, such issues often revolve around self-confidence. "Top women in sales are often working upstream in organizations where most of the salespeople are male," says executive coach Faith Ralston, who runs Play to Your Strengths, in Minneapolis, Minnesota. "This can be challenging." It gets hard for women to find role models and even harder to trust instincts that diverge from the herd. "Too many women try to be like the boys," says Ralston. "Successful women salespeople are uniquely themselves as well as uniquely female."

Ralston also works to build leadership skills for women, partnering with corporate clients and Awesome Women, a nonprofit group in the Twin Cities. She's developed a grid for training based on the suits in decks of playing cards. Women tend to be strong in what she calls "Heart talents," or reading between the lines and developing trusting relationships with both customers and employees. That allows women to leverage a broad array of resources. But women often need to develop their "Diamond and Club talents." The Diamond talent helps salespeople see possibilities in order to come up with the Big Idea for a customer. The Club talent helps in deal making so salespeople can successfully reach higher-level executives.

Another difficulty for women in sales is that they can "get a little unfocused," explains trainer Manfer. Once a woman has achieved some success, she may resist the necessary give and take and become too inflexible. She will decide, "This is how it's done," says Manfer, rather than continuing to take cues from the customer. He puts it down to fear.

If the woman backs up and starts the sales process anew, she's worried she'll lose the sale. "Confidence is the ability to solve problems for the customer," he says. "But women sometimes are afraid the sale will get away from her if she negotiates."

The girl stays in the picture

On January 7, 2008, Americans nationwide learned that playing the gender card had migrated from the land of politically incorrect onto the competitive fields that can close the deal.

Barack Obama had just swept the Iowa presidential caucuses, much to everyone's surprise. Momentum was with him as the New Hampshire contest heated up. And what happened? Hillary cried.

That's it! A few tears from the nation's first credible woman candidate for president and Hillary not only won New Hampshire and found her "authentic voice," but went on to wage one of the fiercest primary competitions in US history. The tears welled at a Portsmouth coffee shop when voter Maryann Pernold, 64 at the time, said to Hillary that as a woman Pernold knew "it's hard to get up every day and get ready and get out of the house in the morning." She asked Clinton how she managed to do that every morning to face the relentless pressures of the campaign trail. Off guard, Hillary's eyes filled, her voice choked, all caught on camera, and we suddenly saw Hillary the vulnerable instead of Hillary the invincible. "This is very personal for me," she said.

There it was: Two penultimate "girl" moments caught on camera that ran 24/7 on all media outlets and continue to be replayed nearly a decade later. First, there was the teary visible emotion, and, second, candid admission that the quest was personal. Do men ever acknowledge their professional ambition as personal? On the contrary. What women always hear instead is, "Don't take it personally."

For decades, women in the workplace were continually warned that crying on the job was the cardinal sin, no matter how bad it gets. In the 1992 movie, *A League of Their Own*, which featured women baseball leagues during the World War II era, the Tom Hanks character, manager Jimmy Dugan, personified that strict prohibition. When one of the women players starts sniffling because of his insults, Dugan reacts with utter male disbelief and frustration: "Are you crying? Are you crying? ARE YOU CRYING? There's no crying! THERE'S NO CRYING IN BASEBALL!" Why? Because it's way too "feminine," meaning "weak." Tears telegraph that a woman worker isn't "man enough" to make tough choices. Showing overt feelings and cracks in composure automatically clouds judgment and leads to bad, that is, "emotional" decisions. So, tip of the hat to Hillary, however unintended, such strictures and perceptions are eroding. Certainly, it's still pretty much a no-no to burst into tears in the office, but workplace conventions about sex keep evolving. Professional behavior and customs are slowly but inexorably shifting, absorbing changes in sex roles and the edited etiquette of gender equality.

From explicit to gender-neutral

In the 1970s, Southwest Airlines unveiled, in more ways than one, a brand-new look for its flight attendants, aka "stewardesses." SA's women of the skies began roaming the aisles in white go-go boots and tight hot pants. The airline trotted out a special campaign, unimaginable today, to market its new look: "Sex sells seats," its ads boasted. Since then, as "girls" became "women" and "secretary" grew into the more respected "admin," a host of occupations have been shuffling the gender card deck.

Male nurses in hospital uniform are not quite as immediately assumed to be doctors and vice versa. Basketball players of both sexes have seen their uniform shorts get longer and looser as the times turned sex-conscious, likely because as the sexes began working alongside each other off the playing fields, sexy tight attire became uncomfortable and inappropriate. Pantsuits for women, whether TV news anchor, intern, CEO or political candidate, now are de rigueur business attire. Masters of the universe may still exclude women associates from bonding rites on the links or at the club. However, those same guys are making deals on the sidelines of soccer fields while cheering their daughters' goals. More to the point, seeing those daughters grow up and face hurdles because of their gender has opened many Boomer men's eyes to subtle bias in workplaces that they previously never noticed or thought to change. Even office romances, long considered shocking breaches of business decorum, have turned into a big yawn, absent any coercion or imbalance of power that becomes sexual harassment, obviously. Many companies have now amended HR policies with guidelines that explicitly define acceptable forms of employee dating.

"We've been taught to be gender-neutral in the workplace," says Theresa Zagnoli, who runs a communications consultancy in Chicago. "But most of those rules had to do with language, touching and artifacts, like hanging up a pinup calendar in your office. The rules didn't—or couldn't—include nonverbal behavior, like tipping your chin a certain way or looking into someone's eyes or smiling." Nowadays, says Zagnoli, whose clients are mostly male lawyers seeking help with communications or jury selection, "we're much more comfortable with both kinds of behavior."

Men and women mostly shrug off gender differences these days: Men are from Mars, women from Venus, everyone says knowingly, without addressing the issues of power or status also played out in sex roles. On the surface at least, gender today is defined more as style than the substance invoked in the past.

Is it okay to make eyes at a prospect?

In recent years, marketers have learned to develop messaging that accentuates demographic differences, carefully signaling "inclusive" but mostly targeting new customers and unexploited markets. Once uniformly plain vanilla, ads and campaigns now speak directly to distinctions of age, race, religion, sexual orientation, national origin and more. Assuming no whiff of bias or offensive expression, consumers shrug it off as Marketing 2.0 if not actual progress.

That would seem to foreshadow the next step for gender: If we're relaxed about gender differences in professional settings, and if sex roles and the language of gender is just another option in the marketing toolbox, then is it okay to harness sexual wiles to build the business relationship and the sale? It depends on who's answering the question.

A growing number of entrepreneurs, sales trainers and communications coaches say that being overtly womanly or distinctly manly can be used to your advantage in winning business. Others are sure that such selling tactics are at best risky and inappropriate or, at worst, a throwback to the days of rigidly defined and discriminatory sex roles. Obviously, most of the new-gender discussion delves into women's behavior because they've been integrating existing male sales ranks. As women gain positions of power, they must work out the balance between acting "feminine," whatever that may be nowadays, and combating old sexualized prejudices. In this terrain, there's little consensus about where the borders are drawn, what steps over the line and which behavior or customs actually can help close a sale. What is clear is that relying on sex advantages to pitch business requires very sensitive antenna for timing, personality and circumstances.

The sexual dynamic for women is always implicit anyway and might as well be leveraged, in professional ways of course, says consultant Zagnoli. "Men are higher up on the food chain and power comes from their presence." That makes it more straightforward for men. With women, the sales cycle represents power as well, but there's a difference, she says. "Power is sexy, strength is sexy and success is sexy. A woman brings all three to the table, by the way she dresses, talks and the language she chooses. Women don't have to go into active sexual mode to sell," but they can't escape it.

By contrast, Erin Wolf, partner at management consultancy SuiteTrack in Atlanta, is convinced that any hint of flirting or sexual dynamic in a sales meeting is a bad move. With earlier experience working at Goldman Sachs, Accenture and other global companies, Wolf markets a corporate speaking tour called "Lessons From the Trenches: A Woman's Guide to Winning the Corporate Game." She's certain that when women use such selling tactics, they "run the risk of falling back into stereotypes that we have fought long and hard to climb out of."

Most experts lie somewhere in the middle, such as Jeanne Worrick, who detailed her two-decade career of selling in the male-dominated petroleum industry in her book, *Sell Like a Girl*. "I wouldn't go so far as to say that sex closes the deal in the obvious sense of batting the eyelashes, but women have much better intuitive abilities and listening skills," says Worrick. "They read prospects better and so can often anticipate their needs. Men are focused on getting the business and winning. Women tend to be consensus builders and want to make sure the customer is satisfied. Women tend to look beyond the initial closing to the long-term relationship with the customer." Yet Worrick well understood the persuasion of sexual messages when she pursued a sale: "I paid very close attention to what I wore going on my initial call and what I wore to the close," she says. "I was more sexy initially and more serious and in for the kill for the closing. Just the opposite of what you might think."

It comes down to nuance and circumstances, sums up Ashley Swartz, founder of enterprise video platform Furious Corp. "Flirting with a client is a gray matter. In a literal sense, you can't use sex to get the business." Like most women working with the evolving etiquette, she has developed her own rules and style. With clients in the male-centric video game industry, Swartz is often the only woman in a room full of men. She remembers, "When I walked in for a meeting at a huge video game publisher that made the largest online game, everyone paid attention to me. I was probably the first woman they'd seen in a long time," Swartz jokes. "I was wearing heels but I was dressed without showing anything inappropriate. I don't think it's my responsibility to wear a muumuu to a business meeting so I won't distract them." However, Swartz also is not above using the attention. Just to be clear, she says, "I flirt with women too. When I say 'flirt,' I just mean being pleasant and having a genuine interest in what someone else says. It's not about putting my boobs in someone's face."

Until more men grow accustomed to females with power, every woman will have to negotiate her own path when selling to men. Undoubtedly, inserting sex into the sale is a double-edged sword. Plus, say trainers, women in particular often lose the distinction between a prospect and a purchaser. Male prospects may find it harder to say no to a woman than to another man. As a result, women in sales are offered stalls or "think-it-overs" instead of a decision. They end up wasting time that would be better spent in looking for new opportunities.

Women gravitate to innovative sales

Entrepreneur extraordinaire Paula Jagemann-Bane has a knack for hard work and pure plays. A self-described geek, she made her first few million at age 28 during the dot-com heyday, as employee No. 33 at legendary startup UUNET, one of the first commercial Internet service providers. As VP of Investor & Public Relations and chief of staff to the CEO, stock options, natch, were part of her compensation. UUNET went public in 1995, ranking just behind Netscape as the second biggest IPO of that year, and then later was acquired by telecom giant WorldCom in 1996 (and ultimately part of Verizon). Jagemann-Bane walked away wealthy. She was not even 30. For a while, Jagemann-Bane rested on her smart laurels but soon noticed a market niche she decided to fill.

The big selling idea

The story goes that during a family visit in 1997, Jagemann-Bane was showing her brother-in-law's kids how to navigate the Internet by searching for office supply sites, mostly because that was the business their dad was in. It turned out that none of the big office supply companies were then selling online.

Jagemann-Bane decided to jump in. In 1998, investing a half-million of her own money, she launched OnlineOfficeSupplies.com, an ecommerce company that represented brick-and-mortar suppliers. By 2000, the online business was pulling in $20 million a year and she sold it a year later to focus on software development in the supplier industry.

Neither the times nor the software development industry were particularly woman-friendly. Yet after raising $89 million in capital, Jagemann-Bane steered the new company, eCommerce Industries, Inc. (ECI²), to success, even as the post dot-com climate turned inhospitable (the company has now become ECi Software Solutions). She focused on providing technology solutions to small and midsized businesses in industries with strong reseller channels, including janitorial-sanitary products, office products and industrial paper. "I started my company in one of the more difficult vertical market climates," she says.

Looking back, Jagemann-Bane recalls "in the beginning, ECI² predominantly served the office products industry, which was dominated by older men who were not necessarily savvy about technology. I was perceived like a girl trying to sell Girl Scout cookies, not as the head of a technology company that could deliver small businesses efficiencies that they had never seen before. I think my background as a true technologist helped. So did our repeated marketing and PR efforts. I also spoke at industry events, gave interviews to industry publications and quickly gained a reputation as a new leader in the field. It took time. It also didn't hurt that I golfed!" By the time Jagemann-Bane sold the company in 2006, ECI² was valued at roughly $90 million.

Giving back and hardly retired

Jagemann-Bane consistently contributes to business and techpreneur communities, including such involvement as heading up a small-business technology incubator group near her Maryland home. She sits on several boards, is a high-level volunteer for several women's technology and small-business mentoring groups and has been an advisor for the Kauffman Foundation's eVenturing group.

As of late, Jagemann-Bane has decisively moved into the healthcare and wellness arena, pioneering yet another market in her own focused way. In 2011, considering herself "retired," Jagemann-Bane was serving on the board of the Frederick Memorial Hospital in Maryland, and found that breast cancer patients had serious challenges in finding all the homecare health items they required. After trying to buy the items herself online, Jagemann-Bane learned that it took about five hours to unearth all the products—not exactly how a breast cancer patient wants to spend her time. Jagemann-Bane figured she could devise a better solution.

Nowadays, the serial entrepreneur is founder and CEO of Someone With Group, a home health and medical supply online storefront. Jagemann-Bane sees help for the millions of breast cancer patients as just the beginning. She expects to expand her online services for other cancer patients as well.

Women sell by doing what comes naturally

Last, one of the strongest tools in women's sales arsenal is storytelling, which has come back into strategic vogue to help a company stand out, boost business and attract customers. Instead of pushing more slogans or promises into today's noisy channels, marketers are choosing to draw in customers and investors with the more persuasive and quieter power of narratives. Personalized fables and founder legends can warm prospects and lead to buy-in more effectively than other marketing, including case studies or testimonials. Viral stories on social media have also fueled marketer interest. And since telling stories is how women empathize and build connections generally, telling a business tale becomes an organic sell for them.

"Stories inspire us," explains Sunny Bonnell, cofounder of Motto, a branding agency in South Carolina's Myrtle Beach region. "They are the emotional glue that creates meaningful experiences between brands and their audience." Stories speak directly to the human condition, to our hardwired emotions and instincts. It's feelings that truly seal a deal.

"Decision-making is an emotionally driven process," says New York communications coach Jane Praeger, who runs Ovid Inc., and teaches "strategic storytelling" to business students at Columbia University. "When people make a business decision, they start with emotions, and then post-rationalize the decision with facts. There's a lot of science behind why storytelling is so effective," says Praeger, citing the work of neuroscientist Antonio Damasio to prove her point. Head of the Brain and Creativity Institute at the University of Southern California and a bestselling author, Damasio investigates the neurobiology of mind and behavior, particularly decision-making. One of his projects focused on people who had suffered damage in the part of the brain that rules emotions. Turned out, that damage rendered them incapable of making even the simplest decisions.

The once-upon-a-time backstory

Just any old tale won't do, of course. Commanding mindshare and memory comes from authentic and compelling stories that twang nerves and heartstrings. An effective company fable captures and conveys the emotional DNA of a brand, offering value and an experience. Smucker's jam, for instance, combines a heart-tugging message of consistency and caring in its founding family tale. Steve Jobs infused the Apple brand with a story of wizardry and populist must-have. Then there's the emotional bond forged by the Snugli baby carrier, invented in the 1960s by a former Peace Corps volunteer named Ann Moore who saw how mothers cared for babies in traditional cultures. Carmakers continuously embroider their narratives with stories of families creating lifetime memories or couples pursuing adventures.

Business stories abound for startups. By definition, entrepreneurs are emotionally engaged and running the gauntlet of challenges and change. To begin shaping effective stories, owners ought to think about the original spark for the business and the excitement of beginning. Launch days are usually fruitful and filled with anecdotes, including facing unanticipated obstacles. Overcoming failures and the special intervention or encouragement of a mentor or client or relative makes for interesting stories. Then there are the Defining Moments, such as the first deal or client that cleared the runway for the business to take off.

Obviously enough, good stories begin with personal challenge, move through struggle and conquest and end in triumph. But they also should include some dramatic movement. Take your listeners on a journey, advises Suzanne Henry at Four Leaf Public Relations in Charlottesville, Virginia. "To shift from being merely an anecdote to being an actual story, a person needs to have experienced change," she says, explaining that's where many business storytellers fall down. "They give the conclusion (the message) without the context (the story)." In addition to a basic outline, stories need details to make them sing, and work hardest and best when the narrative is relevant as well as emotional. Connecting the business product or service to why an entrepreneur launched is the first place makes listeners appreciate the wares even more.

Once the story is stitched, entrepreneurs must hone versions for each constituent audience and channel. The 60-second sound bite in interviews or online videos should distil the same essential emotions and details as the long-version tale in the company press release and the informal one on the website. "Owners also should prepare a conversational version to share at networking events and in casual meetings with investors. But it's not wise to get locked in and walk away. Stories need to change to incorporate a customer's changing experiences with the brand. For instance, Facebook began with the story of "connecting to students," but has now scaled up to "sharing."

"Stories shouldn't be a sales pitch," reminds Ron Cappello, CEO of Infinia Group, a New York branding agency. The goal is to craft such an effective story that the listener is transformed from mere customer into brand evangelist who can't wait to tell the story to others.

12

Negotiations: Not Happening vs. Not Yet

Her way: **When faced with no, women give in more readily.**

His way: **When faced with no, men think, "Not yet."**

In November 2010, Andrea Servadio and her partner Brandy Han opened doors to one of the first premier dog care spas in Los Angeles. Fitdog Sports Club, where "Dogs come first," is a 3,000-square-foot facility located in Santa Monica. It features recycled rubber play areas, tested nontoxic toys, grooming and training services, a modern ventilation system that recycles oxygenated air every five minutes, organic snacks, as well as private spaces for "members" to nap, feed and take breaks during their cage-free daycare. The ratio of handlers to dogs is a competitive 1 to 20, and dogs are taken for a couple of hikes a day on nearby beaches and hills. Canines are elite clientele here.

Managing partner Servadio had been working hard on the business plan for six months and her timing for the opening was prime. Shortly after Fitdog's debut, a half-dozen other high-end pet facilities opened around Los Angeles. Competition quickly turned fierce as the trend toward treating pets like family, known as "premiumization" or "humanization," revved up in the area. Reviewing the competition after launch, Servadio and Han decided Fitdog's point of difference was the care and focus on the dogs, not the humans, as well as their "boutique setting." "Large spaces are scary to dogs, even big dogs get lost in them," says Servadio. "They can't get comfortable. We want to accommodate the dogs and we're attuned to what they want when they sleep overnight. Dog owners want to see a lot of luxury care in facilities because it's their perception that at home their dog prefers to sleep in a bed and watch a big-screen TV. But the dog only wants to be in the bed because the owner's there. Dogs don't prefer beds over other accommodations."

Finding cause for paws

Besides leading the pack of local rivals, the Fitdog debut was in line with market trends, such as the expanding upscale Camp Bow Wow national chain, which launched in 2000 in Denver and now has 100 locations and more than 200 franchises. Largely owing to premiumization, the pet services industry has experienced impressive growth, even during the bad economy. In 2015, the American Pet Products Association forecasts $60 billion will be spent on pets in the US, double that of a decade ago. The biggest proportion, $23 billion, goes for food but supplies and pet services, such as grooming and boarding, will reach $14 billion and over $5 billion respectively.

The pet product boom is directly influenced by what humans crave, not animals. Veterinary procedures include chemotherapy, MRIs and hip replacements. Diet supplements offer glucosamine and Omega-3. Human-grade pet food is gluten-free and buoyed with antioxidant superfruits. Designer accessories feature Burberry and Hermès apparel as well as Sealy dog beds made of orthotic memory foam. Luxury grooming and boarding options are growing, with hotel-style accommodations as special pet-friendly options stack up at major airlines. Servadio is well positioned.

Despite being clear-eyed about the need for a solid legal foundation for Fitdog, during the on-ramp to launch, it was Servadio's passive approach to negotiating the facility's rental terms and lease that led to problems. She acknowledges being too hands-off and giving in too soon, which nearly stopped the enterprise in its dog run. As a result, Servadio is coping with a seven-year handicap.

Unleashing Left Coast life

At age six, growing up in a beachside town south of Portland, Maine, Andrea Servadio decided she wanted to work with money. "I didn't know anything about deals, but I was good at math," she says. After her parents divorced and her dad moved to Denver, she decided to make the change to Colorado, graduating from the University of Denver in 2000. Next stop, New York, to become an investment banker.

Servadio worked her way up in investment banking at several firms, mostly structuring deals in the oil, gas and transportation sectors. In an industry still notoriously hard on women—"my college finances classes were only 10% women"—she earned vice president status in only four years. When the 2008 financial crisis hit, Servadio had just started a job at Fortis, then a Benelux-based banking firm. The company was forced to break up and let go most of the staff, but not Servadio. "I kept trying to get laid off, but my boss kept asking me to stay," she says. "It was depressing. Banks didn't have any capital. There was no deal flow and no way to move on in the new environment. I was just sitting around doing market comps"—comparing prices and structures of financial transactions.

Servadio stuck it out for several months but eventually quit. With money saved from the good years, she headed west. "I always wanted to move to California, because of the weather. I figured I'd go out and maybe write screenplays or something—anyway relax and figure out what to do." It was May 2009. She was 31.

Resettled in Santa Monica, Servadio and partner Han, who'd also left an investment banking position, soon checked out daycare options for their beloved Jack Russell terrier, Brecken. Nothing seemed to match the services they had used in Manhattan. "They were not as nice and the staff didn't seem as educated about dogs," says Servadio. "They weren't clean. They didn't give dogs their own spaces for overnight stays. We tried three different places and every time Brecken came back tired or sick or with an eye infection. We were starting to get discouraged." Los Angeles clearly didn't offer the luxury dog daycare options found in New York, likely because of lifestyle and climate differences. That's when the notion of launching a premier facility took hold.

Over the next several months, Servadio and Han toured more than a dozen dogcare centers. "We checked out services, looking for ideas, doing comparisons of price and services." In January 2010, after putting together a business plan, the couple went through the drawn-out process of applying for a SBA-guaranteed loan through a local bank. The financial mood at the time was all about pulling up the drawbridges and guarding the doors. Banks were not at all interested in lending, least of all to a luxury pet care startup. "They just laughed at us," says Servadio. No doubt, the women's financial training came in handy. They kept at it and eventually secured a SBA loan through a large commercial bank as well as another smaller loan though public small business resources.

Not knowing what you don't know

That was where their comfort zone ran out of terrain. The next and largest hurdle was renting space. "That was my hardest couple of months," says Servadio. "We've negotiated lots of contracts over our careers, but we didn't know the market terms for leases in Los Angeles. We needed someone who does local real estate." In addition, the owners of the space they wanted were both particular and uncomfortable about renting to a pet facility. Untutored in LA real estate, the founders didn't sit in on the contract negotiations and left the agreement terms to be structured by their real estate lawyer. But they had hired on the cheap to save money and then, instead of staying hands-on in the negotiating process, they focused elsewhere, and simply accepted the deal. "We knew more about legal terms in contracts than the lawyers we hired, but we weren't spending time on it and they weren't getting paid enough." After going through three different lawyers and three months of negotiations, Servadio still wound up with unfavorable terms on a seven-year lease. If they had pushed harder or refused to give in to unfavorable terms or kept looking at spaces, they probably would have got a better deal. But they gave in. "The only reason we got the lease at all here was because the owners' real-estate rep believes in doggy daycare. We had no history of business. Our financials were strong, but we weren't millionaires. He put his faith in our model."

"We're living with this lease," Servadio says. "It's expensive and we're on the hook the whole time." Lessons are clear: Stay close to the negotiating table and be clear about the agreement goals. Remember that hiring good representation will pay off in the end. "Mistakes won't be replicated," says Servadio with conviction.

Trading across the gender divide

Despite the fact that women are credited with stronger relationship skills, they typically leave money on the table in negotiating situations, whether salary in corporate organizations or pricing, fees and funding options for entrepreneurs. Sometimes that's because women pursue perks other than dollars, such as flexible work schedules or more free time or greater equity so they readily compromise on money. Even so, they don't usually win as much as they can at bargaining tables. Gender matters in negotiations.

When professional women and men are divided into two groups and tasked with the same strategic goal of nailing a deal through negotiation, the all-male and all-female teams rely on noticeably different tactics. Business professor Deborah Kolb and lawyer Carol Frohlinger have looked into those differences. Now a professor emerita, Kolb specialized in women's business leadership and used a gender lens to research and teach negotiating skills at Simmons School of Management in Boston, which offers the country's only accredited MBA program exclusively designed for women. Her work led to a practical career guide for women, *Her Place at the Table: A Woman's Guide to Negotiating Five Key Challenges to Leadership Success*, released in 2004, coauthored by Kolb, Frohlinger, and a third coauthor Judith Williams.

Seeing the need for women to better advocate for themselves during negotiations, and having tracked rising interest from employers to recruit and retain women, Kolb and Frohlinger expanded their book into a corporate training firm, called Negotiating Women. Clients have run an institutional gamut, from Pfizer, T. Rowe Price and Ernst & Young to the New York City Bar Association and University of California. In 2014, Kolb left the firm and Frohlinger assumed ownership, broadening the negotiating focus into a general advisory firm to advance women's leadership.

Negotiating Women research reveals that when men and women have equivalent access to data, they are equally adept at negotiating. In other words, such skills are not a sex-based trait. But when background information is hazy, or the negotiations represent a new situation, women tend to give in more promptly. In the face of no, women are more likely to walk away than men.

Even famous women with clout back up in negotiations. Recently, Oscar-winning actress Jennifer Lawrence acknowledged that she gave in too quickly on salary negotiations and so was paid less than her male co-stars in *American Hustle*. One reason women give in more quickly may be because they're relatively new to owning businesses and may not have as much practice in running operations or closing deals. More importantly, however, men usually have stronger professional networks and access to a broader bench of mentors than do women. Deeper comparative information of the players and the field gives men the decided advantage. Confident of the going rate, men can keep pursuing the yes. They're primed to hold out for what they know are appropriate or relevant positions, say, about compensation, pricing or time-money deliverables. That's why it's key for women entrepreneurs to join coaching groups or peer associations. By recognizing tendencies to make immediate concessions, women can avoid sabotaging their efforts. "They need to talk to people like themselves," urges Kolb.

Deals done under the table

Besides sitting down at tables without enough competitive information, women also tend to ignore the dynamics of something Kolb has dubbed the "shadow negotiation." This consists of issues that neither side has actually put on the table but are nonetheless being negotiated, especially around power and status. "Most people think the issues to be decided are in a business context," says Frohlinger. That translates into such items as price, terms of delivery, improvements, timelines, quantity or quality, staffing and so on. "That's the substance of the negotiation," says Frohlinger. "But people don't often spend enough time on the interpersonal dynamics." That means the personalities of who's at the table, which bargainer has leverage or clout, who commands attention and gets heard, who acts as leader—overall, the "how" rather than the "what" of meetings.

Typically, it is within these personality and power dynamics—the shadow negotiation—that gender gets engaged. Interviews conducted by Negotiating Women with hundreds of professional women found that "women could nail the issues and mount a strong argument for their case. Where they stumbled was in managing the shadow negotiation." Paying attention to the sub rosa deals will allow them to uncover hidden assumptions, expectations or agendas that may be derailing the agreement, no matter what participants say they want. Contemporary business life has added other factors. Increasingly, bargaining parties and their representatives face each other across different lifestyles, cultural backgrounds, values, religions, languages or business practices and ethics. That too influences the perceptual or implicit negotiation going on that may veil real motivations or issues.

Negotiating in a new light

Some "strategic levers" can help small businesses and less powerful bargainers move negotiations forward with stronger opponents. When big-deal clients keep delaying meetings or ignoring phone calls or asking for yet more time or presentations, Kolb suggests owners create incentives to push the client to talk turkey. These may include adding value to the deal, raising the stakes or costs of inaction or finding allies who can persuade the client to act. Similarly, when faced with postponements, Kolb recommends taking charge of setting the agenda for time, place, dates or discussion rather than passively waiting for a response.

"Small business owners tend to draw an arbitrary line in the sand between when the sales process ends and the negotiating process begins," says Frohlinger. "But if you ask enough questions early in the sales process, you can get help in the final negotiating stage." For example, say an owner asks a client early on about what's most important or worrisome to him in the proposed deal. And he responds, "What keeps me up at night is that the supplier will disappear or won't deliver on time." That's a clear signal that your negotiation session should build in strong guarantees and incentives for reliability and deadlines.

Once again, the outcome often depends on how much confidence a woman feels and demonstrates during the negotiations. Is she in command of that seat at the bargaining table? "If a bargainer doesn't move to direct the shadow negotiation, she can find the agreement tipping against her," observes Kolb. Managing under-the-table influences means becoming an effective advocate of the proposed positions. "A bargainer's advocacy essentially defines her claim to a place at the table. It tells the other side not only that she is going to be an active player, but that she will not and does not need to settle for less than she deserves."

Dissed if women do, doomed if they don't

However useful and revealing, Frohlinger and Kolb's analysis doesn't account for the outright bias when bargaining parties meet, nor does their work address the judgments made about women who decide to ask for more. Cultural and social stereotypes inform lots of noisy perceptions but that static goes high volume during the adversarial tensions of a negotiating cycle, no matter if it's about compensation, a contract or even who's putting the kids to bed tonight. When negotiations are in play, gender appears to hit nerves harder and flare tempers faster.

It'd be tough to find a successful woman on the planet who hasn't at some time been called "pushy," "aggressive" or worse because she signals she's unsatisfied with whatever it is she's already got and dares to ask for more. This entrenched dynamic for women doesn't seem to quit, even at the higher echelons and in supposedly enlightened workplaces.

In spring 2014, a particularly public rendition of this Pushy Woman Syndrome ignited at the dignified Gray Lady herself, the *New York Times*. Then executive editor Jill Abramson, the first woman ever appointed to the paper's top news post, had been in place for less than three years when she was summarily canned. In her stead, management named the first African American, a man, to the position—hard to fabricate a bias argument here. But afterward, in the wake of waves of insider media shock at the abrupt dismissal, reports surfaced that Abramson was not fired because of her poor performance but owing to her "brusque personality," and her inquiries into pay disparities. As journalist Ken Auletta detailed in a *New Yorker* story that May:

> As with any such upheaval, there's a history behind it. Several weeks ago, I'm told, Abramson discovered that her pay and her pension benefits as both executive editor and, before that, as managing editor were considerably less than the pay and pension benefits of Bill Keller, the male editor whom she replaced in both jobs. "She confronted the top brass," one close associate said, and this may have fed into the management's

narrative that she was "pushy," a characterization that, for many, has an inescapably gendered aspect.

No kidding. In the immediate aftermath, Abramson refused to comment. *Times* publisher Arthur Sulzberger, Jr., also tried to remain above the fray but was compelled by the ongoing furor into releasing a staff memo that announced "misinformation" about that pay gap. Could be. Auletta cites a friend of Abramson as saying the pay gap was bridged only *after* Abramson complained. More likely. To date, Abramson has publicly said little about her version of events. In the fall of 2014, she granted an interview to *Cosmopolitan* that shed little light. Acknowledging that Sulzberger had stated that he had problems with her management style, Abramson emphasized that she's "unashamed" of being fired and that "... young women should not feel stigmatized if they are fired." She also had some negotiating advice for women:

> My advice on getting a raise is what everybody's advice is: to become a confident negotiator, but that is so hard. My admiration for women who are good at that is unbridled. Women in general have a harder time talking about money with their bosses. It's part of that syndrome, like you're so lucky just to have the job.... Men never chalk up their success to luck but women often do. In my experience, men more often than women brought up money and talked about it and pressed for what they wanted in terms of salary before they agreed to be promoted.

Odds look good that Jill Abramson will have the last word. She's been teaching at Harvard and, early in 2015, inked a reported $1 million book deal that will cover the future of media. No doubt, her news will be fit to print.

___

Gender blowups

It's not just what and how much a woman asks for that colors the tone of a negotiation. Emotional reactions also are perceived differently. When men get angry during the horse-trading, it's usually viewed as a strategic tool. Outbursts are considered the bargainer's signal that he's passionate and intense about an issue or goal, rather than signs that he's losing it or out of control. When women get emotional, they're labeled "hysterical"— the gender term nonpareil. Men are told to "Calm down." Women are told, "Don't get so upset." There's a significant difference.

A couple of studies by Catherine Tinsley at Georgetown University's McDonough School of Business and Emily Amanatullah at McCombs School of Business at the University of Texas at Austin, found substantial backlashes against female negotiators in business who were "assertive" and "self-advocates." Colleagues thought such women were dominant and arrogant and didn't want to work with them because the women were too pushy and not feminine enough. In some cases, when women initiated negotiations instead of waiting for men to start the proceedings, they were financially penalized, and received much less than they requested. The researchers found no backlash for male negotiators, whether the men were characterized as "self-advocating" or not.

It may not even be strong opinions or digging into positions that trip up women at the bargaining table. Linguistics professor Deborah Tannen's research into cross gender communications shows that as kids, girls sit close and face each other. Boys, on the other hand, tend to keep space between them and often look away. Tannen's assumption is that men may see women's natural negotiating body language, moving close or leaning forward, as too aggressive or inappropriate. To reduce that impression, some experts suggest women may get a better reception by sitting side by side and not looking at the man directly when discussing anything touchy, such as feedback about performance, especially during negotiations.

Boosting the confidence quotient

Whenever the question of performance comes up for women entrepreneurs, the research quickly moves to the issue of confidence in negotiations particularly, and in business ventures generally. The go-to expert in how to maintain business confidence both in individual leaders and throughout organizations is Rosabeth Moss Kanter, and her philosophy for success is clear: "The goal of winning is not losing two times in a row," she says succinctly.

A Harvard Business School professor, bestselling author and internationally acclaimed strategic consultant (repeatedly named to lists of the "50 Most Powerful Women in the World"), Kanter systematically explores the decisions, policies and performance that lead to success or failure. She documents these in-the-field examples in her book, *Confidence: How Winning Streaks and Losing Streaks Begin and End.* Using case studies and on-the-ground research, Kanter looks at the factors that build and restore business confidence as well as how to create a company environment that will foster success.

For starters, most people have an erroneous idea of what confidence is. "Confidence is not a mood or a feeling of pessimism or optimism. It is the expectation of positive outcomes," says Kanter. "It's the belief that your ideas, work and efforts will become successful. Even when things are tough and there are bumps in the road, you have the confidence to hang in there and keep trying. You expect a favorable outcome." Translating those expectations into tangible business decisions and day-to-day operations is the hard part. Winning streaks in sports are easy to define because of measurable score results. But a winning streak in business "is a set of continued successes, a series of unbroken wins," explains Kanter. "Even when there are minor setbacks, you bounce back and continue to achieve your goals. By contrast, a losing streak is going into a decline. Some losing streaks can accelerate so fast they become a death spiral," she says.

The gender divide in confidence then is all about women's lower expectations. "Women have just as much drive in business as men do, and women now believe in themselves more, which in itself is a confidence builder," says Kanter, pointing to the rising numbers of organizations that mentor women in business. But men expect to succeed more readily than women do, and that's been the reality up until recently. "In the past, men had natural access to cheerleaders, contacts and colleagues they could call on to help them. We are now seeing an acceleration of those networks and personal confidence for women." Like most supporters of women's leadership, Kanter believes they can better build confidence by surrounding themselves with other women who are advocates of their success.

"Another drag on women's confidence is how often they wait until they have the perfect solution or plan," says Kanter. In those cases, "their punishment for failure is a lot more severe than it should be. They become discouraged by the first fumble and are then defined by that—they keep losing. Women need to be tougher about difficult setbacks. They need to connect themselves to successful people and ignore discouraging voices around them. Showing up is the first rule of success." Tapping into the advice of peer groups and women's business associations can help.

Creating a winner's circle

Women owners can significantly improve their negotiating skills by tapping into the expertise of someone who's already jumped the hurdles—that is, by working with a mentor. Ideally, a mentor is a seasoned business veteran, either in the community or the industry, who viscerally knows what it feels like to walk in the mentee's shoes. The purpose of the relationship is to advance the protégé's interests and goals, and both sides need to understand that. Mentoring isn't a gripe session or a flurry of phone calls to manage a crisis or a deal. It's a formal process, with regular meetings and a system for reviewing progress and performance. As a mentee, a female entrepreneur agrees to heed the mentor's advice and work toward change, typically not an easy task. If she's unwilling to implement the advice, then everyone is wasting their time.

Identifying the right mentor throws up several challenges. First, as we've seen, the sexes do not experience the business world in the same ways, whether as client or supplier, manager or marketer. That means the relationship, when the mentor is male, can turn complicated or confused. Next, widespread success for women-owned businesses is still in its first generation. Fewer women can mentor the up-and-coming generation. As a result, female business owners might consider enlisting a few or a series of mentors, both men and women, who offer differing viewpoints, skills and tutoring. Entrepreneurs might also focus on specific issues depending on a mentor's expertise, say, to ramp up technology or to hone negotiation skills.

Evidence shows that women work with mentors more often and for longer periods than men do, and that the relationship pays off. A study of male and female corporate presidents and vice presidents that compared career-building mentor relationships, conducted by Susan Schor, who was a Pace University management professor at the time and is currently an Eileen Fisher executive, found that women averaged more numerous and longer mentor relationships than did men. All the women in the study had one to four mentors in their careers, while only half of the men had any at all. The multiple mentor approach clearly is effective for high-achieving women.

Mentoring works best when the participants are simpatico, matching in social style and values as much as possible. Like all partnerships, the relationship relies on trust, chemistry and commitment. The advisor's star power also is a factor in the choice. High-profile mentors may be able to open doors and promote a young business, while credentialed mentors can talk up a mentee's company in the right places to the right people.

Next-stage mentoring

Mentor relationships aren't only for newbies or startups. They can be invaluable for veteran owners in taking business to the next level. For example, the Committee of 200, a powerful Chicago-based organization of female business owners founded in 1982, runs the Protégé Program for women entrepreneurs with high growth potential. An intensive, 24-month program for women entrepreneurs with revenues in the range of $5 to $15 million, the C200 initiative helps women improve leadership skills and learn more about venture capital, private equity, human resources and finances.

Sarah Shaw, whose Los Angeles handbag business went under because of naive underpricing even while sales were booming, believes mentoring might have saved her company. That motivated the start of her current Entreprenette coaching consultancy. She wants to help women build businesses. "You're on your own island starting a business," says Shaw. "A mentor can show you how to do things so you can be as savvy as possible. You get help with all the different aspects of how the business works. Then, even if you choose to delegate tasks, you still understand it. For instance, if you hire a PR person and you don't know the first thing about it, you won't know if they're doing a good job and you won't be able to help in any decision for an action plan they take. You'll be 100% relying on their expertise. I did that in my business and I often ended up getting the short end of the stick. It was really detrimental to the growth of my company."

Nowadays, says Shaw, "I think of myself as a paid mentor."

13

Success: Satisfaction vs. Size

__Her way:__ Winning is feeling recognized, being valued and making a contribution.

__His way:__ Money is the primary yardstick.

When they began dating back in 2000, Jessica Rovello and Kenny Rosenblatt got to talking about the games they had loved to play as kids in arcades and who was the better player: Think Ms. Pac-Man. Rovello challenged Rosenblatt to a game but arcades, of course, were long gone and they were unable find a video game online to settle the score. It led to a brainstorm. Why not launch a development studio to create those classic arcade games for Internet play?

The result is Arkadium, based in New York with an outpost in Simferopol, Russia, and now a leading developer of casual games. In contrast to "enthusiast" or "hard core" video games, casual games offer simple and streamlined play with puzzles, trivia, card games, wordplay and board games like Atari or Donkey Kong, solitaire and mahjong. Hundreds of casual games are developed each year, although the top 20 generate most of the revenue.

Arkadium now boasts a library of over 300 games, serving billions of game plays to millions of unique gamers across multiple distribution channels, including online and Facebook, via mobile and for custom clients such as CNN, Comcast, the *Washington Post* and AARP. "If you've played a game online in the last 10 years, it was probably one of Arkadium's," claims the company's promotion. Revenue has increased every year. "Our goal going forward is to keep putting out great products and remain highly profitable," says Rosenblatt. The surprise? The couple did not raise first-round capital or Series A financing until 2013, a dozen years after launch. "We went one way when the rest of the world went another," says Rosenblatt. The cofounders also retain majority control.

The couple, who've since married and had three kids, extol the benefits of their pay-as-you-go growth strategy. "A lot of 20somethings who think about starting a company are trying to make a bazillion dollars quickly and be the next Mark Zuckerberg. It's like a reality show," says Rovello. "But not taking any financing and growing organically for as long as you can means you get to maintain control of your business." Bootstrapping also gave them time to "become the business people we needed to be at each stage of the business."

Retooling for Plan B

That was hardly the first plan. At the turn of the 21st century, Manhattan's tech-heavy Flatiron district was still swimming in dotcom fever and investor cash, especially for cool content ideas. Rovello and Rosenblatt were poster-perfect for the era's entrepreneurial profile. At 25, each already had new media track records: he in engineering, business development and implementing networks and database systems; she as a broadband marketing executive and the online marketer who produced the website for the breakout indie film, *The Blair Witch Project,* one of the first campaigns to flex the power of viral. Their expectations mirrored the exuberant times. "We gave ourselves six months and if nothing happened, we'd abandon the idea," says Rovello. After tapping $15,000 from their 401(k) retirement accounts, they launched in 2001.

"I had a business plan and I was going around to mentors and advisors to raise $1 million," says Rosenblatt. But the advisors quickly pointed out the company had zero valuation and therefore no leverage—neither product nor employees. "We had nothing but thirty pages of paper and they said we'd get eaten alive by the terms." So the couple put their heads down and began building a business on their own.

The year of launching dangerously

Their strategy was to develop a game or two and then again look for funding. But in 2001, other unimaginable hurdles were in store. First, of course, the dotcom bubble burst, big time. "No one wanted anything to do with a dotcom," says Rovello. Next was 9/11, which, among its searing horrors, brought the economy to a standstill. The pair took side jobs building websites for $5,000 a shot, didn't take salaries while paying employees and kept developing product. "We believed in it," says Rovello. They wanted more than just a quick payout. They wanted to create a quality product.

To save money, they outsourced development of their debut game to $2-an-hour programmers in India—in retrospect, a rookie mistake. The couple had never before designed a game and the developers weren't much better. After six months, the programmers' software still crashed their system and little was delivered. On September 11, when the towers came down, Rovello and Rosenblatt were in Chandigarh, about two hours' drive north of New Delhi, desperately trying to fix the errors. They lost a year and began again.

"It was a good lesson," Rovello says today. "It taught us that you got what you paid for." Soon after, they hired developers in the Ukraine (now Russia), this time first commissioning $100 and $200 projects to test skills and deliverables. That evolved into a solid relationship, ultimately leading to the Arkadium office in Simferopol.

Nevertheless, two years after launch, with games at last ready, the company still wasn't sustainable. Lots of people liked to play games; few would pay for play. Arkadium was circling the drain. "At that point, we were married and thinking about starting a family," says Rovello. "We thought we had six more months before one of us had to get a job. We didn't want to be held hostage by our dreams." They were literally saved by a phone call. An executive from R. J. Reynolds Tobacco Company called to ask if they had any casino games for the website. Rosenblatt said sure. Arkadium had none.

The couple shifted into high gear, creating a poker game proposal and winning the bid for $250,000, which netted $50,000 after costs. R. J. Reynolds gave them more work and, at last, Arkadium was moving into the black, albeit with a different business model. The company focused on creating custom games for corporations rather than online play for consumers. "We had to go where the money was," says Rosenblatt. "Being self-funded, we didn't have $10 million to spend to find a business model. We had to be profitable or we'd be out of business. It made us disciplined."

Playing for keeps

Virtually nonexistent a decade ago, casual gaming has mushroomed. Mobile gaming on tablets and smartphones is likely to generate over $30 billion in global profit in 2015—with China and the US the biggest markets—and may soon eclipse traditional consoles as the primary gaming method, according to industry researcher Newzoo. Social casino games alone make up more than a fifth of the top 20 grossing iOS games in the US as people take to mobile's convenience and the "pick-up-and-play" ease of casual games during commutes or other downtimes. Players number about 200 million around the world, with, to the surprise of many, women age 35 – 55 the dominant demographic.

Arkadium has maintained solid B2B or custom corporate sales and ramped up to 150 staff in its two offices in the US and Russia. As the consumer market expands, the company has been moving back to the direct retail business. It takes several months to develop a quality casual game title, so the couple is always looking ahead to what Rosenblatt calls "the fruits of that labor." Meantime, neither one is thinking about exit strategies. "Our goal is to be the biggest casual game company in the world," says Rovello. "We want Arkadium to be synonymous with the best talent, the best product and the best profits."

By running the company as married partners, Rosenblatt and Rovello play to their individual strengths. "It's a case of divide and conquer," says Rosenblatt. "I focus on technical engineering, business development and sales, while Jess covers operations, marketing, production and PR"—a fairly typical husband-wife owner divide except that Rovello oversees all game production. She also acts as Arkadium's public face. In 2010, Rovello was named to *Crain's New York Business* 40 Under Forty, an annual list of regional winners who've achieved major success before turning 40.

Making it, male vs. female

Given the familiar gender divide in business—men take on analytics and numbers; women supervise staff and marketing—perceptions have formed around female aspirations that are difficult to shake. Because women don't focus as often or as hard on financials, received wisdom has concluded that women aren't as ambitious as men and don't or won't compete to win. In other words, women aren't tough-minded or relentless enough to achieve "success," as it's traditionally defined.

Certainly, we've seen that women entrepreneurs tend to start and run smaller businesses than men do. In tracking women-owned entrepreneurial startups, the Kauffman Foundation acknowledges the recent rapid spike in women's startups. However, the 2009 study downplays women's impact by noting that their firms record lower survival rates as well as lower levels for size, growth, earnings and profits. Kauffman researchers conclude that female-owned firms simply aren't as interested in growth as male-owned firms. More recent studies echo this "lack of interest" to account for women's smaller companies.

But if you look through a gender lens, there's a more compelling spin to that data. "The interesting thing about women entrepreneurs is that many of them may be purposely starting businesses as a lifestyle choice," said Kauffman Senior Fellow Alicia Robb, when the findings were released. "The number of women-owned businesses growing faster may reflect that women are going into business as a viable way to move out of the traditional employment market and gain flexibility. It's hard to know if those kinds of businesses are where they want to be."

Numbers support Robb's interpretation of women's choices. Their startups continue to proliferate at a robust pace. Although smaller, the sheer volume is boosting the economic impact of women-owned companies. Nearly 1,300 new women-owned businesses launch every day, double the rate in 2010, according to the 2014 "State of Women-Owned Businesses Report," commissioned by American Express OPEN. However, women still aren't growing those companies. "...Women-owned firms only employ 6% of the country's workforce and contribute just under 4% of business revenues," says the report.

Yet the times are in flux and the growth gap may be narrowing. Employment in women-led firms has been expanding, and while those real numbers remain low, employment at male-led firms actually is contracting. Projections indicate that this trend will continue. The Guardian Small Business Research Institute predicts women-owned firms will generate as many as 5.5 million new jobs by 2018. That's more than half of the 9.7 million new jobs all small businesses are expected to create and about a third of the more than 15 million total new jobs projected for 2018 by the US Bureau of Labor Statistics. Women's smaller companies over the years may also stem from their blocked access to lenders and funders, which has only lately begun to ease. Why try so hard to tap outside sources for growth when rejection is the probable result? Like

Arkaridum when financing options dried up, women owners may simply put their heads down and build for the future.

Size is a male measure

Company size and revenue are hardly the only markers for achievement, but rather the traditional metrics men like to measure. "Maybe size is not what drives a female entrepreneur but relative profitability, impact on society, company culture, employee satisfaction and other values," CEO Maxine Clark told *USA Today* in a 2008 interview. The founder of Build-A-Bear Workshop in 1997, Clark grew the company into 400 shops worldwide and upward of $400 million in revenue, then stepped down in 2013 to focus on public education in the St. Louis, Missouri region. She credited Bill Gates as an inspiration for using her business success for larger purposes.

Today's multifaceted women are well aware that daily business needs must make way for other parts of their lives. That tradeoff is often for family, and usually made willingly. A 2012 survey of 258 entrepreneurs conducted by business professors Kimberly Eddleston at Northeastern University and Gary Powell at Lancaster University in the UK, examined male and female entrepreneurs' satisfaction with their families and the role families played as owners built businesses. The researchers looked at "how positive facets of their family experiences, family-to-business enrichment and support nurture their satisfaction with work-family balance." Their findings corroborate obvious day-to-day business dealings. "Overall, results supported feminist theories that depict entrepreneurship as a gendered process," said the researchers. Women entrepreneurs nurtured their satisfaction with work-family balance by "creating work-family synergies." Integrating business and family experiences enriched the women. Men, on the other hand, were satisfied with work-family balance by "obtaining family support at home." That is, the men preferred someone who cheered them on while keeping the home fires burning and the personal wheels turning.

Caretaking isn't the sole reason women owners trade off time and money in the business. They may be tending kids or relatives and cooking family meals, but they're also training for triathlons, taking trips to Morocco or Machu Picchu, carving out time for surfing or Master Gardening classes, all in addition to working and meeting with clients. "Men tend to start a business to be the boss and grow the business as large as possible; women start businesses to be personally challenged and to integrate personal and business goals," reports the National Women's Business Council 2012 annual report. By choice and design, then, women may build enterprises that grow slowly, expand deliberately and bring in the "just enough" revenue and professional achievement to keep them satisfied. Plus, women's firms often change as their lives do. "When I first started, I did not have a business plan, I had a life plan," says Julia Billlen, who launched Warmly Yours, her Chicago-area company, in 2000 to provide electric radiant heat products. Today, the business is a much larger entity, operating as a full-dress heating supplier of floor heating and snow melting systems as well as radiant panels and towel warmers. "I'm content," says Billen.

For women entrepreneurs, this notion of "work above all else" doesn't compute. They either can't afford or don't want to ignore other responsibilities and options.

Success is a journey, not a target

Stories of women edging into entrepreneurship as a life-changing solution or an experiment rather than a selected path to glory are a recurring theme. "My husband passed away when I was 39 years old," says Karen Swim, now 51, and owner of Words for Hire, a marketing and PR agency for small and mid-sized businesses based in Sterling Heights, Michigan. "I had been off work for two-and-a-half years caring for him," she says. After her husband's death, she returned to the corporate world. Within three months, it was clear she needed to make a different choice. "I launched my own business because I wanted to earn a living and also have a life," says Swim.

These days, after a decade of running her own firm, Swim finds that feeling successful or not depends on what's going on in her life. "The wonderful thing about having your own business is that you get to define success and redefine as needed," she says. "Success is not about having it all but having what you want, whether that is a multimillion dollar empire or a small business that allows you to work with select clients. It is individual to each woman."

In addition to her main communications business, Swim also works as a business coach and mentor. "I've noticed and learned from the different approaches of men and women entrepreneurs," she says. "In the early years of my business, I fell into a common trap of not trusting myself. I personalized the financial transactions and nurtured others without nurturing my own business." Over time, she learned how to make the right decisions for the business, which she thinks men tend to do better than women. "My biggest obstacle is most often me," acknowledges Swim. "As a business owner, it's not the economy or outside forces that are the biggest challenge but your own mindset and how you perceive things. There have been times that I have allowed fear—of change, failure or even success—to hold me back from taking a big next step. I am constantly a work in progress but each time I grow I realize that the real obstacle was internal."

Money isn't pink or blue

There's that confidence factor again. All too often, because of women's frequent preference for mission over money, they face challenges that arise from lack of funding, whether from lenders or investors. "Definitions of success also influence goals," reports the NWBC's "Launching Women-Owned Businesses onto a High Trajectory." "Many women business owners believe that they cannot both grow a business and fulfill their values-based goals. So, they often default to focusing on the mission rather than growth goals." In contrast, men view business as a competition. Success flows from big hits and money is the primary yardstick. As a result, men usually prepare for bigger risks. They tend to sprint toward the imaginary finish line that represents a big reward. Their focus is on winning and cashing out. Wisely, men will craft exit strategies early on and then embrace the risks that are needed to get there.

However admirable a women entrepreneur's values and practices may be, it's money that oils the machinery of business. Women must learn how to become comfortable with integrating profits with purpose. The recent surge in social entrepreneurships, most of which are launched by women, has led to a host of workshops, conferences, seminars and the like that offer business-grounded remedies for women's disconnect. Bridges are being constructed, but in the interim, reality is biting. Female owners could use more lessons in what's required to clear the hurdles and impress the money guys.

Harvard professor Rosabeth Kanter suggests three ways women can "overcome the residue of discrimination and prejudice they face from funders." First, they need some early successes, so they can show bankers and venture capitalists that their business proposition will pay off. Next, they need to have big ambitions and not settle for a small niche. "They should think in the largest possible terms, not just locally," she says. Then, they need to overcome the historical bias that women will drop out. "They need to show they're in it for the long haul. The worst thing is that women in business continue to sell themselves short," says Kanter.

Before even approaching funders, women must research the kind of backing that will best suit their business. Financing comes in many types, from short-term credit lines all the way to the sale of a portion of the company. Each approach has its pros and cons, depending on the business model and needs. Owners can tap any number of sources to help work through the scenarios, including peers at groups like the

National Association of Women Business Owners or from the SBA and its Small Business Development Centers. A candid talk with the company accountant or financial manager is a good start.

Creating the on-ramp for funding

When getting ducks in a row to seek funding, before anything else, women entrepreneurs must ensure that their business plan is impeccable and clear, the business financials are buttoned up, any required licenses, permits or certifications are current and outside contractor and employee agreements are legal and tidy. After that, four missteps commonly crop up when women stray from the path that impresses investors, and these can easily be sidestepped.

The first is presenting a business model that doesn't appear scalable. Businesses that can grow fast by providing solutions to big, far-reaching needs or problems are the ones that attract VC money and infusions of capital in the way of loans and other investments. Lately, biotech healthcare, financial services and both business and consumer apps and software have been investment winners. Yet even when women-led firms are in the tech sector, these mostly tilt toward service provider businesses, which are fueled by selling time not products. To persuade potential investors, an owner must demonstrate how the company can reach a size large enough to be worth the investment.

Next, women frequently don't think through a clear exit strategy or explain how investors will get their payoff. Women may view the business as a long-term or lifestyle choice, but investors want big profits—fast. Owners must craft a strategy that will get money out of the business and to the investors, whether by becoming publicly traded, partnering with a larger firm, being acquired, or via some other exit. As part of the process, women may not present a strong enough analysis of revenues and profitability, which is the score investors keep.

Third, women owners focus on the market instead of their product.

Most lenders and investors have endured hundreds of pitches, evaluated scores of companies and are versed in trends and economic conditions. They want to get excited by a solution, not a problem. Women typically expend a lot of effort on the market opportunity rather than talking up key benefits and attractions of their product or service.

Last, at early stages, women owners tend to think their business is worth more than it is, likely because they've invested so much in it, including sweat equity and money from friends and family. Unrealistic valuations scare off investors or cause women to balk at ceding higher percentages of ownership that would actually attract funding. Future projections don't really count when it comes to securing capital early on. It's all about cash flow and the money needed to move forward or break even.

Looking for funding demands research and education. Seekers need to align their funding requirements with appropriate investors and groups. For instance, owners should know an investment firm's primary areas of investment, the geographical areas it covers, how prospects are identified and what specialties it favors. The best strategy is to treat fundraising like a sales process, as a pitch to a client. That means sending out emails, leaving phone messages and creating bullet-point presentations that define the preferred deal parameters. Women also often need to cast a wider net to break out of the insulation of women-only groups. The smart move is to head wherever the deals are done.

Green-tuning business

Even so, mission and money have moved toward each other at a pace few could have anticipated a few years ago. Who imagined eco would become quite so ka-ching? Sustainable business now embraces much more than being virtuous about recycling or reducing energy use. Going green encompasses rising business values and corporate citizenship seen around the globe, including being accountable and active about protecting the health of humans and the habitat. Operating with a triple bottom line—

people, profit and the planet—further fuels profits and brand loyalty. "Cost savings are evolving into revenue generation," says a management consultant who focuses on the arena. "Sustainability is next-generation business thinking because it creates value, attracts customers, retains employees and improves capital and funding," she says.

Multinationals are not the only businesses jumping onto the green bandwagon. With fewer resources and staff, small business owners also see benefits. A 2012 Office Depot tracking poll found 61% of US small businesses were trying to go greener while 70% anticipated going green over the next few years. Those numbers include millions of women, who increasingly are joining the trend by launching and growing businesses that reflect their needs and values. They're creating and marketing sustainable, child-friendly and nontoxic products, often postponing profits to get their products right. We've come a long way.

Mass-marketing sustainable

"When I started this business, the word 'sustainability' wasn't around," says Patricia Boswell, creator of Safonique, a biodegradable, all-natural laundry detergent. Sold as a liquid concentrate in 50-ounce eco-friendly pouches, Safonique retails at an affordable $7 for 50 loads—competitive with eco-brands like Seventh Generation and Method. Safonique also features aromatherapy, a lavender scent made from pure essential oils. The detergent has no enzymes, phosphates or residues that can damage septic systems or clog plumbing. "The word 'green' wasn't around either," says Boswell, whose business is based in the Bronx in New York City.

Launched as a liquid in 2001, Boswell had been developing the Safonique environmental product for years. In the early '90s, she experimented with an all-natural powdered form for the baby market, released in 1996, while she continued to fine-tune ingredients and packaging. She was always attracted to the manufacturing pipeline. "I didn't have a chemical degree but I was focused on biodegradable," she says.

A decade of working in Avon's product manufacturing division gave Boswell a good idea of what could be done and how to do it. "I had the opportunity to work with engineers and chemists, so I knew it wouldn't be difficult to make the changes I wanted," she says. "I knew I could make a better product." Her goal was to make an affordable, healthful product that cleaned efficiently. "Of course I was ahead of my time in a lot of ways," she says.

Validation for that innovation came later. Boswell has since been named a top entrepreneur by *The Small Business Wall Street Journal* and invited to serve on Walmart's Sustainable Value Network Team. She's also been chair of the advisory council for the Institute for Sustainable Enterprise Business Incubator at Fairleigh Dickinson University. In 2004, Safonique won the Best New Beauty and Health Product from the Food Marketing Institute. Better yet, her product now sells nationwide in more than 600-plus retail locations, including Walmart, Jewel, Shop-Rite and Stop & Shop chains.

Nonetheless, growth for Safonique has been slow and sporadic. After more than fifteen years, Boswell is still working on expanding the line, owing to a combination of family commitments and her fervor to get the product exactly right. She also has faced a number of individual challenges.

The triple threat pioneer

Hurdles to developing a successful green product were a lot higher when Boswell began marketing Safonique as a wholesale product. For starters, no one cared about saving the environment. "Retailers would ask why I was doing this," she remembers. "They were mostly puzzled or disinterested." Female entrepreneurs were scarce. As Boswell developed her product through the 1990s and into 2001, women business owners were still uncommon, particularly in the male-dominated field of mass-market product manufacturing and with a product outside the mainstream to boot. Add to that, Boswell is African American. Without dwelling on it much, she acknowledges that race certainly made it more difficult for her to find traction as a wholesale manufacturer.

As if those three strikes weren't enough, Boswell also moved around a lot because her husband, now retired, worked as a men's college basketball coach. The family, with two kids, followed his jobs, which meant Boswell couldn't set up a stable base of business operations. Multiple moves had pros and cons, she says. "As I went around the country, it allowed me to really evaluate my skills and what else I could do besides working for a corporation," says Boswell. "In walking around supermarkets, I saw so many opportunities for change, including household cleaning products." She began research on Safonique when her son was four, testing ingredients in a series of kitchen sinks as the family moved to different universities. "Traveling around the country also allowed me to understand needs about the environment in different communities among different women," she says. Then adds, "Being around coaches allowed me to zone in on how coaches think and how a loss doesn't mean a loss but just gives you focus for the next game."

Boswell is now poised to expand. Late in 2014, Safonique was recommended for use at 68 women and children's centers throughout Louisiana, and that's led her to investigate the market for similar facilities in other states. Nearly two decades after she first developed her all-natural product, Boswell is calmly focused on the future: "If you're a true entrepreneur, trials or tribulations do not bother you," she says. "You just keep moving. You know how to stick to your guns."

A different idea of success just might save us all

Of all the women you'd least imagine would be leading the charge toward more balance, advocating for giving all the parts of our lives better breathing room and integrating work into our lives rather than the other way round, Arianna Huffington wouldn't float to the top. But that's exactly what she's been doing since 2007.

Greek-born, Cambridge-educated, famous author and entrepreneur, Arianna Huffington has long been one of those ubiquitous women achievers. She was one of *Time* magazine's 100 Most Influential People more than once. She's cofounder and editor-in-chief of the respected *The Huffington Post*, which netted her $100 million when it sold to AOL in 2009, four years after launch. She comes across in every interview and profile as a driven mover, shaker and networker. But one day in 2007, Huffington woke up on the floor of her home office in a pool of her own blood with a broken cheekbone and a gash over her eye, the result of hitting the edge of the desk when she passed out from exhaustion and lack of sleep. Ultimately, after countless medical tests, from brain MRI to CAT scan to echocardiogram, nothing was found to be organically wrong. Except, of course, there was. Huffington had many hours in doctor waiting rooms to ask herself some searching questions: "Is this what success looks like? Is this the life I wanted?"

Answers surfaced in a book she released in 2014, called *Thrive: The Third Metric to Redefining Success and Creating a Life of Well-Being, Wisdom and Wonder*. "Our relentless pursuit of the two traditional metrics of success—money and power—has led to an epidemic of burnout and stress-related illnesses, and an erosion in the quality of our relationships, family life, and, ironically, our careers," writes Huffington on her Thrive website. What she urges is a redefinition of success, supporting that with research from the fields of psychology, sports, sleep medicine and physiology that commends mindfulness and unplugging. She defines the third metric as wellbeing, wisdom, wonder and giving.

Asked to share a single piece of advice for women who want to succeed, Huffington has said: "Don't just go out there and climb the ladder of success. Instead, redefine success. Because the world desperately needs it." In the coming decades, that's exactly what women are poised to do, even while launching and growing businesses on their own terms and in their own ways.

PART IV

Afterword

''My advice to everyone expecting to go into business is to hit often and hit hard; in other words, strike with all your might.''

— Madam C. J. Walker

14

Release Your Inner Woman and Succeed

Today, women entrepreneurs are uniquely positioned to expand global innovation, grow national economies and redefine male models of leadership and business. By recognizing and relying on their characteristic gender traits, women can unquestionably change the future.

"The untapped potential of women-owned firms is equivalent to the discovery of an entirely new technology or the birth of an industry. We have the opportunity to create millions of new jobs and add trillions of dollars to GDP," sums up a strategic action plan developed by nonprofit Quantum Leaps and IBM Corporation's Market Development division, which encourages women to grow businesses. "As our world becomes 'smaller' and 'flatter,' there is a tremendous opportunity for us," declares this plan, entitled "The Roadmap to 2020: Fueling the Growth of Women's Enterprise Development."

Every day, the need grows for a revised model to bridge the many gender gaps, whether in pay, in power, in profit, in politics, or in the daily routines of life and commerce. It is vital to honor men's virtues and smarts and risk-taking and good intentions. But we can no longer accept male modes of work as sole standards for success. I believe that by raising the value of women's ways of working and experimenting, we will move into a better 21st century. Respect for sex differences and strengths, as well as open-minded education about how each sex can benefit from the other's best practices, is the true challenge of implementing diversity.

Right now, women entrepreneurs are the best and most immediate way to effect real social and economic change. When women are seen as leaders on their own terms, as the norm rather an exception, and in greater and greater numbers, the indicator on the society's scale moves. Perceptions, policy and parity all improve. But that can't happen without advocacy and engagement. Women need to put on their big-girl pants and own up to taking charge—of money, of business, of their lives. They need to acknowledge that money is transformational, not simply transactional. They need to see its emotional effects as well as its financial value.

Around the world, in developing countries and industrial ones, women today have the most education and opportunity than in any time in history. We ought to leverage that—together.

Corporate ladders are limiting and too rigid. They run out of rungs to balance on and climb, for both sexes, but certainly far sooner and lower for women than for men. They never bend or change direction. By launching businesses that define women's individual ideas of success— and we now know how dramatically that diverges from male versions of success—women will rewrite the rules for families and society and the generations to come.

PART V

Linking to the Crowd

In startups with five or more females, 61% were successful and only 39% failed. When females are engaged at senior levels—founders, board members and executives—companies have a greater chance of being profitable, going public and being sold for more money than they raised.

— *"Dow Jones 2012 Women at the Wheel"*
Dow Jones Private Equity & Venture Capital

15

Ways and Means: Online Resources that Help Women Start and Run Businesses

Categorized by groups, products and services, these resources will enable women-led businesses to launch and operate more effectively while providing key connections to likeminded organizations, experts and communities. Keep in mind that all such tools and groups shape-shift over time. While the listing is up-to-date at publication, it's a good idea to review sources and gain testimonials or references before making commitments. In addition, the Web embraces literally thousands of such resources in each category. This filtered listing therefore reflects broad women-owner interests and support, outlets to gain ongoing information, and networks for small business and women entrepreneurs.

Index

DIGITAL TOOLS

Business Owners Toolkit (bizfilings.com): Small business information and guidance based on the business publishers CT Corporation and CCH, Incorporated, including legal, tax tools and management specifically geared to the small business owner.

Event guides: To learn what's happening in your town or to set up a hosted business meeting and send out invites, try Meetup.com or TheFetch.com.

Marketing tools: Affordable customer contact and survey platforms can send out e-news, event notices, social media campaigns or online surveys, such as ConstantContact.com, iContact.com, MailChimp.com, SurveyMonkey.com, Zoomerang.com. **Crowdsourced providers** put customized needs out to online bid to thousands of worldwide freelancers offering design, writing, marketing, animation and video services at very low costs, including 99Designs.com, Swiftly.com, Fiverr.com, DesignCrowd.com. Options for **DIY tech** mobile and online tools are proliferating, such as this Vistaprint trio of Webs.com to build a website; Pagemodo.com for social media; and ContactMe.com, a contact management system. One-stop tools for **social media management** provide online and mobile dashboards to engage, create, schedule, manage and track social outreach across accounts. Hootsuite.com, TweetDeck.com, Como (como.com) and Huzzah Media (huzzahmedia.com) are examples of streamlined, affordable platforms that can create customized mobile apps for business.

Microsoft Office templates (office.microsoft.com/en-us/templates): Hundreds of free online templates for business needs created for Microsoft Office applications, from financial management to business plans, invoices to marketing materials.

SurePayroll (surepayroll.com): A division of Paychex for small businesses, offering online services and solutions for payroll, 401(k) plans, health insurance, workers' compensation, employee screening and more.

US Small Business management (sba.gov): The Small Business Administration site offers tools, templates and guidance for day-to-day business issues, including leadership, growth, exports, operations, exit strategies, healthcare and more. **Disaster preparedness** (ready.gov): A FEMA channel, Ready Business provides tools to create a plan to prepare for business-killing hazards, including floods, fires, hurricanes, tornadoes and earthquakes as well as pandemics. **Hiring interns** (dol.gov; search "internship compliance"): Department of Labor Fact Sheets clarify what is and is not legal to comply with federal and state regulations for unpaid intern help.

Virtual assistants: Nonprofit trade organization **International Virtual Assistants Association** (ivaa.org) lists independent contractor members who work from remote locations with a searchable directory that connects clients to a wide range of admin, creative and tech talent. Voice-recognition virtual assistant app **SpeakToIt Assistant** (speaktoit. com) answers questions, performs tasks, notifies you of events and more.

ENTREPRENEURSHIP TRAINING AND MENTORING

Association of Women's Business Centers (awbc.org): This nationwide network of more than 100 Women Business Centers offers training, mentoring, business development and financing opportunities to over 100,000 women entrepreneurs every year.

Center for Women's Entrepreneurial Leadership and **WIN Lab at Babson College** (babson.edu; search "CWEL" and "WIN Lab"): The Center focuses on women entrepreneurs with programs, events and research and includes the recently launched WIN Lab to offer select Babson women students and alumni a yearlong accelerator program.

The Committee of 200 (c200.org): Headquartered in Chicago, this membership organization is open to women owners with highly successful companies and its more than 400 members collectively generate more than $1.4 trillion in annual revenues. The C200 Protégé Program selects high-potential women entrepreneurs for a 24-month mentoring process.

Double Digit Academy (doubledigitacademy.com): A fee-based short course in New York for women entrepreneurs seeking to secure venture capital and large angel rounds founded by entrepreneur and funder Julia Pimsleur.

Ewing Marion Kauffman Foundation (kauffman.org): A Kansas City, MO, private foundation with roughly $2 billion in assets dedicated to worldwide entrepreneurship programs, workshops, events, content, tools, research, education and exploration.

ExxonMobile Women's Economic Opportunity Initiative (exxonmobile.com; search "women"): Launched in 2005, this global initiative helps women in developing countries with training, mentoring and networks.

General Assembly (https://generalassemb.ly/): Established in 2011, this global educational group offers classes, workshops, full-time programs and online educational programming for digital skills, including Web development, user experience design, digital marketing and data science.

Goldman Sachs 10,000 Women Initiative (goldmansachs.com/10000women): A global initiative of the investment bank's foundation that provides women entrepreneurs worldwide with business and management education, mentoring, networking and access to capital.

infoDev's Women's Entrepreneurship Program (infodev.org/gender): A World Bank program at 127 centers, infoDev supports entrepreneurship in the developing world, promoting women in business with incubators, social networking and technology consulting.

The Level Playing Field Institute (lpfi.org): Based in Oakland, CA, with ties to Stanford and UC Berkeley, this nonprofit was founded in 2001 to eliminate barriers faced by women and people of color in the STEM industries and offers workshops, programs and other preparatory courses in computer sciences.

MicroMentor (micromentor.org): A free online platform developed by the Aspen Institute that connects entrepreneurs to a wide range of volunteer mentors, offering convenient sessions conducted by phone, video chat, in person or email, depending on preferences.

The National Association of Negro Business and Professional Women's Clubs, Inc. (nanbpwc.org): Founded in 1934 by New York City realtor Emma Young, this national organization for professional African American women works to bolster communities and provide training for entrepreneurship, leadership and technology.

Network for Teaching Entrepreneurship (nfte.org): This nonprofit works with students in low-income communities nationwide and around the world to teach entrepreneurship and leadership skills.

US Small Business Development Centers (usa.gov; search "sbdc"): Hosted by nationwide universities, colleges and state economic development agencies with public/private funding, the 1,000 SBDC centers provide free consulting and low-cost training for small and mid-sized businesses. **SBA Office of Women's Business Ownership** and **Women's Business Centers** (sba.gov; search "women's business"): Established in 1979 to oversee a network of Women's Business Centers (WBCs) throughout the US that provide management and technical support, especially for underserved women owners, including training and counseling in many languages to help women start and grow businesses.

Webgrrls International (webgrrls.com): Founded in New York City in 1995, this worldwide membership group has been at the forefront of the women's movement online, offering affordable workshops, community, bootcamps, networking and classes in software and coding in cities coast to coast.

Women Accessing Capital (womenaccessingcapital.com): Under the aegis of Women Impacting Pubic Policy, this national program educates women business owners on accessing capital, with courses that teach appropriate types of funding, obtaining capital and managing business finances.

- **Women's Business Enterprise (WBE) Certifying Groups**

Center for Women and Enterprise (cweonline.org): A nonprofit established in 1995, this group helps women start and grow businesses throughout Massachusetts and Rhode Island, offering education, training, technical assistance and WBE certification.

National Women Business Owners Corporation (nwboc.org): Created in 1995 to bolster women's competition for government and corporate contracts by developing standards and policies for WBE certification.

State and local government certification: Each state and most major cities offer WBE certification and each has different regulations. Check websites for state and city government procurement procedures and/or state departments of state to learn about applications and contracting opportunities.

US SBA Federal Women Owned Small Business Program Certification (sba.gov; search "WOSB") and **Women-Owned Small Business Federal Contract Program** (sba.gov; search "WOSB"): Effective 2011, federal contracting opportunities for women-owned small businesses (WOSBs) were expanded, authorizing contracting officers to set aside certain federal contracts for eligible WOSBs or economically disadvantaged women-owned small businesses (EDWOSBs). To qualify, owners must first register as a vendor and then complete the certification application before any bid.

WEConnect International (weconnectinternational.org): This global nonprofit helps women-owned businesses succeed by educating and certifying WBEs based outside the US and by connecting owners to multinational corporate buyers.

Women's Business Development Centers (wbdc.org): Headquartered in Chicago, this nonprofit has 14 offices across nine Midwest states to offer certification and support for women owners with workshops, conferences and mentoring.

Women's Business Enterprise National Council (wbenc.org): Founded in 1997, this national nonprofit now is the country's largest third-party certifier. WBENC advocates for women suppliers to large corporations and offers assistance to women entrepreneurs, providing formal MatchMaker programs that connect corporate members with its certified enterprises (WBEs).

US Women's Chamber of Commerce (uswcc.org): An approved third-party certifier for WOSB for federal contract programs, the chamber helps women gain access to government contracts and offers tools for growth.

FEMALE-FRIENDLY FUNDERS

• **Educational and nonprofit**

Angel Capital Association (angelcapitalassociation.org) and **Gust** (gust.org): Searchable directories of accredited angel investors and groups.

Angel Resource Institute (angelresource.org): A nonprofit with education and best practices info for early-stage capital and angel investing, including workshops, research and programs.

Astia (astia.org): Linking investors and entrepreneurs to fuel social innovation, this global nonprofit supports men and women owners with programs and resources, including the **Astia Fund,** which provides capital for high-growth women entrepreneurs.

Center for Venture Research (paulcollege.unh.edu/cvr): A research arm of the University of New Hampshire's business school, the Center studies early-stage equity financing and offers detailed data about angel investors and deals.

Crowdnetic (crowdnetic.com): A technology and data solutions provider for the global crowdfinance marketplace, this online hub has timely information about the field as well as events and similar services.

F6S (f6s.com): A network of worldwide resources for founders to find global startup programs, apply to accelerators, pitch investment funds, post or apply for jobs, get free deals and grow.

Investors' Circle (investorscircle.net): A well-established nonprofit early-stage impact investor that focuses on funding social venture and sustainable firms around the country.

Keiretsu Forum WISE (keiretsuforum/search "women"): This global investment community established the Women Investing in and Supporting Entrepreneurs committee in 2007 to encourage involvement of women angel investors and entrepreneurs in early stage ventures and holds year-round events and an annual Summer Solstice.

Pipeline Angels (pipelineangels.com): A nonprofit angel investing bootcamp for women that focuses on investing in women social entrepreneurs with pitch summits and training programs nationwide.

Women's PE Briefs (womenspebriefs.com): Weekly private equity newsletter about women investors.

National Venture Capital Association (nvca.org): A trade association and lobbyist for US venture capitalists that includes research and statistics about current VC investments.

Women's Venture Fund (womensventurefund.org): Founded in 1994, this nonprofit organization helps women in the New York and New Jersey region to obtain loans and financing.

• **Angels**

37 Angels (37angels.com): A New York-based network of women-only angels that focuses on male- and female-led startups and also offers a fee-based training bootcamp for novices.

Belle Capital USA (bellevc.com): An early-stage angel fund focused on women-led startups in IT, tech-enabled products and services, life sciences and clean tech sectors.

Broadway Angels (broadway-angels.com): A women-only angel group with an IT focus.

Empire Angels (empireangels.com): This New York network's members are mostly in the financial services industry with a focus on technology that serves financial institutions or FinTech startups.

Golden Seeds (goldenseeds.com): A network of angel investors, along with a smaller VC fund, this is one of the largest funders for early-stage women-led businesses nationwide.

Joanne Wilson (GothamGal.com/investments): New York-based Wilson invests in early-stage, mostly women-led companies and stays hands-on and dedicated, offering advice and access to her network of funders and advisors.

Phenomenelle Angels Fund (phenomenelleangels.com): Based in Wisconsin, this network focuses on women and minority Midwest businesses in tech, consumer goods and services and communications.

Prosper Women Entrepreneurs (prosperstl.com): A for-profit angel investor and nonprofit mentoring network launched by local women leaders, including Build-A-Bear Workshop founder Maxine Clark, to bridge the entrepreneur gender gap in the St. Louis, MO region.

Women's Capital Connection (womenscapitalconnection.com): A Kansas City, MO-based angel network that invests in early-stage women-led startups in the region.

• **Venture capital**

.406 Ventures (406ventures.com): This Boston-based venture funder invests in early-stage technology companies and maintains hands-on engagement.

Aligned Partners (alignedvc.com): Women-founded, this early-stage fund invests in IT companies, mostly cloud-delivered and mobile services.

Aspect Ventures (aspectventures.com): Launched by two women VCs, this fund focuses on early-stage companies to increase opportunities for women-led startups.

The Build Fund (corp.aol.com; search "BBG"): Still ramping up, this $12 million venture fund from AOL will focus on early-stage investments in women-led consumer Internet startups, including ecommerce and media.

Ceres Venture Fund (ceresventurefund.com): This Chicago-based fund has an all-woman team and focuses on high growth, early-stage companies in the Midwest with interests in healthcare, IT and business services.

Cutting Edge Capital (cuttingedgecapital.com): Based in Oakland, CA, and certified as a B Corp, this woman-founded investor supports social and out-of-the-mainstream ventures with Direct Public Offering deals or small company offerings direct to the public with smaller returns and lower buy-ins.

Cowboy Ventures (cowboy.vc): A community of advisors and team members led by several women, this seed stage fund focuses on technology and products that "re-imagine" work and personal life in large markets.

EDF Ventures (edfvc.com): Based in Ann Arbor, MI, this VC firm invests in early-stage healthcare companies developing technologies that address large problems or transform markets.

F Cubed (femalefoundersfund.com): A hands-on New York investment group of three cofounders that provides seed stage funding to women entrepreneurs and works to open doors for women founders.

Forerunner Ventures (forerunnerventures.com): An early-stage women-only investment group that focuses on innovation in retail and consumer experiences.

Illuminate Venture (illuminate.com): This Oakland, CA-based venture funder steered by high-profile VC Cindy Padnos, is known for its gender-blind reviews and focus on the enterprise cloud and mobile computing space, especially SaaS (software as a service) applications and Big Data solutions.

Isabella Capital (fundisabella.com): Based in Cincinnati, OH, this VC firm focuses on early-stage companies in IT, healthcare, retail and consumer goods and communications, particularly with female leaders.

Next Wave Ventures (nextwave.ventures): Founder Alicia Robb, a Senior Fellow with the Kauffman Foundation, launched this initiative in partnership with other women-focused venture funds to offer education and training for women angels and to build a diversified portfolio of investments.

Northwest Social Venture Fund (nwsvf.org): A Portland, OR-based impact fund that focuses on social business ventures for deals up to $250,000.

Women's Venture Capital Fund (womensvcfund.com): Based in Los Angeles and Portland, this VC firm invests in women entrepreneurs, with a focus on fast-growth digital, green and sustainability startups.

Version One Ventures (versiononeventures.com): This Canadian-based firm, founded by well-known tech entrepreneur Boris Wertz, works as a "micro" venture fund, with early-stage investments and a focus on consumer Internet, ecommerce, SaaS and mobile opportunities, and, lately, women-led ventures.

• Crowdfunding

Equity-based

AngelList (angel.com): One of the largest equity-based crowdfunders for startups, this group includes options for syndicate deals, or a group with a lead investor who usually negotiates terms with the startup.

Crowdentials (crowdentials.com): Designed to help companies raise capital and comply with JOBS Act requirements, this pay-to-play platform offers SaaS applications that verify investors, ensure security and retain privacy during campaigns.

Crowd Fund Capital Advisors (crowdfundcapitaladvisors.com): An advisor for public and private sectors on using crowdfund investing technologies.

EarlyShares (earlyshares.com): A combination rewards- and equity-based platform that offers access for accredited investors to private startup opportunities.

FundAthena (fundathena.com): Founded in 2015 to serve the new SEC Reg A+ marketplace, the firm focuses on mid- to late-stage businesses with gender diverse management.

Portfolia (portfolio.com): Founded by Trish Costello, cofounder of the Kauffman Fellows Program, this online platform connects individual investors and affinity groups with private entrepreneurial companies.

Lending-based

KivaZip (kivazip.com): A crowdfunded lending program established by well-known microfinance lender Kiva.org, this "character-based lending" leverages an entrepreneur's friends and family as first-tier funders, then reaches out to the crowd.

Rewards-based

Indiegogo (indiegogo.com): Launched in 2008 and one of the best-known rewards-based platforms, this crowdfunder has attracted millions of contributors and thousands of campaigns, especially from the creative and social justice communities.

Fund Dreamer (funddreamer.org): This Los Angeles platform focuses on bringing more women and diversity groups into the tech and business worlds, maintaining a low 1% campaign fee.

MoolaHoop (moola-hoop.com): Designed for women entrepreneurs who want to raise funds for micro and small businesses.

Plum Alley (plumalley.co): This New York-based platform is dedicated to raising money for women-led enterprises and innovation.

• **Lenders**

Lending Club (lendingclub.com): Founded in 2007, this peer-to-peer online platform offers alternatives to traditional banking systems, with lower interest rates to borrowers and better returns to investors.

OnDeck (ondeck.com): Also launched in 2007, this technology-enabled Main Street lender focuses on small business, evaluating applicants based on their performance rather than credit ratings.

Opportunity Fund (opportunityfund.org): A California nonprofit social enterprise that provides microloans for Bay Area small businesses.

Prosper (prosper.com): The first US peer-to-peer lending marketplace, this platform has more than 2 million members and has funded over $1 billion in loans. Borrowers list loan requests between $2,000 and $35,000 and individual lenders invest as little as $25 in each loan listing they select.

Tory Burch Foundation (toryburchfoundation.org): This private foundation established in 2009 by fashion mogul Tory Burch supports economic empowerment of women entrepreneurs and their families, offering access to affordable loans, entrepreneurial education, networking programs and mentoring support.

NETWORKING AND SUPPORT SYSTEMS

Association for Enterprise Opportunity (aeoworks.org): A national membership organization that assists underserved entrepreneurs in starting, stabilizing and expanding businesses.

American Express OPEN (americanexpress.com/smallbusiness): An American Express marketing arm, offering resources, content, credit card and travel services for small business owners plus specific OPEN for Women services, including the CEO BootCamp.

Better Way Moms (betterwaymoms.com): This online magazine and community helps mothers balance work and family, offering workshops, retreats and advice for home-based businesses.

Dell Women's Entrepreneur Network (dell.com; search "DWEN"): A Dell corporate initiative, the US and global DWEN supports and connects female entrepreneurs with networks, sources of capital, knowledge and technology.

Empower Lounge (empowerlounge.com): Based in Austin, TX, an online community and network for women entrepreneurs, with guides for sale and peer stories for women owners.

Founding Moms (foundingmoms.com): A collective of online resources and offline workshops and events that support mom entrepreneurs with mentoring, networking and growing their business with help from peers and business experts.

Global Women Inventors & Innovators Network (gwinn.com): A London-based worldwide network with regional activities to increase women-led enterprises by partnering with governments, industry experts, organizations and educational institutions.

Mightybell (mightybell.com): This online software platform lets organizations and individuals create communities and networks, particularly for self-employed pros, and participates in the American Express OPEN CEO BootCamp.

National Association of Women Business Owners (nawbo.org): Established in 1975, this membership group promotes and supports women entrepreneurs with 5,000 members and 60 chapters across the country. It was the organization that was instrumental in securing passage of HR 5050, the Women's Business Ownership Act in 1988.

National Center for Women & Information Technology (ncwit.org): Based in Boulder, COLO, this nonprofit community of 600 universities, companies, nonprofits and government groups works to increase women's participation in computing and technology and promotes IT careers for female high school students.

Project Eve (projecteve.com): A digital publisher and online community of 18 million monthly viewers for women in business, offering mentoring, networking and support.

United Succes (unitedsucces.com): An international membership network for established women-owned businesses that offers connections, support, peer and expert advice.

Watermark (wearewatermark.org): A Bay Area networking group of senior women executives and entrepreneurs focused on developing and supporting leadership roles for women.

Women 2.0 (women2.com): The world's largest membership community for next-generation women technology leaders, offering educational content, programs, networking and events in cities across the country.

Women Entrepreneurs Grow Global (womenentrepreneursgrow-global.org): A social enterprise founded by author and international trade consultant Laurel Delaney that offers support and information to help women-owned businesses move into the global marketplace.

Women in Technology (womenintechnology.org): Located in the Washington DC area, this professional association for women in the tech industry offers a peer community, support, programs and resources to advance women in technology from the classroom to the boardroom.

Women Presidents' Organization (womenpresidentsorg.com): A nonprofit membership group for women who run multimillion-dollar companies with peer-to-peer advisory groups and networking to help accelerate growth.

Venture Mom (venturemom.com): A peer-to-peer site for moms looking to start an income-generating enterprise that allows for family, including ideas, advice, profiles in success as well as products and services for sale.

PURPOSE-BASED BUSINESS PLATFORMS

B Corporation (bcorporation.net): A socially responsible organization that evaluates and certifies B Corporations, which commits profitable businesses to heed social and environmental standards.

BALLE (Business Alliance for Local Living Economies; bealocalist. org): A membership community of 50,000+ entrepreneurs, business networks and funders committed to growing the values-based economy.

Boundless Impact Investing (boundlessimpact.net): A research and advisory platform that helps members maximize the social impact of their investments.

Conscious Capitalism (consciouscapitalism.org): Advocates and teaches how businesses can do good while turning a profit.

DigitalUNdivided (digitalundivided.com): A social enterprise that offers programs to encourage increased participation of African American and Latina women digital entrepreneurs.

Green America (greenamerica.org) and **Green Business Network** (greenbusinessnetwork.org): This nonprofit business network of 3,000 firms works toward environmental and sustainable practices, offering tools, programs and certifications to help companies go green.

Innov8Social.com (innov8social.com): This is a guide to impact innovation, social entrepreneurship and legal and policy issues in the field, with interviews, event recaps, tools and features.

L³C (americansforcommunitydevelopment.org): A for-profit type of LLC corporate structure, the Low-Profit Limited Liability Company puts social mission before turning a profit and is currently approved in Vermont, Illinois, Louisiana, Maine, Michigan, North Carolina, Rhode Island, Utah, Wyoming, The Oglala Sioux Tribe and the Crow Indian Nation of Montana.

Skoll Centre for Social Entrepreneurship (sbs.ox.ac.uk/ideas-impact/skoll): Founded by social entrepreneur and former eBay president

Jeff Skoll, the Centre is part of Oxford University's Saïd Business School and promotes social entrepreneurship worldwide and holds an influential annual forum.

SOCAP (socialcapitalmarkets.net): This platform that connects social venture investors, entrepreneurs and social impact leaders hosts an annual event in San Francisco that draws more than 10,000 attendees.

Social Venture Network (svn.org): A community for social entrepreneurs that encourages collaborations and peer-to-peer connections to support the triple bottom line of people, planet and profit.

Young Women Social Entrepreneurs (ywse.org): A nonprofit membership group that advocates for young women social entrepreneurs and leaders, providing training, access to resources, peer and mentor support, and networking, with chapters in SF, Portland, NY, LA, Washington DC, Miami, Atlanta and Africa.

RESEARCH AND ADVOCACY GROUPS

American Association of University Women (aauw.org): Based in Washington DC, this national membership organization, founded in 1881, promotes women and families with research, advocacy and lobbying.

American Alliance of Micro Business Women (aambw.com): This advocacy and community group offers tools, resources and lobbying for issues that affect microbusinesses and the self-employed.

Business and Professional Women's Foundation (bpwfoundation.org): The first national organization to support professional women, this nonprofit battles sexual discrimination in the workplace and develops programs and workplace policies that meet the needs of working women, communities and businesses.

Catalyst, Inc (catalyst.org): Established in 1962, this well-known nonprofit focuses on increasing opportunities for working women and female entrepreneurs while operating as an execuitive recruiter and research group.

Center for International Private Enterprise, Women (cipe.org/topic/women): Leveraging programs and international partnerships, CIPE works with worldwide women's business associations to advocate for reforms, support women's participation in local economies and educate women entrepreneurs.

Center for Women in Business (uschamberfoundation.org/center-women-business): This arm of the US Chamber of Commerce Foundation supports women business leaders with research, events, mentoring and peer-to-peer networks.

Diana Project (babson.edu; search "diana project"): Launched in 1999 by five women business scholars, this research project is a multiyear, multi-university study of global female business owners.

Gendered Innovations (genderedinnovations.standford.edu): A policy and research project at Stanford University, this institute investigates how sex and gender—biology and cultural influences—affect business, health and medicine, the environment, engineering and science.

Global Banking Alliance for Women (gbaforwomen.org): A global consortium of member financial institutions that partners with McKinsey & Company, to develop programs that provide women entrepreneurs worldwide with access to capital, markets, education and training while advocating for women's economic role as consumers, investors and job creators.

Global Entrepreneurship Monitor (gemconsortium.org): Initiated in 1999 as a Babson College and London Business School partnership, this is the world's largest annual assessment of individual entrepreneurial activity with an annual budget of $9 million that covers 75% of the world population and 89% of global GDP.

Million Women Mentors (millionwomenmentors.org): An engagement campaign to mobilize corporations, government entities, nonprofit and higher education groups to become active participants in mentoring girls and young women in STEM fields.

National Economic Council (whitehouse.gov/NEC): Established in 1993 as an economic advisory group for the President, the NEC and the Council on Women and Girls researches and advocates for women in business.

National Women's Business Council (nwbc.gov): A nonpartisan federal advisory council for women entrepreneurs, offering advice and counsel to the President, Congress and the SBA on economic issues important to women business owners.

National Women's History Museum (nwhm.org): A privately funded digital resource (currently raising funds for a physical site on the National Mall in Washington DC), the NWHM researches women's history and curates online exhibitions, including in-depth investigations of women entrepreneurs.

Quantum Leaps (quantumleapsinc.org): A nonprofit policy group that provides research and collaborations with global women's business associations, governments, NGOs and corporations to improve access to money and markets for women entrepreneurs worldwide.

Re: Gender (regender.org): Formerly the National Council for Research on Women, this nonprofit connects individuals, institutions and groups with a gender lens on women's identity and economic wellbeing.

The Small Business & Entrepreneurship Council (sbecouncil.org): A research and small business nonprofit lobbyist that encourages initiatives and legislation to support entrepreneurship and small business growth.

The WAGE Project (wageproject.org): A nonprofit working to end discrimination against women in the American workplace and to achieve equality in pay for women.

Wellesley Centers for Women (wcwonline.org): One of the largest gender-focused research organizations in the world, the Centers develop theory, communications, training and studies that affect women's lives and concerns.

The Women's Entrepreneurship Committee (csb.org/project/wec): Part of the nonprofit International Council for Small Business, the WEC manages an award for best academic paper on women's entrepreneurship, and drives communications and marketing for research, education and practitioner communities.

Women Impacting Public Policy (wipp.org): A nonpartisan organization that educates and advocates on behalf of women-owned businesses.

STARTUP LABS AND BOOTCAMPS

These labs require applications. Some are rental spaces or membership fee-based while others require equity from resident startups.

1871 (1871.com): A Chicago nonprofit community and coworking space for digital startups with low rents and networking benefits accessed via application.

500 Startups (500.co): A global community of startup investors, mentors and four-month accelerator programs in Mountain View and San Francisco, CA as well as Mexico City.

Angelpad (angelpad.org): Founded by ex-Googler Thomas Korte, this Silicon Valley mentorship program helps Web-technology startups build better products, raise funding and grow businesses. Since the 2010 launch, AngelPad companies have raised over $200 million in funding and generated over $400 million in exit value.

Blackstone Entrepreneurs Network (blackstoneentrepreneursne-towork.org): A charitable foundation of well-known global investor Blackstone, this initiative works in several regions to identify and repli-cate four program models that accelerate businesses and create jobs.

Centre for Social Innovation (socialinnovation.org): A coworking space, community and launchpad for social entrepreneurs offering programs, speakers, experts and tech networking, this lab launched in 2004 in Toronto and now has 100,000 square feet in four locations in Toronto and New York City.

Founders Space (founderspace.com) Based in San Francisco, this group connects founders, angels, VCs and advisors to provide startups with education, resources and networking while focusing on disruptive models and new markets.

Founders Institute (ft.co): Based in Silicon Valley, with chapters in 40 countries, this is the world's largest entrepreneur training and startup launch program, offering four-month part-time programs. The Institute has helped launch nearly 1,300 companies in five years.

Google for Entrepreneurs (googleforentrepreneurs.com): Funded by Google, this worldwide initiative launched in 2011 and partners with startup communities in 125 countries to build "campuses" where entrepreneurs can learn, connect and build companies.

HealthBox (healthbox.com): An accelerator program launched in 2012 with facilities in Boston, Nashville, Chicago and London, this lab focuses on growth and solutions for the healthcare industry.

Impact Hub (impacthub.net): A global incubator and startup lab network with 7,000-plus members in 54 worldwide locations, including the Bay Area, New York and Philadelphia, offering programs, community networks and mentoring for social change entrepreneurship.

Innovation Depot (innovationdepot.net): A business incubator that focuses on emerging biotechnology/life science, IT and service businesses, operating in partnership with the University of Alabama at Birmingham.

Interise StreetWise 'MBA' (interise.org): Based in Boston, this award-winning nonprofit organization offers a nine-month educational and networking program to help existing small business owners ramp up by developing a three-year strategic plan.

MergeLane (mergelane.com): Dedicated to boosting and investing in women, the MergeLane business accelerator is based in Colorado.

NewME (newme.in): Launched in 2011, an online platform with Silicon Valley experts and mentors provides support for "out of the box" entrepreneurs or newbies without investor or accelerator connections. NewMe does not automatically take equity in its member firms.

Pace Entrepreneurship Lab (paceelab.com): Part of New York's Pace University, the Lab offers undergrad and postgrad students workspace and a learning environment to collaborate and innovate ideas and company formation. Pace also hosts an annual pitch contest.

PIE (piepdx.com): A Portland, OR, accelerator and mentorship program suited for a wide range of startups and hosted by the well-known ad agency Weiden+Kennedy.

The Refinery (refineryct.com): Based in Connecticut, The Refinery focuses on startups in the region that target the underserved market of women, both as consumers and as entrepreneurs.

Springboard Enterprises (sb.co): One of the first women-facing bootcamps, Springboard offers nationwide programs, accelerators, pitch presentation coaching and access to funders to build women-led tech companies. Since 2000, 545 women-led firms have participated in its accelerators and, to date, its portfolio companies have raised $6.5 billion in financing.

Startup Health Academy (startuphealth.com): A global, long-term coaching program and peer network for healthcare entrepreneurs reaching seven countries and 35 cities, with a goal of building 1,000 health companies over the next decade.

Techstars (techstars.com): One of the largest startup accelerators with locations in Austin, Boston, Boulder, Chicago, London, New York City and Seattle, this three-month program selects only 10 or so startups per location, investing seed funding as well as offering mentoring, access to capital and expert networks.

Y Combinator (ycombinator.com): One of the most prestigious Silicon Valley facilities, this three-month accelerator provides coaching, mentoring, seed funding and expenses for startups and access to funders later, mostly for first-stage scalable tech ideas.

• **Contests**

Cartier Women's Initiative Awards (cartierwomensinitiative.com): In 2006, Cartier partnered with the Women's Forum, INSEAD Business School and McKinsey & Company for this annual global business plan competition to support women entrepreneurs, with six winners and prizes of $20,000 each.

EY Entrepreneurial Winning Women (ey.com; search "winning women"): An Ernst & Young annual national competition and executive leadership program to identify and support a select group of high-potential women entrepreneurs and businesses.

Global Social Venture Competition (gsvc.org): Founded in 1999 by MBA students at UC Berkeley's Haas School of Business, this worldwide MBA student business plan competition for social ventures awards $50,000 in prizes.

New York StartUP! (nypl.org; search "startup competition"): An annual business plan competition of $15,000 managed by the New York Public Library's Science Industry and Business Library (SIBL) with partner Citi for New York City residents.

White House Demo Day and **InnovateHER** (whitehouse.gov; search "demo day" and "innovate her"): Initiated by President Obama in August 2015, this "contest" focuses on selected startup stories from diverse founders to support entrepreneurs with SBA and private sector funding and accelerator and incubator mentoring.

YouNoodle (younoodle.com): An online platform that helps startup founders get advice, prizes and opportunities from a network of startup competitions, connecting entrepreneurs with advisors and investors, while fast-tracking startups into accelerators and other programs.